'I enjoyed BACK CRACK BOY and LIAM AT LARGE enormously. They are wonderfully accurate pictures of working-class life on Merseyside in the Thirties, and of the tight network of family and friends which made such a harsh life bearable. One of the tragedies of town planning on Merseyside is that in the wholesale removal of families to new housing estates, they broke up their sustaining networks.

I know just how Liam must have felt when he first got into a bath. I had had baths as a young child; but the wonderment of a real bath when, during the war, we moved out of Liverpool to a frowsy little bungalow in the Wirral, a home with an ancient but workable bath, made me feel like a film star.'

Helen Forrester

SQUARE PEG IS THE CONTINUING STORY OF LIAM, BEGUN IN *BACK CRACK BOY* AND CONTINUED IN *LIAM AT LARGE*.

D1350670

Also by Joseph McKeown

BACK CRACK BOY
LIAM AT LARGE

and published by Corgi Books

SQUARE PEG

Joseph McKeown

CORGI BOOKS

SQUARE PEG
A CORGI BOOK 0 552 13328 0

First publication in Great Britain

PRINTING HISTORY
Corgi edition published 1988

For Pat and Joe

This book is set in 10/11 Melior

Corgi Books are published by Transworld Publishers Ltd., 61–63 Uxbridge Road, Ealing, London W5 5SA, in Australia by Transworld Publishers (Australia) Pty. Ltd., 15–23 Helles Avenue, Moorebank, NSW 2170, and in New Zealand by Transworld Publishers (N.Z.) Ltd., Cnr. Moselle and Waipareira Avenues, Henderson, Auckland.

Printed and bound in Great Britain by
Cox & Wyman Ltd., Reading, Berks.

Contents

Chapter
1	Demob Day	7
2	Oh Bonko!	25
3	The Rat Race	44
4	Dinny	60
5	Reunion	70
6	Fate Takes a Hand	86
7	Walking on Eggshells	98
8	A Slight Squall	110
9	Future Planning	122
10	Windfalls	135
11	The Great Day	149
12	Biddy	161
13	P.T. Walla	174
14	Madame Gymnastica	191
15	Home Leave	214
16	St Benedict's	231
17	My Dear Teresa	254
18	Nemesis	267
19	God's Will	284

1

Demob Day

The second of June 1947 was a glorious day in more ways than one, as I drew the curtains in my quarters for the very last time and let the sunshine stream in, the day all servicemen had, and would dream about until the citizen army was finally disbanded: our personal 'D' day . . . Demob day.

In a semi daze, from a combination of deep sleep and a rough night in the mess the previous night, I sat on the edge of my spartan bed and tried to come to terms with the fact that at long last I had finally got my 'ticket'. By early afternoon I would be a civvy again. A civvy! I was at once elated, despondent and, to be quite honest, just a bit scared. I was leaving institutionalised security, good friends . . . No, almost brothers who had, for seven long years, shared all that they had with me, even, in times of dire stress, their very lives. Suddenly I had the odd feeling of not wanting to go, and gave myself a private telling off. Don't be so damned daft, I told myself irritably, of course you want to go. You want to be home, don't you? Damn it all man, you've thought of little else since you came in, same as everyone else. Come, on, for God's sake, take your finger out and don't be so flamin' daft, will yeh?

'Ah yes,' an anxious voice, deep inside me, answered, 'it's all very well. I know I want to go home, but what about a job, eh?'

'Oh come off it,' insisted the first voice, 'you've got a job and you know it!'

'Y'mean the railway? You know damned well I mean the railway. They've kept your job open for you, haven't they? What more d'you want? Jam on it?'

'Porterin! I want something a bit better than that after this lot, mate.'

Back came the disturbing voice in a flash. 'And who the hell d'you think you are? King Tut? Don't kid y'self, mate. You've nowt much to offer in Civvy Street, so don't get cocky. You're not the only one comin' out, y'know, so stop feelin' sorry for y'self. Do as you've always done, just flamin' well gerron with it, OK?

Breakfast in the mess enhanced rather than diminished my mental conflict, as my fellow sergeants pulled my leg unmercifully. Then followed a round of the camp, handshakes, good wishes, and open envy that I should be the lucky one to go. My final interview was with the CO, to wish me luck and throw me a broad hint that the Army offered a great career, if I cared to sign on the dotted line for the full twenty-one years. The pick-up was at the guardroom where, with three companions, I slung my kit into the truck, and with a final nostalgic look round, we left.

I was surprised and disappointed at my state of mind as we drove away. Nor, apparently, was I alone in this. My companions seemed no happier than myself, and it was a silent journey to the station. However, the mood changed dramatically, thank God, as we boarded the train. It was packed and everyone, by the sound of it, in an advanced state of demobitis, as we picked up speed for York and our final release.

Well-oiled, and with happiness spreading rapidly throughout the boisterous compartments, the final arrival in the great city became the biggest Sunday school outing I had ever been on. Eternal friendships, which would last but a few hectic hours, were sworn as the beer flowed freely throughout the journey. But as we quickly found out when the train stopped and

8

we tumbled out, we were not civilians yet, as MP's and Army Transport staff rounded us up and herded us into waiting trucks. Minutes later Red Caps and their acolytes eased us into the huge hall for documentation and on to Aladdin's cave beyond. This cavernous kitting-out section was festooned with garments of every description and filled with chattering, half-dressed troops, trying on the unfamiliar clothes. Never in all my life had I seen so many clothes, with uniformed 'shop assistants' trying their damnedest to satisfy their 'customers'. There were suits galore, and in any colour you wanted, provided it was either some shade of brown or blue, and double-breasted. Over-coats were available in the same colour scheme, plain or belted, mackintoshes, boots, shoes, shirts, every-thing and, with the sales talk, there went a constant warning as we neared the end of the line: Watch out for the spivs when you get outside. They'll skin yeh!

'What's all this, then?' I asked the sergeant in charge of the footwear section.

He grinned. 'You'll see 'em,' he warned. 'They're there every day, tryin' to kid blokes into partin' with their demob kit.'

'You're jokin'.'

He shook his head. 'You'll find out, mate. They're on to a bomb there, I'll tell yeh. You flog it to them and they go straight on the black market and skin some other poor sod. They've got to be on a winner, haven't they?'

'What are they offerin'?'

He looked at me in surprise. 'You're not partin', are yeh? I've told yeh, they'll skin yeh.'

I winked. 'Not if you can get me a spare box they won't.'

He laughed. 'Got yeh. You won't be the first. 'Look,' he added, 'I'll slip you one at the end of the queue, OK?'

A thought occurred to me as I tried on my new shoes. 'By the way, do they open the boxes on the spot?'

9

He shook his head. 'Not as far as I know. No time. The scuffers would 'ave 'em. Any road, they know what's in them, don't they?'

I grinned happily. 'Do they now?' I replied with a wink. I felt a presence looming near me and looked up to see a tall, ginger-haired RE corporal. He tapped the issuing sergeant on the shoulder.

'Cin yeh no' get one fer me, Sarge?' he asked in a broad Scots accent.

'Sorry Jock,' replied the sergeant, 'I daren't. I'm still in, y'know. I can only do one now and then.' The corporal's face fell.

I gave him a wink as he looked down at me. 'Don't worry, Jock. We'll split it, OK? Have you got anythin' to put in it to make the weight?'

'O aye,' he said, delightedly reaching into his kitbag.

I laughed. 'Right, you're on, then. You take my box on the way out and I'll flog the duff one.'

'Right y'are then,' he replied delightedly, as I turned to the sergeant.

'What are they offerin', Sarge?' I queried.

He shrugged. 'Dunno really. Ten, fifteen, twenty quid. Depends what you can screw them for I suppose.'

'Hae Jimmay,' broke in my new friend, who seemed to call everyone Jimmay! 'Ye'll no mind if I screw 'im, will yeh? — After all, he'll no expect a bargain frae a Scotsman, will 'e?'

We burst out laughing. 'You're right mate, he won't. 'Look,' I added, 'you'd better stick your name on your box, otherwise we'll get the whole damned lot mixed up, and my kit sure won't fit you, will it?'

He looked down from his six foot two and agreed.

'Oh by the way,' interrupted the sergeant as I packed my snazzy blue suit and matching overcoat, 'if anyone asks about the spare box – yeh don't know me, OK?'

We nodded agreement and prepared the 'spare'. Safely packed with what we could find, and the weight

10

matched to a nicety, we picked up our kit, passed through the final documentation and stepped out into the brilliant sunshine. According to plan, I hung back with our boxes while Jock, with kitbag and official cardboard box, sallied forth. He had not gone ten paces when a sleek, brilliantined figure accosted him. A heated discussion followed. A couple of times he made to move off and each time the bloke grasped his arm. At last money changed hands and Jock, face serious, walked off. I met him round the corner, a broad grin on his face.

'How'd it go?' I queried, handing him his own box.

He held the money up triumphantly. 'He'll no be pleased when he opens it,' he said gleefully, counting ten one pound notes into my hand. 'We'll hae a wee dram to celebrate,' he announced.

I looked at him apologetically. 'Sorry Jock, I don't drink.'

He gazed at me, shocked. 'Yeh dinna drink? Nae I canna believe that . . . Not even a wee dram?' he continued coaxingly. I hesitated. 'Ah come on, Jimmay, we'll nae see each other agin . . . An' it's his bawbees we're spendin'. Come on, ye must celebrate afore ye gae hame.' Still I hesitated. 'My word on it,' he added solemnly, 'I'll nae ask yeh t'have more than one.'

I grinned. What the hell, I thought, it's Demob day.'

He grinned hugely as I capitulated. He kept his word and only asked me to have one, but I couldn't let him buy me one and not treat him back, could I? So I had another, and so it went on, and I'm damned, even now, if I can remember just how and when we did part, except that I found it difficult to sing, as I walked with a kitbag on one shoulder and a large brown box tucked under my arm. I often wondered whether Jock remembered. I would dearly have liked to see the spiv's face when he opened it up. Still, there was nothing wrong with the box!

11

*   *   *

My memory of York as a city is a complete blank, but I was happy when I stood in the bows of the ferry boat, with the cool Mersey breezes gradually clearing away any fuzziness, watching the familiar sights of the river. This was the part of the journey home that I always loved, crossing the river, for, as the brown waters slid beneath the keel I knew that home was the next stop. But this time it was special. This time I would not have to go back. This time, with fifty-six glorious days' leave to come, I could come to grips with the future . . . But the doubts would return.

Fifteen minutes after the boat tied up, I was outside our back door. I knew exactly what the scene would be indoors, for it would be visiting day. Aunts Min and Sarah would be there for sure, drinking tea and putting the world to rights. Who else might be there I wasn't sure, but they would, without doubt. I slipped quietly into the yard and it wasn't until I opened the back kitchen door that they heard me. The scene as I came into the kitchen was exactly as I had pictured it. Mam rose with a cry of delight as I came through the door and gave me a big hug. Aunt Min, more like a Toby jug than ever, beamed as she struggled to rise. Waving her down I crossed the kitchen, kissed her podgy cheek, then turned to the doom-laden oracle of the family, Aunt Sarah, sitting as usual bolt upright in the hard-backed chair, to kiss her leathery, unresponsive cheek.

'There,' said Mam as I straightened, 'get that down you.' I smiled as I took the proffered cup and sat on the end of the sofa. Now I knew I was home.

'Well, what are yeh gonna do then?' Aunt Sarah's blunt question caught me with the cup half-way to my lips.

'Oh for God's sake Sarah!' snapped Mam. 'Give him a chance will yeh? He hasn't even unpacked his things

12

yet, woman.' She was obviously annoyed. I noticed, with a slight shock, the greying hair, the age lines beginning to creep about her eyes and mouth.

Aunt Sarah sniffed aggressively. 'I was only askin',' she said in a hurt tone. 'After all, there's a lot of'm comin' out now, y'know.'

Mam picked up the pot irritably for a refill. 'Of course there's a lot comin' out!' she snapped, taking her eyes off Aunt Min's cup as she poured, and wetting the cloth as she missed it. 'There,' she added, 'now look what you've made me do.'

The slight panic that ensued as Aunt Min expertly wiped the cloth, then pushed a saucer underneath to stop any stain on the table, gave me a breathing space. In the euphoria of arriving home, work had been the furthest thought from my mind, and I might have known from experience that the point would come up early, but not this early.

Aunt Min, ever the soul of diplomacy, turned to her sister-in-law. 'Honest Sarah,' she said peevishly, 'you get worse, you do. Why don't yeh let the lad settle down a bit? 'E 'asn't 'ardly got 'is flamin' 'at off yet. Anyroad,' she added before Aunt Sarah could reply, 'he's got a good job, 'asn't he?'

'Oh?' replied Aunt Sarah, thin sandy eyebrows raising in surprise. 'And where's that then?'

'You know damned well Sarah. The Railway, that's where. He left there to join up, didn't 'e? Aye,' she continued reflectively, 'he could have been exempted there if he'd wanted to, y'know. That was one of them there, y'know . . . er . . .'

'Reserved occupations,' I broke in helpfully, as she floundered.

'Aye that's it, reserved what'sit . . .'

'Yes,' broke in Mam, 'and I'll never know why he didn't take it neither.'

I shifted uncomfortably. The memory of the arguments when I joined up were still clear to me. I tried to

13

edge the conversation off this old family wound and put my foot straight in it again. 'Ah well,' I said half pleadingly, 'y'know why I went, Mam.'

'No I damned well don't,' she snapped.

'For meself,' broke in Aunt Sarah in a pious tone, 'I thought you were daft, I . . .'

Aunt Min, as always, leapt to my aid. 'Alright Sarah!' she snapped irritably, 'that's all in the past. What's done's done. He's home safe and that's all that matters. You can't put old heads on young shoulders at a time like that. Anyroad, you've got somethin' t'talk about, you 'ave. Your Alf did the same thing in the last lot, so you've got no room to talk, 'ave yeh?'

'Aye,' replied Aunt Sarah in a sepulchral tone, 'an' look what 'appened to him. Snuffed it on the Somme, an' 'er with a new baby!'

What she didn't say was that she and Uncle Matt had been left holding that very sick baby when its mother died within six months of her husband, and a very heavy burden it had proved for them, with my cousin Alf, several years older than me, in permanent bad health. Not that his burden got him down, not Alf. He was a born optimist and as happy as his surrogate mother was miserable.

'Ah yes, well you're right there Sarah,' replied Aunt Min soothingly. 'But that's life. What's done can't be undone. I suffered too y'know.'

Aunt Sarah looked at her apologetically. She had momentarily forgotten that Aunt Min's husband hadn't come back either. 'Sorry Minny, I forgot.'

'Oh that's alright,' she answered magnanimously, 'forgerr'it. The main thing is,' she added, 'Li did get 'ome, thank God, and, he's got a job t'go to, 'aven't yeh Li?'

I nodded unenthusiastically. I didn't fancy portering at all, and that's all I would get if I went back. No thanks, poor wages, lugging goods about all day, touching the forelock to the odd passenger who might deign to tip me a couple of coppers. No thank you, I thought savagely, they could stuff that, and for once I agreed with Aunt Sarah when she replied with an authoritative sniff.

'He won't settle at no railway, not now 'e won't, not after gallivantin' about all these years.'

Aunt Min, ever ready to defend me, bridled. 'Course he'll settle, won't yeh Li?' I shrugged non-committally. 'He's not daft y'know,' she continued. 'It's a good job is that. Once you're there, you're there for life, an' that's nothin' t'sneeze at these days, I'll tell yeh.'

Not for me, I thought. But Mam saved me from answering. 'Come on,' she ordered, 'get your tea. I'll go and get some more biscuits.' Before sitting down again she brought me another cup of tea, giving me an old-fashioned look as she handed it to me. 'You are goin' back there aren't yeh?' she queried.

I hesitated. 'Well, y'know . . .'

Concern crossed her face. She smoothed her already neat hair absently, and by the action I knew she was worried. I felt guilty.

'They did make your wages up, y'know Li, when you first joined up . . . And the job is waitin' for you. It's only fair now, isn't it? I mean they have kept it open.'

I felt terrible as I gazed miserably at her. I didn't want to hurt her, but I knew damned well I wanted something a bit better if I could. I fenced, and silently cursed Aunt Sarah. All my plans for when I came home, and what I would do, had gone straight up the creek, all because of one damned silly question. I sipped in silence for a moment as she waited for my answer.

'Well, I've still got all my leave to go yet, Mam. It's a bit earl . . .'

'Oh I know all that, I'm not saying there's any rush like but, y'know—' She left it unfinished but I knew perfectly what she meant. But how could I tell her I didn't want to go back into a rut from which I might never escape? She just wouldn't understand. To her

15

and everyone else in the family it was a good job, something that before the war had been beyond price. I didn't want to commit myself, and took the coward's way out.

'Don't worry y'self, Mam. It'll be alright. Just let me get my bearings for a while. I'll see to everything, honest I will.'

Aunt Sarah noticed my hesitation with glee. 'There,' she said triumphantly, 'I told yeh, didn't I?' Her face beamed as all her worst fears seemed to be realised. 'They'll all be like this y'know, unsettled like. It's the war y'know, always the same,' she added authoritatively.

I could have kicked her as Mam's face showed worry again. Why the hell couldn't she keep her mouth shut?

Aunt Min stepped straight in. 'Luk Sarah,' she snapped, 'it's none of your flamin' business. He knows what 'e's doin'. You just leave 'im alone.'

I was grateful to her, but it was all too late. Mam, already worried and edgy at this unexpected obstacle to her desire to see me settled, still stood waiting for an answer. I could hardly refuse to go back, but neither was I ready for that kind of a decision, and anyway I just didn't want to go back there. I gazed at Aunt Sarah, willing her to shut up, but no, with the sensitivity of a bulldozer she ploughed on regardless.

'Well,' she continued, 'stands to reason doesn't it? 'E's seen somethin' different with all this gallivantin', an' it's unsettled 'im. Wants somethin' better, that's what he wants.' I was in complete agreement with her. That was precisely what was up with me, although I daren't say so. 'After all,' she added, 'he is a sergeant, y'know!' With this clincher to her argument, she shrugged her thin shoulders and rested her case.

I glanced at my sergeant's stripes. She could be right. Maybe I did fancy myself a bit. However, what I thought was irrelevant just then, because Mam stood there like a bird of ill omen, waiting for an answer, and I knew she wouldn't wait too long.

'Well?' she said, her tone a mixture of sorrow and anxiety.

Again I fenced. 'Well what?'

She grimaced. 'Well, are you goin' or aren't yeh? That's what.'

I looked at her pensively. I knew she was anxious, and felt a traitor. She was right of course, it was a good job, steady, pensionable and safe ... But that was seven years ago! Life had changed, I had changed. I had seen and wanted better.

'Well?' the word came out like a bullet. She was at the end of her patience.

I was about to capitulate when Aunt Min, glancing at the clock over my head, clapped her hand to her mouth. 'Jesus!' she gasped, 'luk at the time.'

Mam was also shocked and all thoughts of me and my problems were momentarily forgotten. I breathed a sigh of relief at the sudden activity. Aunt Sarah, with her hat always on, was soon ready, but poor Aunt Min was definitely not built for speed.

'Hey Li,' she called as she struggled in the chair, 'give us a hand, will yeh?' I laughed and dashed across to shove her off the chair. 'I'll be alright now, luv,' she gasped, leaning against the table. 'Once I'm on my plates I'm as right as ninepence.' But her innermost thoughts were saved until I helped her on with her coat, as Mam went into the back kitchen. 'Now don't upset y'mam,' she whispered. 'You'll never know how she's worried about you these past years. Now you just go down there tomorrer, even if you don't take the job, alright? She's not daft, y'know. Promise now?' I nodded. She prodded me good-naturedly in the ribs as we walked down the tiny hall. 'Now don't you take any notice of that one,' she added, nodding at Aunt Sarah who was just going through the door. 'Guaranteed to put 'er foot in it she is.'

I laughed quietly as we caught up with her. 'OK Aunt Min, don't worry. Everything'll be alright, honest.' I turned as I heard the back door bang. 'That's me dad, I'd better go.' She nodded, and waddled down the path, stopping as I called after her not to forget to keep off the beer. 'It'll only make you deaf!'

She responded in the usual way to this normal parting advice from me, by cupping her hand over her ear . . . 'Y'what?' she shouted with a grin. In high good humour she joined a scowling Aunt Sarah.

I closed the door and dashed back to greet Dad with a mixture of quiet excitement and anxiety. After a rough time with the women I hoped he wouldn't broach the same subject, at least not yet. Filthy dirty from the shipyard, he was half-way through stripping his boiler suit off when he stopped to greet me.

'Hi yeh!' he said, holding his hand out with a grin. 'You're 'ome then?' He leaned back to inspect me. 'You've lost a birra weight!' he opined.

I grinned but said nothing as he removed his overalls and turned to the sink to wash. Behind, me mam was busy at the stove getting his dinner out. She passed no comment over the job, but I knew he would as soon as he was settled, and he wouldn't be so easy to turn aside.

Within minutes all three of us were sitting at the table, a bad sign in itself because Mam never sat down to a meal with us. She was usually too busy in and out of the kitchen, seeing to everyone else. I stabbed spasmodically at my plate, waiting for the question I knew must come. It did, as Dad sliced a sausage with the concentration of a surgeon.

'What're yeh gonna do then?' he asked, looking up. Mam, cup half-way to her lips, sat silent, an anxious look in her eyes.

'Well y'know, I'm er . . . Well I've only . . .'

'He's goin' down to the Railway tomorrow, aren't yeh?' she broke in, without taking her eyes off me.

Hell! I thought, here we go again! 'Well er, I thought like er . . .'

'You don't seem very keen,' he said, taking a slice of bread, with a sidelong look at me. I shrugged.

'He isn't,' confirmed Mam, sweeping a few invisible crumbs off the table with her hand, a sure sign of irritation with her.

I braced myself as he looked at her, then nearly fell off the chair in surprise.

'What's all the rush about?' he asked her quietly.

She gazed at him, forehead furrowed. 'What d'yeh mean?' she demanded.

'What I say,' he replied evenly. 'He 'asn't been 'ome five minutes, 'as 'e, so what's the rush?' I could have kissed him as she rose irritably and stalked into the back kitchen. Thank God he was looking at his plate and missed her expression. 'Anyroad,' he continued, 'let's 'ear all about it, y'know, how they demob yeh an' all that. Must've felt funny comin' out after all that time.'

I smiled. He would never know how funny it felt, but I was more than happy to launch into everything that had happened. This was how I had pictured my homecoming, and my happiness was complete when Mam, still annoyed but knowing Dad too well to push her questions, joined us at the table with a fresh cup of tea. For an hour or more we sat talking and laughing as I regaled them with the details of the day; but then, with the meal over and the table cleared, Dad made himself comfortable in his chair, and with a Woodbine glowing between his fingers, the question of the future again reared its head. This time I knew there would be no escape. The trouble was, I didn't really know what I wanted to do, myself.

'You're goin' down there, then?' he asked.

'Course 'e's goin' down,' broke in Mam, leaning on her elbows at the empty table. 'It's only fair, isn't it?'

'What d'yeh mean, only fair?' he queried.

'Well,' she replied with a look at me, 'they made 'is wages up when 'e first went in, didn't they? They've kept their jobs open an' everythin'. Of course it's only fair he goes back, isn't it?'

'Oh aye,' he answered thoughtfully, 'I'll go along with yeh there. But there's a bit more to it than that, luv.'

'What are yeh talking about?' she demanded in surprise, as I looked from one to the other, amazed.

I never dreamt he would take this attitude. Prudently I kept my mouth shut in case I put my foot in it.

'Well,' he said flatly, 'he's norra lad now, is 'e?'

'What the 'ell's that got t'do with it?' she snapped exasperatedly. 'It's a regular job, isn't it? What more can 'e ask for?'

'Oh yeah, I'll give you that . . . But it's his life, isn't it? It's up to him what 'e does, not us. Anyroad,' he continued, as she gazed at him in astonishment, ''e's got plenty of time yet — aven't yeh?' he added, turning to me.

'Oh yeah,' I replied enthusiastically, 'fifty-six days. I can even rejoin at my old rank if I do it before that's up, I . . .' I stopped in horror as their whole attitude suddenly changed and they looked at me in shocked surprise.

'Y'what!' cried Mam.

I could have kicked myself. It would break their hearts if I went back. I back-pedalled rapidly. 'Ah I was just kiddin' Mam, honest. I wouldn't join up again,' I lied, 'not unless I was desperate, like.'

Dad looked at me thoughtfully. I wasn't kidding him. 'Oh I don't know so much,' he said quietly, 'I've gorr'an idea you like the life. You seem to, anyway . . . We're not daft y'know.'

'No, honest Dad, I want to settle, no kiddin'. It's just a bit strange that's all.'

A fleeting smile crossed his craggy face. 'I'll believe yeh,' he said disbelievingly. 'But still an' all, I think your mam's right. It might be just as well if you went and had a quiet luk round the station and see how you feel. You don't have t'go back to the Railway but, as your mother says, they've been fair, and it is a steady job. You could do worse, y'know.'

I looked at him in alarm at the sudden change of tack.

He caught my expression and waved his hand at me. 'Oh don't worry lad, we won't push yeh. As I said, it's up to you, then if yeh don't fancy it, well, fair enough. But think about it. It might be worth havin', while you're lookin' round for somethin' else.'

I nodded doubtfully. Oh, I knew what a steady job meant to them, alright. Whole families had gone through sheer hell before the war, because nobody could land one. I had no illusions about that.

'But then again,' he continued before I could make any comment, 'you're young. You did well in the Army with yeh stripes, so it's only natural you want t'get on if yeh can. I'd be the same meself.'

I gave him a grateful look. At least he was trying to understand, but Mam, ever practical, gave a disgusted cluck.

'That's all very well!' she snapped. 'But 'e's got no trade, no nothin' t'get a good job, has 'e?'

I looked from one to the other as they began to get a bit irritable.

'Well 'e's not daft, is 'e?' he snapped back.

Her answer came back pat. 'I know damned well 'e's not daft,' she replied in growing exasperation, 'but 'e's got no certificates to prove 'e's not daft, 'as 'e?'

There was no answer to that one. As usual, she had hit the nail dead centre, and that was my problem. Oh yes, I had some fancy ideas alright. I knew I wanted something better than a dead-ender, but what? I could just imagine myself going for an office job. The interviewer need only ask me one question to sink me without trace! 'What are your qualifications?' Exit Liam!

For the first time since the subject came up, I felt

21

uncertain. If only I could have been like Declan, my late brother-in-law, with a degree. Poor old Declan. I fell silent.

'What yeh thinkin' about?' asked Dad curiously.

'Oh, just about what me mam said, y'know, qualifications and that. Tell you the truth I was thinkin' about Declan. Oh by the way, when is our Teresa coming home?'

Mam shrugged 'Tomorrow, I think. She knows you're out this week so you can bet your boots she'll be home as soon as she can get.'

I grinned. Teresa and I had always been close. 'How is she?'

Again Mam shrugged, her mobile face changing as the conversation got round to my youngest sister. 'Not at all well, Li. To tell you the truth, I don't think she'll ever be the same again, God help her.'

Dad's eyes dimmed a little as she spoke, and I knew the hurt was gnawing at him again as it did to all of us. Poor Teresa! Fate had certainly used a double-edged sword against her in the 1941 blitz, less than a year married to one of the nicest blokes to come out of Trinity College, Dublin. It had been a strange and unlikely story of love for a lowly housemaid and a man beyond her class. She had left her service in Dublin because she knew the vast difference between them. But Declan had followed her, taken digs in the town, and pursued her with relentless determination. No one had given them a cat in hell's chance of success, but their feelings were deep. They married and bought a house, the first in the family to have owned a house and, with his background, Declan had easily landed a good job in Liverpool. Their future seemed assured and strewn with happiness, but fate decided otherwise. I can still remember vividly the terrible frustration I felt as I sat crouched in a dug-out, far away in a strange land, reading Dad's letter months after the event. Declan had been killed on his way home from

22

work on the Liverpool side, by an aerial torpedo that took practically a whole street and countless others with him.

But that was only the start. The baby Teresa carried, and to which everyone looked forward with excitement and pleasure, was stillborn. But still fate would not relent, for within a week of the tragic birth, as she stayed home in Mam's safe hands, her own house was blown to smithereens in another raid. She never recovered properly. A suspected childhood weakness in her heart reappeared, minor problems built up into major ones, until she was but a caricature of her former self. But one thing she did not lose — her spirit. The present break with Uncle Mick in Manchester would do her a power of good, but I would be glad when I could wrap my arms round her again and see for myself just how she was.

'Well,' said Dad heavily, breaking in on my sombre thoughts, 'there's not much we can do about it. God's will, I suppose.' Then, with unaccustomed bitterness in his voice he added savagely, 'An' a bloody fine sense of justice he's got, too!'.

'Pat!' ejaculated Mam in a shocked voice, 'That's blasphemous.'

'Aye, maybe,' he replied sombrely, 'but they didn't deserve that, did they?'

Knowing he would only get upset, I changed the subject hastily to my other sister and her family. Both of them cheered up at once as they described the antics of my tiny niece Patricia, the apple of Dad's eye, and Patrick, just a couple of years older than her. According to Mam he could charm a bird off a tree, while Seamus, the oldest of their three children by some years, seemed to have retained his position as the family 'buggeroo'. As Mam said, he was the 'other end' of his father, my squat and fiery brother-in-law, Jimmy.

'Are yeh goin' round there t'night?' asked Mam, 'Kids'll be disappointed if yeh don't, y'know.'

23

I hesitated. If I didn't go round and see my brother first he'd only take the hump. Dad laughed when I said so, then issued a warning to keep off politics when I did see him. According to Dad he was so far left these days, it was a wonder he didn't fall off. I promised to keep off the subject, but Mam had a warning too.

'And keep off unions too,' she reminded me. 'Y'know what 'e's like.'

It was a warning I didn't really need. I knew my brother Con only too well. On one of my very few leaves we had parted brass rags on the subject. With promises made, and anxious to see the children's faces when I gave them their presents, I rose to go.

Mam stopped me. 'Aren't you gettin' changed?' she asked, pointing to my uniform.

I laughed. 'Why should I? I've worn it long enough haven't I?'

Dad gave me a quizzical look. 'What about yeh demob suit?' he asked. 'You're a civvy now, y'know.'

I grimaced. 'No thanks, I'd feel funny in that. I'll wait 'till I've had a few dummy runs in it. I feel more at home in this.'

'Please y'self,' he replied equitably. 'Don't be too late, will yeh? We'll have a talk about the Railway when you get back, if yeh like. It's up to you.'

I had hoped that the matter was dead for the present, but it wasn't. I shrugged. 'OK then, see you later . . . Tarrar.'

2

Oh Bonko!

I felt bug-eyed and weary as I strolled with relentless determination towards my old station. I didn't want to go, but it was all part of the deal I had struck with Dad the previous night. Never one to stay up late, I had been surprised when I returned to find him alone, except for a fresh pot of tea, two cups and a gleam in his eye.

'Where's Mam?' I asked unnecessarily.

'She's gone up. Thought we'd have a natter if you're not too tired.'

And what a natter it was. We went through the pros and cons of my possible future with a fine tooth comb. He didn't push, he didn't criticise. With just a word here and there he listened intently, then came the questions, and after a while the comments, until I had a fair idea of which end up I was. I went to bed painfully aware of my academic shortcomings in the way of any ambitions for a better life.

Perhaps the most surprising thing was that Dad had felt exactly as I did now. He had always wanted what I now wanted, but for him it had simply been a non-starter. For me, however, the game was wide open, if I had the will to work at it. The only thing he actually baulked at was a return to the Army. For reasons that I was well aware of I knew that, deep down, he hated soldiers. The war was different, but now it was peacetime the hate and distrust had returned. But even on this he was more flexible than I had ever known him.

If that's what I really wanted, then so be it, it was my life. He also knew that there I was in charge of something,. however small, and it fulfilled in many ways my niggling desire to escape the rut. The decision, he emphasised, would be mine, and no one elses. I would also, he reminded me, have to come out sometime and face Civvy Street.

I had much to think about as I walked; but first, the station master! That was all part of the deal. Dad, like Mam, was a great believer in fair play.

I was still musing as I walked through the great arched gateway and into the cavernous gloom beyond. The noise was appalling, and the stench of oil and grease assailed my nostrils as I stopped reflectively under the station clock and looked miserably around me. On the rare leaves I had had during the war, this battered, bomb-wracked building, less than a mile from home, had seemed like the gateway to Shangrila, but now, with not a familiar face in sight, and with the prospect of spending the rest of my working life there, it suddenly took on the forbidding aspect of a prison.

The long, half-glazed roof, still open to the sky over the greater part of its length from bomb damage, its smoke-blackened girders seemed even blacker than I remembered them. The platforms, once so spick and span under the eagle eye of old Benyon the station master, were now littered with debris. The white lines, painted along the platform edges to assist passengers during the blackouts, had mouldered to a dirty yellow. Even the trains themselves, once swarming with cleaners the moment they came to rest after a journey, were now grubby and unkempt. I wandered, unchallenged by any ticket collector, on to Number One platform, where I had spent so many happy hours. Now it was a dump!

'Train's gone, mate.'

I turned as the gruff voice behind me crashed into my thoughts. God! I thought, gazing at my informant, it's a good job old Benyon's not about. This bloke's feet wouldn't touch the floor on his way to the office! One hand in his pocket, cigarette hanging from the corner of his mouth, uniform cap on the back of his head and stains on his jacket, he looked a sight.

With little sign of animation, he gazed at me through bleary eyes. 'Gone,' he repeated, rolling the cigarette from one side of his mouth to the other.

'Yeah, so I see,' I replied with a glance at the empty line. He shrugged, turned, and coughed his way down the platform. Bloody hell, I thought as I watched him go, this place has gone down the nick and no mistake! I did a quick calculation as I watched him stagger away. If I came back to work, I was liable to be stuck here or somewhere like it until I was sixty-five. Flippin' hech! I thought. Thirty-seven years! Mentally I recoiled. Oh no, not on your flamin' nelly. But for my promise to Dad, I would have walked out there and then. Deeply despondent, I eased my way towards the clock to have a quiet smoke. Minutes after stubbing the dog-end out under a highly polished boot, I headed for the station master's office.

The interview was short and to the point. After a wait of nearly ten minutes, I was ushered into the august presence of the great man. If my seven years experience of hairy sergeant majors was anything to go by, this feller — tall, thin, and with wispy red hair atop an irritable face from which two deep blue eyes stared suspiciously — was a right 'backstud'. He hadn't been born, he'd obviously just been issued! By long habit I stood automatically to attention while he drummed his long fingers and stared silently at me from behind his littered desk.

'Ex-service staff I gather?'

I nodded. 'Sullivan, sir.' I gave him my details.

A curt nod to one of the clerks produced my file from another room. I winked at one of the girls who were present. She tittered, drawing a frown from the boss as

27

he thumbed impatiently through my file, then glanced at me without warmth. If I hadn't had my cap still on, and no escort, I'd have sworn I was on a charge.

'Porter I see?'

'Yes sir.'

He gazed at my file, then stabbed it with his finger. '1937!' he snapped.

I looked at him puzzled. 'Sir?'

'1937,' he repeated irritably. 'You were on a disciplinary charge, insulting a passenger.'

I remembered the incident well. The passenger had been a well-dressed toff of about my own age at the time, the sod! I hadn't really told him off, I just told him the truth, that was all. I was still on the carpet, though. I remained silent. There was no answer to that one.

'That won't do Sullivan!' he snapped.

I thought of the porter I had just been talking to. Why the hell wasn't he out there with some real discipline? However, I bit my tongue in case I said too much. He dropped the subject, but evidently wouldn't forget it. He asked me when I was discharged and when I intended to resume duties. The thin eyebrows knitted irritably together as I explained that I still had fifty-six days' leave to come.

He nearly snapped my head off. 'Quite, quite. I'm well aware you have leave, Sullivan, but you haven't answered my question. When do you intend to resume duties?'

It wasn't the questions but the way he put them that got under my skin. He spoke as though I was dirt.

With difficulty I smothered my rising temper. 'Well I don't know exactly at the moment, I just came to let you kn . . .'

'Quite!' he snapped. 'But you have a date in mind, of course?'

I felt the amused glances of the staff around me, and it made me madder. The only thing that prevented me from telling him to stick it where Paddy stuck his ninepence was my promise to Dad. I stuck it out . . . Just.

'Well, I thought I would come and see you just before . . .'

He flicked an invisible speck from his uniform jacket, then impatiently moved his ornate cap, with the magic words STATION MASTER embroidered on it, from one side of the desk to the other. I got the message alright. My job was there, as the Railway had generously promised all staff who managed to dodge the flack and get home in one piece. But he, personally, wasn't interested in me, either as a person or as a future underling. Where a few doubts about not going back had niggled at me when I walked in, his attitude made my mind up. The words were out before I could stop them.

'I don't think I'll bother,' I said, surprised at my own calmness.

He glared at me, then flushed angrily in the shocked silence around us. Confident now, I stood myself at ease and looked straight into the cold eyes as he spoke.

'I would remind you, Sullivan, that . . .'

With nothing to lose I stopped him short. 'Mr Sullivan now, sir!'

His mouth thinned into a straight line before he spoke. 'I would remind you Mr Sullivan,' he began slowly, 'that I am the sta . . .'

I smiled in quiet elation. There was damn all he could do to me, and I felt happy for the first time since waking that morning. 'I told you,' I broke in quietly and dropping the 'sir', 'I don't think I'll bother. I've reported back as I was supposed to, but I think I can do better elsewhere. Someone else can have it.'

He fixed me with a ferocious look as I turned to go. It was all heady stuff, but I didn't push it. Instead I smiled, thanked him for his time, then, with a last look at his grim, angry face, walked out on to the station

29

concourse. I felt happy yet scared; I had just cut my own throat as surely as though I had taken a knife to it. The next problem was to tell Mam. Dad would understand, but Mam? . . . I needn't have worried.

Fifteen minutes later I walked into a reception committee headed by Aunt Sarah. One look at my face told them all they needed to know.

'There!' said my aunt triumphantly. 'What did I tell yeh? I knew it.' She looked and sounded like Cassandra finally getting a prediction right. But what did surprise me was that neither Mam nor Aunt Min seemed at all surprised. In fact there was a hint of a smile round Mam's mouth as she poured me a cup of tea. I looked at her and shrugged.

''Ere, get this down yeh,' she said. 'You've been, that's all that matters,' she added, as I took the cup and perched myself on the end of the sofa to await the inquest. Aunt Sarah was at it before I had swallowed the first mouthful. She warned me that I wouldn't get another chance like that.

Aunt Min looked at her, amazed, and spoke without thinking. 'Well,' she ejaculated, 'of all the bloody 'ypocrites! You were the one . . .' She reminded her of what she had said when I first arrived home. Aunt Sarah pursed her lips in retaliation as Mam lost her patience.

'Oh never mind all that!' she snapped. 'What's done's done!' She looked at me. 'What 'appened?' she asked.

I knew from long experience that nothing but exact detail would do, and I obliged. We were still at it half an hour later, when the doorbell went. I slipped down the hall and, opening the door, got a terrible shock. It was Teresa. God, she looked rough! Without a word I wrapped my arms round her and in silence we clung to each other. It had been nearly two years since I had seen her and I was devastated. Always small, petite and full of bounce, she seemed to have shrunk even

30

further, and the blue-grey eyes, so like Mam's, though bright had a vague, haunted look about them. I could have wept.

She must have felt my tension and, still with her arms around me, tilted her head back and smiled at me. 'It's alright, luv,' she said soothingly, 'don't worry. I'm alright, honest I am. Just a bit tired, that's all.'

'Who is it?' Mam's enquiring voice floated to us to break the spell.

'It's our Teresa,' I called back. There was a scramble in the kitchen, and seconds later Mam, quickly followed by the others, were on their feet and waiting at the kitchen door as we entered. My job and I were quickly forgotten.

Despite the shock of Teresa's appearance and my act of Hari Kari over my job, the first official day of my leave, with Teresa home again, was a happy one. From there on, however, as far as I was concerned, things deteriorated rapidly, with only my diminishing leave quota cushioning me from the harsh realities of finding a job. For all the talk of plenty of work about, as I renewed old acquaintances around the town, in my scheme of things there was nothing, just the same old dead-end labouring jobs, and they in turn meant only one thing: into the rut again, and that I didn't want. Within a week I was in the depths, and twice Mam pulled me up short.

'What the hell's up with you?' she asked, as I sat disconsolately staring into space on a miserable, wet day.

'Nothin',' I replied defensively.

'Well!' she snapped back. 'If that's what yeh luk like with nothin' wrong, then Christ 'elp yeh when there is! Now you liven y'self up a bit. You're makin' everybody flamin' miserable. You want t'be 'ome, don't yeh?'

I had looked at her, shocked. 'Of course I want t'be home,' I protested, careful not to upset her. 'Fancy askin' a question like that!' Damn and blast it. Like

31

everyone else in uniform, I had dreamt of nothing else, for God's sake! Then it gradually dawned on me, I was the stranger. They hadn't changed, but I had. The realisation made me feel worse, a traitor even, but it was no use, I'm damned if I could shake it off. And as each day passed, with nothing in sight and problems building up, I missed the old companionship more and more. I missed the nights in the Mess, giving and taking orders, being responsible for something. Even being shot at had its own peculiar excitements.

Not that I didn't have company. The house was, as always, like Crewe station as relatives, friends and neighbours came and went in endless succession. But of my own age group, most were still scattered, and those who weren't seemed different. I hadn't even laid eyes on Dinny who, through his job in the shipyard, had remained at home. But if I knew Din, he'd be round before long.

By Saturday I was at rock bottom, all illusions gone, as I tramped the town in search of something decent. If only Antoinette had been there, everything would have been different. The very thought of her made me fifty times worse. Damn the flaming war! Only for that we would have been married by now, maybe even with a couple of kids. God almighty! What a waste of seven good years. I wondered where she was now. The last I heard of her, she had packed college in and joined the Wrens. With all those hairy matelots around, I wasn't very pleased when she had informed me, and said so. Then, after a few months, with me on the move abroad, the letters stopped coming. I went out on my first and only blinder and that was that; but oh, how I missed her still.

As for Dinny, he must have been raking the stuff in, with overtime and God knows what all. I remember tackling him on embarkation leave, about still being in the shipyard.

'Not been called up yet, Din?' I had queried, as we sat in his favourite pub.

32

He had grinned. 'Doesn't luk like it, does it?'

'Are you gonna join up?'

He had given me a quizzical look. 'Come off it Li, I'm down the Yard aren't I? Navy work, essential y'know.'

'Well I know you're not a flamin' conshie so . . .?

'No,' he had replied with a wink, 'an' I'm no' flamin' daft neither! I tell yeh, I'm on essential work. No good 'avin' sailors with no bloody ships, is it? No Li, if they want me, mate, they'll call me up. I don't mind one way or the other, but if they're waitin' for me to volunteer, they'll wait a helluva long time, I'll tell yeh.'

I hadn't seen hide nor hair of him since. No one knew where he lived, because they had been bombed out, but Dad said he was alright and, according to him, he was quite a leading light in the Union these days. I laughed when Dad told me. Trust Dinny! He was as crafty as a bag of monkeys. As for the rest of my old school mates, well, one or two just didn't make it to their 'tickets' as I had been lucky enough to do, and the rest were scattered God knows where. The more I thought about it the more fed up I got because, despite my diligent search for something decent, time was rapidly running out. A final decision had to be made, whether to stay out and take a chance, or duck back into the safety I knew, with my present rank. I also knew if I did, it would bring great sorrow to Mam and Dad, even though neither of them would say a word to stop me. And Teresa — well, I shuddered to think. Oh God, I thought as I sat in the empty house, why can't I be content?

*   *   *

''Ello, and what are yeh dreamin' about now?' asked Mam. I looked up in surprise as she and Teresa came in through the kitchen door. I hadn't even heard them coming back from Benediction, so lost in thought had I been.

'Thinking about the Army, I'll bet,' opined Teresa as she removed her coat.

'No, no I wasn't, honest,' I lied, not wishing to upset them. 'Just been havin' a quiet read, that's all. Must've dozed off, like.'

'Pull the other one,' suggested Mam sarcastically.

'Where's me Dad?' I asked, changing the subject. I couldn't fool her.

'Gone t'see your Uncle Matt, then they're goin' round to the club for half an hour.' She gave me a long look. 'Thought you'd 'ave come to Benediction with us t'night,' she said with a note of disappointment. I shifted uncomfortably in my chair, trying to find an answer. 'You always used t'go!' she added accusingly. 'You used to like Benediction.'

I looked from her to Teresa. She was right, I used to love it. The nicest service in the Church, but a lot of water had gone under the bridge since then.

'Yeah, you're right. It is a lovely service, but er — well, y'know?' I trailed off lamely. But she knew alright; I wasn't half as holy as I used to be. In fact, to be honest, after what I'd seen I wasn't holy at all!

'Well,' I said defensively, 'I went to Mass this mornin' didn't I?'

Teresa came to my rescue. 'Ah, give him a chance, Mam. He's not settled yet is he?' Mam just gave me a look, then vanished into the back kitchen. She was worried, and I was worried because she was worried.

'What's up Li?' asked my sister quietly, as she came and sat alongside me, 'Fed up?'

I nodded miserably and answered with a question. 'How are you feelin' . . .? Any better?'

She shrugged. 'Oh, don't worry about me Li, I'm alright. Going for some more tests next week. Perhaps they'll sort me out then.'

I gave her hand a squeeze. 'I hope so luv. It must be rotten for you.'

She smiled resignedly then her expression became

34

serious. 'It's you I'm worried about, Li. What's up with you? You seem, oh, I don't know — restless — like a fish out of water. Are you sure you're alright?'

Keeping my voice almost to a whisper in case Mam heard me I told her the truth. 'Honest, luv I'm absolutely cheesed off. There's just nowt t'do. I thought I was goin' to enjoy my leave but, to tell you the truth, I'll be damned glad when it's over and I can get things settled, y'know a decent job. If Antoinette was here it might be different but . . .'

'Yes,' she replied sadly, 'a pity that. She's a lovely girl, I miss her a lot. What happened there, anyway?'

I shrugged and told her what had happened after she joined the Wrens. 'Met someone else, I suppose. I'd nip round and see her Mam but, well, if she is married I'd feel a right charlie, wouldn't I?'

She grimaced. 'You wouldn't be able to see them anyway,' she said.

I looked at her, puzzled. 'Why not?'

'Oh they were bombed out, just after you want abroad.'

I recoiled in shock. 'Oh God no, don't tell me . . .'

She held up her hand to calm me. 'Now don't get yourself all worked up, luv. They weren't killed or anything. Luckily they were out and Antoinette was away. Anyway, ask me mam, she knows all about it. I wasn't too well myself at the time, as you know.'

I gave her hand a squeeze as her eyes misted at her own memories. 'I know, luv, nobody's had it rougher than you.'

She shrugged resignedly. 'It's God's will, Li.' I nodded silently and veered away from the subject. I wasn't seeing eye to eye with God on several subjects at that moment. 'Are you going back Li?' she asked anxiously. 'Mam would be broken-hearted, you know that?' I remained silent. 'Are you?' she persisted.

I held my finger to my lips as I heard Mam filling the tray to bring in, but I couldn't have answered if I'd wanted to because, in shipyard parlance, I didn't know whether I was 'punched, bored, or countersunk.' I had a sudden idea. There was just one member of the old gang I could see. Bonko Armfield. True, he was as thick as two short planks, but he was better than nothing.

'Hey Mam,' I said as she came in, 'does Bonko Armfield still live up the North end?'

'Y'mean young Jimmy Armfield? Yes, as far as I know anyway. Why?'

'Thought I'd nip up there and see him.'

She raised her eyebrows. 'What d'yeh want t'go there for? They tell me it's like a pigsty. Anway it's up t'you, but don't say you weren't warned. Probably at the pub anyway, if I know that lot.'

I looked at her in surprise. 'Does he drink then?'

She laughed. 'Sup it out of a dead man's clog, he would,' she said cryptically.

I changed my mind about going. 'Oh if he's gonna be out, there's not much use goin', then. Still I'll catch him when he comes home from work tomorrow.' They both laughed. 'What's so funny then?'

'Jimmy Armfield workin'!' answered Mam amused. 'He couldn't work in convulsions. You ask our Con. He'll tell you about Jimmy Armfield. Never went in the Army neither, the crafty sod!'

'Yeah well,' I said loyally, 'he's still an old mate. I'll nip round in the mornin' before the pubs open. Might catch him then.'

Mam clucked disgustedly as she poured the tea. 'You'll 'ave t'be bloody quick!' she suggested.

*   *   *

Late next morning with half an hour before the pubs opened, I negotiated the junk-strewn garden and, with the warm sun on my back, knocked gently on the door of Bonko's council house. It was certainly an improvement on his old Dock Road tenement where I had last seen him, although the junk around me didn't augur well for its condition inside, especially the screams of the children percolating through the door. Three times I knocked in growing irritation, gazing at the limp, dog-eared curtains hanging behind the grubby glass, without result. The fourth time I hammered the knocker and the noise inside stopped stone dead. Seconds later Maggie's florid, sweat-streaked face, framed in a halo of tatty hair, appeared round the edge of the half-opened door. Her eyes, deep sunk in the fleshy folds of her face, glared at me suspiciously.

'Well!' she snapped irritably. 'Whaddy yeh want?'

'It's me,' I said, forcing a laugh as I removed my natty new trilby. 'Liam, y'know?' A piercing scream, followed by a heavy thump came from inside, and her face clouded with anger as she turned round.

'Jimmy!' she yelled, 'stop them there bloody kids fightin' will yeh?'

'Ah shurrup,' came Jimmy's voice in reply, 'I'm readin'. Anyroad, 'oo's that at the flamin' door?'

A fleeting homicidal look crossed her face. 'You come'n see f'yerself.' Another scream interrupted her. 'Ooo!' she muttered to herself. 'Those bloody kids. I'll swing for 'em yet . . . Jimmy!' she roared, in a sudden escalation of tone. 'It's wanna yeh mates, come t'the door will yeh?' With the door now fully open in her agitation, I was able to absorb the full effect of her presence. Never a beauty and always generously upholstered, she was now a fat, waddling slut of monumental proportions, with a smell to match.

My heart sank. If this was the doorstep reception I didn't fancy what might follow, but it was too late to turn back now. I was impressed by the sound of Bonko's defiance, although what would happen when I was gone was something else again, from the expression on Maggie's face.

She suddenly got fed up waiting for him to appear and her lips tightened. ''Ang on a minute,' she snapped, and with surprising speed waddled indoors, to be replaced by two unwashed, half-dressed children who, with altercation growing between their parents, gazed at me wide-eyed. With a bang an inner door crashed shut, and a moment later, an artificial beam on his face, Bonko appeared. I was shocked. Never an Adonis, and endowed with just enough sense to come in out of the rain, he had gone even further downhill since I had seen him last. His embryo beer-gut must have cost him a fortune, and already showed signs of expansion, as it peeped cheekily over his low-slung belt.

'Well!' he exlaimed. 'I'll go to our bloody 'ouse. It's you!' With his hand half out to greet me, he stopped as the children crowded round him. 'Gerr'in!' he roared. 'Go on, gerr'in and mind yer own business. Yeh norr'even dressed yet.' The smallest made to protest. 'Git,' he said threateningly. 'Oo,' he continued as they vanished indoors, 'little buggers they are, honest.' His hand came out again and I shook it. 'On leave then?' he enquired.

I shook my head and grinned. 'No. Out now Bonk, coupla weeks ago. Thought I'd drop round, like.'

'Great,' he replied with evident pleasure. 'Come in then, don't stand on the doorstep. I'll get the missus to put the kettle on'

I smiled as I followed him into the fetid front room.

'Hey Maggie!' he shouted as I gazed at the chaotic room. 'Put that there kettle on, will yeh?'

'It's on!' she roared back from the kitchen. 'It's gorra bloody boil, 'asn't it?'

'Well 'urry it up then will yeh? Siddown,' he invited. I made to sit on a dilapidated chair. He reacted in alarm. 'No, no, not there mate. You're liable to go arse over 'ead on that one. It's the kids y'know, little sods. Sit over there on the sofa.'

Watched by four curious faces, ranging from about three to nine years old, I safely negotiated the littered

38

table and sat on the edge of the horsehair sofa and, with two boys and two little girls edging closer, tried to open a conversation. It was murder.

'You're not working then, Jimmy?' I asked, giving him the dignity of his proper name in front of the children.

He grimaced. 'Na . . . Me feet, y'know.'

I glanced at his slippered feet. They seemed alright to me. 'Pity,' I replied sympathetically.

He gave a quick inhalation of breath. 'Oh aye,' he continued, 'fair crease me sometimes Li, you wouldn't believe it mate.'

'Ah,' I said without feeling, 'shame.' From there we moved on to his stomach and another indrawn breath. 'Oh?' I said, without surprise, looking at his beer-gut. 'Plays you up eh?'

His face registered agony. 'Cor bloody 'ell,' he said, 'somethin' cruel Li. You just . . .' He spotted the eldest lad standing quietly facing the wall near the front door. 'Hey Alfie,' he demanded suspiciously, 'what yeh doin' there eh?'

'Nuthin',' replied Alfie without turning.

Jimmy wasn't satisfied. 'If you tear any more of that there bloody wallpaper,' he snapped, 'I'll belt yeh, OK?' With the threat delivered, he was about to turn to me when he spotted the four-year-old girl sitting quietly and knickerless on the floor at the other end of the sofa, gazing at me open mouthed as she assid-uously picked her nose. He frowned angrily. 'Rita!' he shouted. ''Ow many times 'ave yeh bin told about pickin' yeh nose? I won't tell yeh again.'

I smiled to myself. Bonko's *forte* as a lad was just that, picking his nose. Rita stopped, but the quiver on her lips developed into a cry as Maggie came in with the laden tray.

'There!' she said accusingly, elbowing the table debris aside to put the tray down. 'Now luk what you've done. She's cryin'.'

39

Bonko snorted. 'I know damned well she's cryin'. She's always cryin'. Anyroad, gerr'em outside. Lerr'em play in the garden, it'll do 'em good.'

I looked at him, amused. Garden! It was more like an assault course! Maggie began to shoo them out, but as one set the others off crying, the second lad, the image of his dad, objected.

'I wanna butty,' he said belligerently, pushing his luck with a visitor present.

Maggie bent down menacingly, her huge buttocks partly obscuring the view. 'You've just 'ad one,' she hissed.

He persisted. 'I wanna'nuvver one,' he said, lips quivering.

Still bending, she glared at him and bunched her fist. 'You'll gerra thick ear in a minute,' she hissed again. 'Now gerr'out, and quick.' With the remainder of the howling kids he 'got'.

'Hey!' snapped Bonko as she waddled to the door. 'Warrabout the tea?'

She heaved her bulk round and fixed him with a venomous look. 'Warrabout it?' she snapped.

'Well it won't pour it's flamin' self, will it?' he snapped back.

With the youngest child seated comfortably on her bosom, she glowered at him. 'I've only got one pair'f 'ands y'know. You pour it out.' If she had had a neck she would have tossed her head. As it was, she turned like a tank and lumbered through the door, leaving Bonko staring at the empty space. With his authority dented, he levered himself up from the depths of his chair and began to pour.

'Women!' he muttered savagely. 'Honest Li, they get on your flamin' wick. Don't ever get married, mate, it's murder!' I laughed. 'Where was I?' he asked. 'Oh yeah, me stomach. Ooo!' I tried to head him off his complaints without success. 'An' that's not all,' he continued, 'I get this er, whaddy yeh call it, hmn, the doctor did tell me — oh yeah, veteego, that's it, y'know sorta . . .'

'Dizziness?' I suggested helpfully.

'Yeah that's it. Cor blimey, fair chronic it is sometimes.'

'Like when you go to work?'

He missed the sarcasm. 'Yeah, funny isn't it? Don't go out much like, of course, just round t' the pub and the club an' that like y'know.'

'D'you get it then?'

He looked puzzled for a moment, then the penny dropped. He grinned. 'Na, not really . . . Well, they're not far are they?'

I could have kicked the slob, but held my rising temper in check. 'So,' I said evenly, 'what with your feet an' your stomach and the what's it, you can't do much in the way of work then, can you?'

'Na,' he agreed. 'Bloody shame in't it? Mind you Li,' he added, watching my face closely, 'I've 'ad a few days 'ere an' there, like, y'know. Did a coupla weeks with your Con a few months ago, but still y'know,' he added, cheering up a bit, 'when this new National 'ealth what's it starts next year it'll . . .'

'Y'mean this Social Security thing?' I queried.

'Yeah that's it. It'll be great Li — everythin' free! Allowances for the kids, free doctors, new glasses, new teeth and God knows what all else. An' all free! Cor, just right for us, mate.'

Suddenly I felt like banging his head against the nearest wall. I knew I had to get out before I blew. O yes, they would be alright, the lazy sods. I looked at him sprawled in his chair, contentedly smoking his Woodbine, a fat, bovine slob, and thought of some good mates like Tom, cut to ribbons and left to rot in some God-forsaken waddy in the desert . . . For this? I felt my temper rising too quickly for comfort and rose abruptly.

'I'll have to go now Jimmy,' I lied. 'A little job t'do for me Mam.'

41

'Ah, a pity,' he said, half rising. 'I was hopin' we coulda slipped down to the rub-a-dub for a jar like,' he added hopefully.

'Don't drink Jimmy, you know that,' I said with a supreme effort to be pleasant.

'Oh yeah, I forgot,' he replied with regret, as another easy pint slipped from his grasp.

'I'll see you around,' I said heading for the door.

'Pity we didn't know you were comin' Li,' he said apologetically, as I opened it. 'The missus didn't 'ave time to tidy up, like.'

I took a parting look at the shambles behind me as the fresh air swept over me. Tidy up . . . Jesus! I thought, it would take a week to sort out the front room, never mind the rest. I circumvented Maggie standing in the middle of the path as she took the eldest boy by the gansey for something or other.

'Tarra then Maggie, thanks for the tea, luv.' She nodded, glad to see the back of me. If she wasn't, then I was certainly glad to see the back of them. If I knew my people right, there was one helluva row brewing when that door closed again.

Despite the brilliant sunshine I felt at rock bottom again as, head down, deep in troubled thought, I headed home. There was no need for the filth I had just seen, no need whatever! Even in the old days, when things were really bad, it had been very, very few who had let themselves go like that, and even fewer who were not personally clean. The whole damned episode sickened me and, I had to confess, scared me a little. Where, in God's name, was I going to fit in to this brand new world I had come home to? Deep in thought I walked unheedingly, wishing I had never gone to see Bonko. It had depressed me more than ever. I thought of the children, poor little blighters. With parents like that they wouldn't have a cat in hell's chance. Still, the new welfare scheme coming along would see they didn't starve unless, as seemed likely, it was all spent on fags and booze.

I stopped to light a cigarette, and suddenly realised I was nowhere near home. What a daft thing to do, to take a wrong turn in my home town. I laughed to myself as I looked at the vaguely familiar church across the road. Damn, I wasn't even in my own parish. It was St Joseph's, a couple of miles from our church. Instinctively I crossed over and popped in to light the ritual candle. It was deserted, its silence a peaceful balm to my unquiet mind. I said my prayers by habit, without thought or meaning. Gradually the peace and tranquillity laid its gentle hold on me, and my thoughts took on a semblance of order. I calculated calmly that I had about thirty days left in which to set my future course. Maybe, if all else failed I could go back in the Army full time and make a career of it. But what if I did go back and was then posted overseas for several years? Mam and Dad weren't spring chickens any more. If anything happened to them I might never see them again! God, I couldn't have that. If nothing else put me off, that possibility did.

With that out of the way, the challenge was definitely Civvy Street, and it was now! I remembered Mam's advice from the old days: 'When fate's against yeh . . . Spit in its flamin' eye!' God knows, she'd had enough experience of it. I lit three more candles on the way out: one for the family, one for Tommy and Sniffer who wouldn't come back, worst luck, and an extra one for myself, just to make sure I had enough 'spit' for the job. I was sure going to need it.

3

The Rat Race

'Where the divil have you been?' demanded Mam
irritably as I walked into the kitchen.

'Been t'see Bonko' I replied, surprised at her irritation. 'I told you!'

'Aye, I know you did, but 'ave yeh seen the time?
Your dinner was ready hours ago!'

I glanced at the clock and gasped. Two thirty! 'Cor,
flippin' 'ech. I didn't know it was that late. Sorry
Mam.'

'I'm surprised you stayed there all this time,' she
replied as she took my covered dinner out of the oven,
then clucked heavily. 'Look at it,' she continued
disgustedly, as she removed the cover. 'This lot's no
good now.'

I looked at the shrivelled mess. It definitely looked
off, but I objected fiercely when she suggested cooking
something else. 'No, no,' I protested, 'it's my fault. No
need to waste good grub. Just warm it up again, that'll
do me, honest.'

She hesitated as she looked at it. 'No that's OK. I'll
eat it, don't worry.' She laughed as she popped the
re-covered plate back into the oven and turned the gas
on. 'Oh by the way,' she said as she stood up again,
'your Aunt Sarah wants to see yeh.'

I looked at her in surprise. My aunt and I weren't
exactly lovebirds. 'Oh, warrabout?' I asked her as she
came back in with my burnt offering.

She shrugged. 'I dunno. Maybe it's somethin' t'do

with their Alf. Anyway I said you'd pop round in the mornin', alright?'

'Is Alf sick?'

She grimaced. 'Not as far as I know. You're sure that's goin' t'be alright?' she added, pointing at my plate.

I laughed. 'Of course it is. Seen worse in the Army,' I added, spearing a blackened potato. 'It's grub, that's the main thing.' I changed the subject. 'How's Teresa t'day?'

A worried frown crossed her face. 'Well, y'know. she's alright but . . .'

'Now don't worry, Mam,' I replied, hacking at a piece of dried meat. 'She'll be alright, you'll see. The doctors'll fix her up.' She shook her head, unconvinced. 'Anyway I'm home now, so I can take her out now and then, can't I?'

She looked at me quizzically. 'Aye,' she replied, without taking her eyes off me, 'but for how long?'

I tried to simulate surprise. 'What d'you mean?' I asked innocently.

A smile flitted across her face. 'You know damned well what I mean!' she answered. 'You're not settled yet, are yeh? Oh I know. You don't fool me my lad.'

I tried to bluff. 'Ah come on Mam,' I said between mouthfuls, 'of course I am. It's just a bit strange, that's all. Well, it's got to be hasn't it? I'll be alright once I'm fixed up. Don't worry about it now. Promise?'

'No,' she answered bluntly. She paused thoughtfully, then with equal bluntness asked me if I knew what I did want. I hadn't a clue and we both knew it.

I tried to ease her mind and repeated my plea not to worry. 'Look Mam, you've enough on your plate with Teresa, so don't go worryin' about me. I'll make out alright, you'll see.'

She sat down on the other side of the table with a cup of tea. 'How are they round there?' she asked out of the blue. 'Like a pigsty I'll bet?' I nodded agreement. 'I told yeh,' she confirmed. 'The other end of 'er mother, that one, an' Gerty Spencer was always rotten dirty. Oh,' she added with another change of tack, 'have yeh seen Dinny yet?'

'No, not yet. Don't know where they live nowadays, but I'll bump into him, don't worry.'

'I wonder if Con's mentioned to him you're home. He's still in the Yard y'know?'

I told her that Dad had already mentioned it and we went on to discuss this blithe and crafty spirit. She said he was one of the lucky ones to stay in the Yard throughout the war.

'Yeh,' I replied, 'and if I'd known then what I know now, I'd 'ave been right there with him.'

She shook her head. 'Oh no yeh wouldn't. I don't believe that. Anyway,' she added, 'you never liked the place when you were there. Couldn't get out fast enough, could yeh? They tell me he's up to his eyes in union work these days,' she added before I could reply.

I laughed and winked at her. 'Din never gave owt for nowt Mam, you know that. I'll lay ten to one he's got somethin' up his sleeve. He's not one for getting mixed up with union troubles for fun, and that's a fact.'

'Maybe. Good luck to 'im I say, but if he's that well in, perhaps he could get you fixed up.'

I shook my head vehemently. 'No thank you. If I'd wanted t'go down the Yard again, I'd have been there by now. No Mam, I want somethin' with a bit more prospects, y'know, like office work, somethin' like that.'

She frowned heavily. 'An' what the hell do you know about office work?' she asked bluntly.

'Nowt!' I replied with equal bluntness. 'But there's nothin' to stop me tryin', is there?'

'Well,' she answered with a grimace, 'whatever you do, you'll have t'make your mind up, and quick. You haven't got forever y'know!'

She was right. I reckoned I had just about twenty-one days for a decision of some sort, and was glad when the doorbell rang to avoid further awkward discussion. It was Teresa, puffing a bit, but chirpy. Both Mam and I put the same question as she walked in gasping.

'Oh I'm alright,' she said edgily. 'Stop worryin'. Just a bit short of wind. I missed the bus, that's all.'

Mam showed concern, ordering her to sit down and have a cuppa. 'I keep tellin' yeh,' she said as she handed the cup over, 'yeh shouldn't walk so far.'

My sister laughed resignedly. 'Oh Mam, don't fuss, please! God,' she added with a grin, 'anyone'd think I was gonna snuff it any minute!' Mam clucked irritably as she left for the back kitchen and Teresa turned to question me. 'Where have you been?' she asked, as I settled beside her on the sofa. I told her. 'Hmn,' she snorted, 'better you than me, from what I hear. By the way, did me Mam tell you about Aunt Sarah wantin'. . .?'

'Yeah,' I interrupted. 'Any idea warr'it's about?'

She shook her head. 'Dunno. Y'know what Aunt Sarah's like. Said something about Alf digging, I think.'

'Alf . . . Diggin'?' I gasped. 'He can hardly lift a spade, never mind use it . . . Where?'

She shrugged. 'Ice works, I think she said.'

'The ice works? What the hell would he be diggin' in the ice works for? The twit!'

I didn't know it then, but I was just about to enter the rat race again.

*   *   *

As promised, I was there early. Aunt Sarah, for once without her hat on, was having breakfast. Her thin, angular body twisted in the chair as I walked into the kitchen, and for the first time I noticed that her wispy hair was almost non-existent on the top of her skull-like head. She gazed sadly at me.

'Yeh 'aven't gorra job then, yet?' I shook my head, but refrained from expanding. 'Perhaps you can do me a favour, then?' she added.

'I will if I can, y'know that.'

'It's our Alfie,' she continued sorrowfully, ''e's takin' this 'ere flamin' job on. Honest, 'e worries me soul case out, that feller.'

I wasn't surprised at her worry. A semi invalid, with a bad heart only one of his troubles, he was forever taking a dozen and one different jobs on, despite the doctors' warnings. The trouble was, he just didn't like being idle. I told her what Teresa had said about a digging job. She confirmed it.

'But he can't do tha . . .' I began.

'I know bloody well 'e can't!' she interrupted with unusual vehemence.

I had an uneasy feeling about where I was going to fit in in all this, and didn't fancy it one little bit. I wasn't used to digging, either.

'What does Uncle Matt say about it?' I asked.

'Thinks 'e's flamin' crackers . . . Cin yeh give 'im a hand Li?'

I fenced. 'Well, I might get fixed up with a job meself like, might'n' I? I'm lookin' all the time, y'know.' She looked crestfallen and I felt a traitor. In the heavy silence Alf walked in, cheerful as ever.

''Ello,' he said with a grin, 'an' warr're you doin' 'ere then, this time of the mornin'?'

If he thought that she'd sent for me, there would be trouble, I knew. I stepped lightly. 'Oh,' I replied nonchalantly, 'just passin'. Thought I'd drop in, like. Aunt Sarah tells me you've got a job on. That right?'

He forgot all about my frowning aunt as he launched into an enthusiastic description. By all accounts it was a cinch, just a couple of days' work and, according to him, money for old rope. She looked at me worriedly. I

48

was on the spot. Knowing Alf, I didn't want to volunteer, because ten to one it wouldn't be anything like he had described, but I knew she had good cause to worry. He wasn't fit for heavy work and never had been, but he just wouldn't listen. I had no option, despite my misgivings.

'Give you a hand if you like,' I volunteered reluctantly.

'No, you're alright Li. I cin manage it, no problem.'

If looks could have killed he would have dropped dead on the spot. She made to speak.

'Look,' I broke in to prevent a row, 'I'll tell you what Alf, we could nip round there, have a look at the job, then we could have a natter about it. How's that? Give me somethin' t'do anyway, wouldn't it?'

His face lit up. 'Great,' he replied, as Aunt Sarah gave me a grateful look. 'Come on then, it's only round the corner, you'll see. It's a piece of cake. Not diggin' really, just sorta clearin' a cellar out, like.'

Minutes later, having agreed to share the work, we were on our way to inspect the job, and what a job he'd picked! A double hernia job if ever I saw one. One look down the cellar, or what we could see of it, and I began to worry as much as she had. When we opened the trap door leading down to it, there were just two steps visible, the rest was solid junk.

I gazed from Alf to the opening in amazement. 'Bloody Nora!' I exclaimed. 'And how the hell are yeh supposed t'get that out?'

He shrugged without apparent worry. 'Dig into it and barrow it out,' he replied unconcernedly. 'Anyroad,' he added brightly, 'there's a winder under the grid outside. We could chuck some outa there.'

We went round to the cellar window. One glance told me it was impossible to get anything out of that.

'How big is the cellar, anyroad?' I asked as we walked back to the trap.

He mused for a moment. 'Oh, about fifteen foot by

about ten as far as I know, an' about ten foot 'igh I reckon.'

I gasped. 'Cor blimey Alf, that's a helluva lorra junk, isn't it?'

He wasn't impressed. 'Na,' he said airily, 'no problem.'

I could have kicked him. Without success, I tried to talk him out of it, but he was like a mule. He had given his word and he would do it.

'What d'yeh reckon?' he asked.

I told him bluntly. 'You're a mug!' I snapped, knowing I daren't let him tackle it by himself. 'Anyway,' I continued, 'what's it worth?'

'Twenty quid,' he replied enthusiastically.

I couldn't believe it. 'Twenty quid! Yeh kiddin'. Yeh want yeh flamin' bumps read, mate. It's worth more than that.'

'That's not bad for three days' work, Li. Anyway,' he added, 'I gave me word.'

'Three or four weeks, more like,' I retorted scornfully. His face dropped. 'Look Alf,' I said finally, 'I'll give you a hand because if I don't you're gonna bust a gut and you know it.' He nodded disconsolately. 'But first,' I added, 'we're gonna see the boss and up the ante a bit. If I'm gonna get a bloody hernia mate, I want payin' for it, OK?'

He grinned. 'Fair enough boyo, let's go.'

Within minutes, with the agreement that I would do the talking, we faced the short, dapper manager in his office. He wasn't very pleased, but with the option of getting a contractor in, which would have cost a lot more, he finally agreed to twenty each, then put the screws on.

'That includes white-washing too, y'know.'

I looked at Alf shaking his head. 'Did you agree to white-washin', Alf?'

'Not bloody likely!' he snapped back. We would clear it as agreed, I told the furious manager, but the white-washing would come separate if we decided to do it at all. I didn't trust him as far as I could throw him, and he nearly hit the roof when I asked for the agreement in writing. Another five minutes' arguing, and the piece of paper was in my pocket, with arrangements that the job would start the following Monday.

*　　*　　*

It didn't take two or three days, it took damned near a fortnight and, with the weather hot and sticky, choking dust, and every shovelful slung upwards through a two-foot trap door, re-shovelled on to a barrow, then taken down a long narrow passage to the yard to dump, it was the worst job I had ever tackled.

Despite his willpower, within three days Alf was completely bushed, but he would not give in. In the end, with a growing fear that he would do himself some permanent damage, I confined him to keeping the dump tidy in the yard where he could breathe properly. Looking back, I should think it was the hardest twenty quid I ever earned, but I learned a lot — a helluva lot. At one and the same time, all the age-old distrust of bosses renewed itself and I also re-learned that, outside the cosy regimented life of the services, it was dog-eat-dog. The only thing that made the second week bearable was when Teresa, on the Friday after we started, drew my attention to an advert in the local paper. It was made for me. *General clerical work in small expanding business. No experience required!* I couldn't believe my luck. We skipped the cellar the following morning and I was out of the house like a flash, with dreams of semi-gentility large in my mind.

I got it, and was due to start in just ten days' time, after my current job was finished. Without Alf on the shovel it became a race against time but, with the promise of quieter things to come, I flung myself at it, and have avoided shovels like the plague ever since.

*   *   *

Mr Leonardo Castignino was not exactly a quiet person, neither was his buxom wife Bianca. In fact they were crackers. However, their seventeen-year-old daughter, Pasqualina, was just a cracker! And what a cracker!

On the Monday, uncomfortable in my demob suit, but very keen to start, I approached the combined Snack Bar-cum-Ice-Cream Parlour in the main street with a mixture of alarm and anticipation. Knowing that I knew nothing about the job and, despite the advert stipulating No Experience I was more than a little nervous. Castignino, short, neat, and with a heavy black moustache that lifted like a theatre curtain to reveal glistening teeth when he smiled, seemed a decent sort of bloke. He met me at the shop door, and led me, talking non-stop in atrocious English, to the office. My heart plummeted as he introduced me to my new domain with a theatrical flourish.

'You work 'ere eh?' he said with a brilliant smile. 'You like it very much. Very — 'ow you say? — very cosy eh?'

I gazed without enthusiasm at the steel-legged, paper-littered table, jammed into a corner behind crates and boxes at the back of the shop.

He caught the look on my face. 'You not like?' he asked, an edge of surprise and hurt in his voice.

I brightened at once. 'Oh yeah,' I lied, 'it's great.'

The curtain raised again in a flash of white. 'Good, good. Now I go . . . You sort out the papers eh? I come back, maybe one hour.' Again the dentures flashed briefly. 'Today,' he continued, 'is a very beezy day.' With a final lightning flash of teeth he turned and vanished, and all the glory of my new and long desired situation vanished with him, as I sat on the wooden folding chair, and gazed silently at the heap of papers before me.

A quiet panic began to grip me, as I realised that I didn't have a clue where to start, and the glamour of office work became dimmer as I slowly worked through them in the only way I could think of: in alphabetical and date order. I spotted a large, impressive-looking book on a shelf just overhead . . . *Accounts* ran the legend on it. Curiously, I took it down and opened it, then wished I hadn't. Page after page of indifferent script and figures greeted me, in a mixture of Italian and English. Real panic swept me for a second or two. Should I enter the bills I had sorted into the book? And if so, how?

I was still in a wavering trance when the boss returned. He didn't seem very happy, and I knew instinctively that he wasn't going to improve. His garlic-laden breath engulfed me, as he leaned over my shoulder to inspect my efforts. He wasn't impressed.

'What you do eh?'

I felt myself flush and struggled for words. 'Well er, y'know?'

His broad shoulders rose in an agonised shrug as he spread his hands, palms up, like a flower greeting the morning sun. '*Si, si.* But what you do?' I gazed silently at the liquid brown eyes. 'You enter the book, no?' he continued, eyebrows moving up into the deeply furrowed forehead.

'I er, I . . .' I began with a feeling of helplessness.

'Dis book?' he questioned, opening the accounts tome I had run through.

'Aah!' I replied non-committally, then, like a boxer who knew he couldn't come up for the next round, the bell saved me, as a short, buxom, and still vivacious tornado swept into the room.

'What you do 'ere, eh?' she demanded of him. 'I,' she emphasised, tapping her ample breasts, 'do all the work, no? What you do, eh?'

He tried in vain to stem the torrent as her English gave out, then, with arms flying in all directions, he blew. 'Bi–an–ca, Bianca!' he shouted in strangled English. 'Always you come at de wrong time-a eh?' He spread his hands eloquently as she stood, eyes flashing, arms across her chest defiantly. 'Every time I 'ave the work to do you come ... Leonardo you do dis, Leonardo you do dat! ... You no see ... I 'elp Meester Sulleevan.'

A renewed flood hit him straight between the eyes. Even sitting down, I felt like ducking, but there was no stopping her. She had her full say then turned on her heel and bounced out like a well-upholstered rubber ball.

He turned to me in silent fury, eyes rolling, fists clenching and unclenching. 'Weemen. Mama Mia!' I kept a discreet silence. 'Now,' he continued, leaning over me, a little calmer but by no means calm, 'what you do eh? I want deeze,' he picked up a sheaf of invoices, 'put 'ere.' He stabbed his finger at the accounts book. 'You understand?' I smiled, nodded, but didn't. 'And deeze,' he picked up two bills I had put aside separately, 'you make the cheque for, yes? Good.' Again I nodded. 'And then,' he added, stabbing again at the accounts book, 'you put them in there. Easy, yes?' I returned his brilliant smile and came to the conclusion that this was not my vocation, not without a few lessons, anyway. He turned to go, stopped and clapped his hand to his forehead. 'Ah, I forget,' he said, pulling a cheque book from his inner pocket and handing it to me. 'For the payment. No? I come back later.' With a final pat on the back, he left me staring dumbly at the cheque book.

I had seen a cheque book of course, but not very often, and I had never in my life actually handled one. At that moment it was just another, and very unwelcome, mystery which I now attempted to solve, with little success. With two cheques ruined, I gave up and waited for the boss to come back. He wasn't long, and I could see he had taken another verbal bashing. His eyes bulged as he looked at the ruined cheques, and his feelings were relieved in his own language. Then, with immense, and unexpected, patience he tried again.

'You new 'ere, I know,' he said with visible restraint. 'But dis!' he pushed the ruined cheques with his finger. 'No good eh?' Embarrassed, I nodded agreement. 'Look, I show you.' He did. Unfortunately, in his emotional state he left the signature line blank. He gave me a big smile. 'Now you know, eh? Now you make it.'

He turned and left, muttering to himself. Ever pragmatic, I thought that, since he had already made it out I could save wasting another cheque, then spotted he hadn't signed it. No problem, I thought, and signed it for him. The details of the aftermath are too harrowing to record, and lunchtime arrived under a heavy cloud. The first day I must admit, was not a success, and the second was only marginally better, because for the first time I met their daughter Pasqualina.

How can I describe this seventeen-year-old time bomb? Gorgeous, ravishing, divine, and definitely all woman! If the Sabine women were anything like her, it was no wonder the Romans went after them, I thought, as she undulated into the office just about lunchtime on the following day. Things had improved a lot and all I had to do before lunch was to make out an order for two dozen cartons of condensed orange juice to hand to the wholesaler on my way home. Head down, I was just making it out when I felt her presence behind me. I turned, to find my eyes on a level with her navel, and they bulged as I worked my way up. Mesmerised by her animal sexuality, I sat stock still. Seconds seemed like hours, before the silence was broken by her strangely husky voice.

'Allo Meester Sulleevan,' she half whispered, swaying gently, six inches from my startled eyes, a primeval impulse to touch her clawing at me.

'Pas–qual–ina!' came her mother's voice, high

pitched and irritable. She clapped her hand to her rosebud mouth and fled. The spell was broken.

Bloody 'ell! I thought, that was close. Still thinking of her, and regretting I had missed inspecting the undercarriage, I turned and disconsolately completed the order for the orange juice and left.

With it safely delivered to the wholesaler with an urgent request for early delivery, the full impact of Pasqualina's visit did not reveal itself until the following day. The storm broke about two o'clock when, with commendable efficiency, the orange juice arrived. I wasn't actually in the yard when it did, but the screams issuing through the shop as they off-loaded alerted me that something was wrong. Dashing into the yard, I stopped in amazement. There seemed to be crates everywhere, with Bianca rushing about like a maniac, screeching at the top of her voice as the lorry men cheerfully piled them up. Then I spotted the boss, waving his arms in homicidal fury, and gesticulating me into the shop. Words poured from him in an avalanche as I came through the door.

For a few seconds I said nothing, then I blew. 'You told me to order the damned things!' I snapped, rummaging through the out tray for the order copy. I found it and held it up triumphantly, then thrust it into his hand. 'There, read it!'

He did. 'Two dozen crates!' he said disbelievingly.

'Crates?' I took it back and groaned. He was right. I had ordered them.

He shook with anger. 'I say to you two dozen cartons. You say crates! What you do, eh? Ruin me?'

Then I remembered. I was half-way through the order when Pasqualina had come in. Oh God! I thought, that's cocked it up and no mistake. I was right, it had. Strangely calm, Leonardo gazed at me with his big brown eyes, more in sorrow than in anger then, haltingly, he made the understatement of his life.

'You not good at this I tink. Maybe some other kind of work, eh?'

To be fair, I agreed with him. Considering everything, we parted on good terms. If only she hadn't wiggled!

* * *

My early arrival home coincided with Mam's return from the Mother's Union, as usual with Aunts Min and Sarah in support. Teresa, for some reason, had also been with them. The conversation was a predictable question and answer session, with Aunt Sarah in first with her prediction that I had got the sack. Aunt Min leapt to my defence, but I had to admit that Aunt Sarah was right, for once. With coats divested and the kettle on, Teresa nailed me as we sat on the sofa and, with Mam in and out of the back kitchen so as not to miss anything, I regaled them with the details. They went off into fits of laughter as I explained the scene and the reasons for it.

Teresa dug me in the ribs. 'Y'know what you are Li, don't you?' I grimaced and invited her to tell me. 'A square peg, that's what,' she replied bluntly. 'You just don't fit, do you?'

'Aye,' intoned Aunt Sarah solemnly, 'you're right there, luv. 'E doesn't know 'is arse from 'is elbow, that's 'is trouble!' She was right again. We were still laughing when Mam stopped pouring the tea.

'Oh, before I forget,' she said, 'Dinny came round to see you at dinner time.'

'Dinny!' I cried with delight. 'Cor, what a pity I missed him.'

'Oh, don't worry,' she reassured me, 'he'll be round again when he finishes t'night.' Teresa wanted to know more about my ex-job, but I asked her a question instead.

'You're not in the Mother's Union are yeh? I thou . . .'

57

Aunt Min answered for her. 'Course she's not,' she said with a laugh. 'Just came t'the meetin' about the Children of Mary dance. Y'know, the one they hold every year.'

'You're never still in that, are yeh?' I asked in surprise. I thought the Church society was only for unmarried girls, although she had been in it years ago.

'Of course she isn't,' broke in Mam, 'don't be so daft. She's just goin' to help with the refreshments, that's all.'

'Why don't you come?' suggested my sister. 'You always liked a dance.'

'No luv, I don't think so. Don't know anyone these days, anyway.' I tried to change the subject. 'How's Alf, Aunt Sarah?'

She clucked heavily. 'Still knocked up after that damned job. Wouldn't be told, y'know. Anyway,' she continued, 'me an' yeh Uncle Matt's grateful to yeh.'

Again Mam brought the subject of the dance up. 'Why don't yeh go Li? Do yeh good t'shake a leg.'

I laughed. 'No thanks, Mam. Not all that fussy nowadays. I want to get settled before I think about dances and girls. I've got enough problems as it is.

There was general laughter until Aunt Sarah put her foot in it again. 'Yes,' she said. 'Talkin' about girls, whatever 'appened to that there Antoinette?' I could have kicked her. 'I thought you two would have made a go of it?'

'Oh that finished a long time ago,' I replied, hoping she would shut up. 'She's probably married by now. Anyway,' I added, with a change of subject, 'talkin' about the dance, what time does it start?'

'Eight I think,' replied Mam, ''ang on a minute, Teresa knows.'

'What's that, Mam?' asked Teresa looking up from her paper.

'Li wants t'know what time the dance starts?'

Teresa brightened up immediately. 'Oh good. You comin' then?'

'Yeah,' I replied, 'might as well. There's nowt much else t'do.'

'Good,' she said. 'Starts at eight, but I'm going early to get things ready, so you can give me a hand, alright?'

'Fair enough,' I replied with a grin. 'You're on.'

4

Dinny

I glanced at the clock as Tommy Handley's voice boomed from the wireless amid a roar of laughter from the audience, then across the room at Mam sitting at the table, laughing her head off.

'I thought you said Dinny was comin' t'night, Mam?'

She shushed me fiercley. 'I'm listenin',' she said. 'There!' she added admonishingly, as another burst of laughter came from the set. 'Now I've missed it!' She lowered the sound, and leaned forward. 'What did you say?' I repeated my question. 'Well that's what he said, anyway. Perhaps he forgot, or been 'eld up or somethin'.' She turned the sound back up and left me wondering.

It was a long time since I had seen Dinny. Even the year before the war we had drifted apart a bit, because of our move away from the street where we had both been born, he and his numerous brothers and sisters to a new council house at the North end of the town, and us to a bigger house near the park. The move, for me at least, had been a watershed. This strange new world had given me a new perspective. I had also fallen for the girl next door, Antoinette, badly. I didn't know, of course, that I was 'in love', all I knew at that time was that I wasn't sure whether I was on foot or horseback most of the time. The other result of our move from the old street was that, with Antoinette's example, it made me ambitious. Don't ask me why, because I don't know, but it did, and I hadn't damned well got over that, either. I still was and, for a brief moment with the Italian job, thought I had started on my way.

I looked impatiently at the clock again as laughter poured from the set, then sighed with relief as the doorbell rang. Within seconds I was on my feet and opening it, to be greeted with the old familiar grin.

'Hi 'yeh Wack,' Dinny said, sticking a friendly hand out. ''Ow's tricks?'

'Oh not bad,' I replied as I gripped his hand. 'Can't grumble.'

''Ow's yeh Mam?' He had always been fond of Mam, especially the jam butties she used to give him as a lad.

'Fine,' I replied, leading him up the tiny hallway.

Mam gave him a beaming smile as she rose and switched the wireless off. ''Ello Din. How are yeh, then?'

He grinned as he greeted her. 'Oh great thanks. You alright?'

'Oh, not bad,' she answered. 'Cuppa tea?'

He nodded. I watched him in surprise as he sat down on the sofa, pulling his trousers up at the knees. He was quite the dandy these days, neat suit, hair slicked back, but with the same sallow, cheeky face of old. He laughed as he caught my glance. 'What d'yeh reckon to the whistle an flute?' he asked, fingering the cloth.

'Great,' I replied with a grin. 'What lorry did that fall off?'

He gave me a huge wink. 'Gorrit made now, mate. No kiddin'. . .Plenty of work, good. . .' he rubbed his finger and thumb together.

'Not married yet then, Din?' asked Mam with an amused smile.

'Who, me?' he asked, putting his cup on the floor in case he spilt it. 'You're jokin'.'

She pulled his leg about it, then enquired about his mam and dad.

He laughed and shook his head. 'Ah, they don't change much. Y'know me Mam, give 'er a book an' the roof could fall in, she wouldn't notice.'

We burst out laughing. How right he was! Even the police searching the house for loot during the riots hadn't taken her mind off her cheap love story. His dad wouldn't change, either.

As Dinny said, 'Give him a few bevvies, a packet of Woodbines and the racing paper and he's well away.'

Mam chuckled. She knew the Devlins a lot better than most, and for the next hour it was just like old times, laughing, giggling and reminiscing, until Dinny happened to look at the clock.

'Cor, strike a flippin' light!' he exclaimed, 'Is that the time?'

'What's all the rush?' I asked.

'Gorra meet a coupla blokes down the pub. Union stuff, like.'

'What's it all about then?' I asked, feeling a bit fed up that he had to go so soon.

It was bad enough our Con, always on about unions, without spoiling our first get-together for years. I felt peeved.

'Oh it's nothin' much,' he replied with a shrug, 'but I've gorra go. Luk,' he added, getting to his feet, 'why don't yeh come with me. We could 'ave a jar together and . . .'

'I don't drink, Din. You know that!'

He grimaced. 'Still on the wagon eh? Still, that's no sweat, you can 'ave an orange juice or sommat.' He grinned. 'If anyone looks funny at yeh I'll tell 'em you've gorra bad stomach. Anyroad, I wanted a word with yeh. Come on, get yeh coat.'

I capitulated.

'And don't be too late,' warned Mam as we were leaving. 'Y'know what your father's like.'

'What yeh gonna do then?' Dinny asked as we walked down the path.

I sighed. 'Oh God Din, not you as well. Everybody's been askin' the same damned question ever since I got 'ome.'

'I'm still askin',' he replied, ''ave yeh gorra job yet?'

I burst out laughing. He demanded to know what was so funny. I told him I'd had one until dinner time, then launched into the details of the Italian job.

'Cor blimey!' he exlaimed, as I described Pasqualina. 'I reckon I could bring the roses to 'er cheeks by the sound of 'er.'

I'll bet you could, I thought. He had had an eye for the ladies since he was about thirteen. His philosophy was simple: love 'em and leave 'em. He always reckoned that if God made anything better, then he must have kept it to himself. I also knew that he was not going to be daft enough to buy an orchard as long as he could pinch the apples. We were still laughing, when he came back to the subject of work, and for the rest of the way to the pub he tried hard to persuade me to come back to the Yard and work with him. I resisted. That was the last place I wanted to go. If I did, I'd finish up in the rut again. I wanted something better if I could.

'You're a mug Li,' he said bluntly, as we reached the pub door.

I stopped before we went in. Despite my disastrous experience that morning I was, if anything, even more determined to haul myself up a bit. OK I'd got the chop, but at least I'd had a go, and I had learned something. Next time I would be better prepared.

'Look Din,' I said earnestly, 'I've got nothin' against the Yard, you know that. It's a great place, good blokes, plenty of laughs and all that, but it's a dead-end, mate. I just want somethin' better. What's wrong with that?'

'Nowt,' he replied bluntly, 'but 'ow the 'ell are yeh gonna do that without experience or damn all else?'

I snorted irritably. 'Oh you're alright, you're a tradesman. All I'd get is labourin'. That's no flamin' use t'me is it?'

He grimaced, then went straight to the heart of it. 'Well that's up t'you Li, but yeh Demob money won't last forever, will it? An' it doesn't grow on bloody trees, does it?'

Trust him to tell me a hard truth. And he was right. I was getting worried about just that. He tried hard to coax me with the fact that it was nothing like the old days down there. The money was good, they couldn't get enough men for the work in hand, and in his opinion I should grab a job there while the going was good. As he pointed out in a final clincher to his argument, the unions were strong now, no more being sent 'up the road' for your cards at the slightest excuse, oh no.

As he said, 'We've gorr'em now mate, any victimisation and wallop! The 'ole bloody lot's out.' I wasn't convinced, as we walked through the door. It was still a dead-ender. 'Please y'self,' he said, as the pub chatter hit us. 'Come on, let's get the drinks in.'

The babble of voices was deafening, and the air hung heavy with tobacco smoke. Dinny, obviously a regular, was greeted cheerfully on all sides.

'Are they 'ere yet Mick?' he asked when we finally crushed our way to the bar.

'Aye,' replied the barman with a backward jerk of his thumb.

'Right,' answered Dinny, 'give us a pint then Mick, will yeh — the usual. Oh yeah,' he added, 'and an orange juice for me mate 'ere.'

Mick raised his eyebrows in surprise. 'Yeh kiddin'?' he said disbelievingly.

Dinny grinned and tapped his stomach. 'Ulcers,' he said with a grimace, nodding at me.

Mick showed sudden concern. 'Ah,' he said with feeling, 'You poor sod! Gives yeh jip, does it?'

'Flamin' cruel, mate,' I agreed as I took the drink.

Mick stuck his thumb up as we left the bar. 'Oh hey!' he exclaimed, calling us back. 'Tripe boiled in milk, mate, that's what yeh want for that. Bloody marvellous it is, no kiddin'. Basin fulla that, mate, an' you'll think you've bin t'Lourdes. Right Din?' I suppressed a laugh as Dinny nodded, straight-faced. I thanked him. He suddenly thought of another remedy. 'Pobs too,' he said with a knowledgeable wink. 'Them's good, too. Bread an' milk like, y'know. Warm o'course.'

I thanked him again as Dinny dragged me away tittering to himself. 'Thanks be t'God yeh didn't gerr'im started on 'is ingrowin' toenails. He'd 'ave 'ad yeh there all night!'

The fug was no better as we opened the door into a small, more private room opposite the bar. Just two figures sat at a small, bottle-laden table on the far side of an otherwise empty room. It had all the atmosphere of a speakeasy. The two heads looked up suspiciously as we walked over and joined them. One, still in overalls, had a heavy frown on his angular face, the other, about my height and fortyish, with a round face, neatly dressed and equally solemn, tipped his trilby to the back of his head and scrutinised me silently.

'Old mate 'f mine,' explained Dinny, putting his pint on the table and sitting down. 'Just demobbed. Sullivan. Y'know — Con's brother.' The tension eased a little at the mention of Con, and Dinny twisted in his chair. 'Park y'self,' he invited, nodding at the vacant chair beside him. But I knew I wasn't welcome.

I grimaced. 'Oh hell!' I exlaimed in mock annoyance. 'I forgot Din, I'm supposed t'meet me Dad at the club. I'd better skid.'

He grinned at me. He knew I was lying and why. He picked it up neatly. 'Aye that's right, I forgot,' he replied. 'Luk, I'll nip round t'see yeh Saturday night OK? We can . . .'

I shook my head. 'I'm takin' our Teresa to the Town Hall dance on Saturday.'

'What dance is that?' he asked interestedly.

'Children of Mary; y'know, the annual shindig.'

'Warrabout Friday night, then?'

'Great, see yeh then.' I quickly downed my drink and thankfully left.

*　　*　　*

'What was all that about the other night?' I asked Dinny as he walked into the kitchen.

'Oh God, don't ask,' he said with a laugh as he flopped on to the sofa. 'Honest, sometimes I think they're all goin' crackers down there. Just one 'f those arguments, y'know?' I asked him what he meant. 'Oh, inter-union stuff. They're always at it. If it's not one thing it's another.'

Mam, reading the newspaper on the far side of the room, looked up sharply. 'Hey you two,' she said, eyeing us fiercely, 'no politics, y'understand? I 'ear enough of that with Con and y'Dad!' I looked at her in surprise. Even though Dinny was practically family it was still a bit blunt.

But he knew Mam and winked, as he dug me in the ribs. 'That's alright Li, I know just 'ow yeh Mam feels. Look,' he added, 'let's nip round to the club and see yeh Dad. Maybe 'ave a natter eh?'

Half-way to the door I stopped, as I remembered that Con was supposed to be coming round. 'Tell our Con I'll nip round and see him tomorrow afternoon before I go to the dance, will yeh Mam?'

She shook her head. 'He might be goin' t'the football match, y'know?'

I shrugged. 'Well if I miss him, I'll see him after Mass Sunday OK?' We turned to go.

'You're welcome anytime Din, y'know that,' said Mam, picking the paper up again.

'Thanks Mrs Sullivan. See yeh,' he called, as we headed for the door. On our way to the club he explained about the pub meeting, warning me that it was complicated. It was — very.

The two men I had briefly met were, like Dinny,

shop-stewards, one for the sheet-metal workers and the other for the joiners. The 'birr of a talk' I had so nearly scuppered had been one of several opening skirmishes on a point of who did what between the two trades, with Dinny acting as honest broker, trying to calm things down a bit. The problem, as he explained it, seemed to me insoluble yet one, in his opinion, which could prove deadly. It all revolved around the drilling of holes. I laughed as he completed the details and he rounded on me.

'It's no good you laughin', mate,' he snapped irritably. 'This is bloody serious, I'll tell yeh . . . They could strike over this lot.'

'Oh come off it Din, for God's sake. They wouldn't, not over that!'

He snorted. 'Oh wouldn't they just? I've seen 'em out for a helluva lot less, I'll tell yeh.'

Patiently he explained that the real problem was the materials involved, which consisted of aluminium and wood being used in a refrigeration ship which was being fitted out. The trouble was that they were stuck together, with the result that if the sheet metal workers drilled through the aluminium, as was their job, it would also entail them going though the wood, which was the joiner's job, and vice-versa. Both trades would object, and therein lay the rub. It was a real Lulu of a problem over which even Solomon, I told him, would scratch his head a bit.

'Aye,' he answered thoughtfully, 'but some bugger berra solve it before the troublemakers get their fingers in. Otherwise we'll *all* be out!'

As we walked and talked, I felt a growing despair. Was this the world I may be forced to re-enter, if I didn't duck back into my safe and cosy world? God no! The last thing I wanted was argument and trouble. I'd seen enough, more than enough. All I wanted now was a nice, quiet and steady job to build for the future. By the time we finally reached the club, which we had already walked past once as Dinny held forth on a hundred and one aspects of the shipyard and its seemingly interminable problems, I felt punch drunk.

With my hand on the door handle I gave up. 'If it's like that Din, what the hell d'yeh stay there for?' I asked, perplexed.

'Why?' he answered, as though I had taken leave of my senses. 'Because that's all I bloody well know, isn't it? An' anyway, I like it, always 'ave. When things go smooth it's great, you know that. We 'ad some good times there, didn't we?'

'We were lads then Din,' I reminded him.

'What's the difference?' he asked in surprise.

I shook my head and pushed the door open. 'Well, after what you've been tellin' me for the past half hour Din, you can stuff it, mate. It seems to be nothin' but arguments. It's bad enough listenin' to our Con when he gets goin'.'

'Talk of the divil!' he replied with a nudge, pointing to my brother and Dad standing at the billiard table.

They greeted us in high good humour. 'Come on Din,' invited Con with a flick of his head towards the bar, 'I'll get you one in, alright?'

'Oh great!' replied Dinny. 'Make it a bitter, will yeh. I could use one.'

'Dad?' enquired Con. Dad refused; he was waiting for his billiard partner. 'Li — orange juice?'

Dad seemed irritable.

'What's up?' I asked.

He clucked. 'Waitin' for your Uncle Matt. Got the table booked and everythin'. Damned if I know where he's got to. D'yeh fancy a game?'

'Yeah, why not?' Minutes later we were settled into the game, as Con and Dinny returned with the drinks, talking animatedly. They stopped at the table, just as Dad was about to take a shot.

'Hey Dad, what d'yeh think of this lot?' asked Con.

'What the hell are yeh talkin' about?' he snapped edgily.

'Y'know, this 'ere screw business down the Yard.'

Dad held his position and rolled his eyes. 'I think they want their bloody bumps read!' he snapped back. I grinned as I looked from one to the other.

Con's face showed annoyance. 'Yeah but . . .' he began, as Dinny winked at me.

Without moving his position Dad raised his eyes and glared at my brother fiercely. 'Luk Con,' he said with quiet menace, 'I came 'ere t'play billiards, so just leave it, will yeh?' Dinny grinned broadly as Con took both the hint and the hump.

'Come on Din,' he said peevishly, 'let's get back to the bar and 'ave a natter.'

'Politics!' muttered Dad, half to himself, as he finally took the shot, and missed. I remained silent, but I thought a lot, and most of it was about the cosy life of the Army. My mind was almost made up.

5

Reunion

There are days in one's life when events twist and turn so rapidly, and are etched so vividly on one's mind, that a time span of hours seems, in retrospect, like years. The Saturday of the Children of Mary's dance was such a day.

After a restless night, thinking about things in general — the episode with Dinny, the current life in the shipyard and, last but not least, the growing urgency for a decision on my future — I had finally fallen into a fitful sleep. I was awakened, seemingly only moments later, by a frantic scrurrying on the landing outside my room. I was suddenly fully, nerve-tinglingly awake and out of my bed like a flash.

'What's up?' I called in a strangled whisper.

Dad's voice returned in full volume. 'It's Teresa. She's not well.'

I rammed my legs into my trousers and dashed out, shirt half on, half off. Quick though I was, Mam and Dad had been quicker, and as I flung myself into Teresa's room I saw them, tense but quiet, on either side of her bed. Teresa, her small face marble white, lay cradled like a child in Mam's arms, while Dad, tense with worry, stood silent and helpless.

'Sssh,' smoothed Mam quietly, her long, iron grey hair cascading over her white nightdress as she swayed back and forth with Teresa. 'Ssh . . . You'll be alright now. Don't worry, luv. You'll be alright.'

'Should I get the doctor?' I asked.

Mam glanced up, and without stopping her caresses, shook her head as Teresa gasped for breath. 'She'll be alright Li,' she said quietly, 'don't worry. Just get back to bed . . . Go on,' she added, as Dad and I hesitated.

'You're sure?' questioned Dad.

She nodded. 'Just reach me those pills there, and the water,' she added, still in the same quiet voice. 'It'll ease off once she gets them down her.'

Dad moved to get the pills from the chest of drawers as Mam transferred her gaze to me, still in the doorway. 'Go on,' she insisted. 'Get back to bed like I told yeh.' I hesitated. 'I've told yeh, she'll be alright, now stop worryin'. Go on with yeh now.'

With a final glance at the tableau I turned, and with Dad ahead of me on the landing, closed the door. 'How often is she like this?' I asked in a worried tone.

He shook his greying head. 'Oh just now and again, y'know. Just comes on, like. Once she's had the pills, though, she comes round alright, thank God.'

'Hell's bells Dad! It scared the life out of me,' I admitted. 'Just what is the trouble?' She wasn't the old Teresa I knew, but this was the first time I'd seen her like this, and it shook me. 'Just how bad is it Dad?'

Suddenly, without his false teeth, his worried frown, and the scarcely veiled tears for his favourite child misting his eyes, he looked old. This, too, was a shock. To me, Mam and Dad were indestructable.

'It's 'er heart,' he answered slowly. 'She took a helluva batterin' when Declan was killed . . . then the baby . . . then the 'ouse, y'know. Never gorr'over it really. Just wanna them things, isn't it?'

'Yeah, but why should . . .?'

'Accordin' to the specialist,' he continued, 'it's some weakness since she was a kid. The troubles triggered it off again, like. Mind you,' he added thoughtfully, 'she never was strong, but then it seemed to right itself when she went to school . . . until all this 'appened of course. Anyroad,' he added with a deep sigh, 'what-

71

ever the hell it is, there's nothin' they can do about it, so that's that.'

'Have they no idea at all?' I queried.

He grimaced. 'Somethin' t'do with the valves or sommat — that's all we know.' He patted me on the shoulder. 'Go on, do as yeh Mam told yeh, get back t'bed.' I made a step towards Teresa's door to check, but he stopped me. 'She'll be alright, don't worry. Your Mother knows what t'do. Go on, get some sleep.'

For ten anxious minutes I sat up in bed, ears straining for any sound that could give me information. At last Teresa's door opened then closed, and I was out of bed and on the landing like a shot.

'Is she alright?' I asked in a hoarse whisper.

Mam put a finger to her lips. 'Ssh, she's asleep,' she whispered. 'Now get back to bed.'

Thoughtfully I retraced my steps and lay on the bed, but sleep had long escaped me. In its place I had yet another calculation to take into account in determining my future, and my dilemma grew.

*   *   *

By morning, thank God, she was much better, and as cheerful as ever.

'Look,' I said as we sat at breakfast, 'forget about the dance t'night luv, I'll do the refreshments for you.'

'Oh no you won't,' she answered, a gleam in her eye. 'I'm alright. Honest I am.' For a few moments I tried in vain to persuade her to stay home, but Mam intervened as she put fresh tea on the table.

'She's not daft y'know Li. She knows what she's doin', so don't worry y'self. Anyroad,' she added, 'you'll be there to keep your eye on 'er, won't yeh?' I wasn't at all happy but, as Teresa had said, it was no good her just moping around. I extracted a promise from her.

'Alright then, but if you're not feelin' well tell me. Promise?'

'Alright doctor,' she said with a smile, 'I promise.' Her expression changed to one of sympathy as she gazed affectionately at me, head cocked to one side. 'Don't worry Li, please. I'm fine as long as I take the pills. Just forget last night, that's all.' Uneasy, but mollified, I capitulated.

'OK then, I'll stay behind the counter with you, but,' I added, 'you put your feet up till t'night. I'll do the humping about to get the hall ready.' Mam assured me that she would see that she did.

With everything back on an even keel, I spent a busy and enjoyable morning dashing between the convent and the town hall, and by one o'clock, tired and famished, got back home to find Dinny, still in overalls and filthy, waiting for me.

'Hey,' I said with mock severity, 'I thought you said you were comin' round last night, I . . .'

'Yeah, I was,' he interrupted, 'but I got mixed up with that there screw thing, y'know.'

Dad looked up from his dinner. 'They're not still on about that damned thing are they Din?'

'Aah,' he answered, 'they give me a pain in the Diddy. They're never gonna sort this one out, Mr Sullivan, never. It's too damned daft by 'alf.'

'More trouble, Din?' asked Mam, putting my dinner on the table.

'Yeah, the usual y'know . . . But this one,' he added with a grin, 'is a bit more "screwy", like.' He joined Dad and me as we laughed at the pun.

'Screwy's just about right,' opined Dad, getting on with his dinner.

'Anyway, Din,' I broke in, 'if yeh want me t'come out with yeh this afternoon, you've had it, boyo. I'm busy with the dance.'

'That's what I came about, the dance. I've decided to come with yeh.'

'Oh lovely!' exclaimed Teresa delightedly.

'Yeah,' he continued, 'I could do with a good laugh

73

right now, I'll tell yeh, an' I haven't been to a dance for, oh, yonkers.'

'Right,' interrupted Teresa with a laugh, 'you can give us a hand with the washing up. That'll do you good as well.'

For a few minutes it was quite like old times as they pulled his leg unmercifully, but he was more than a match for them, until he suddenly spotted the time.

'Holy sailor!' he gasped. 'Me mam'll think I'm on overtime. I'd berra git, or there'll be nowt left to eat.'

'Oh Dinny!' exclaimed Teresa. 'Don't tell such lies.'

He raised his eyebrows innocently. 'No,' he said seriously, 'straight up . . . Our Mick'll eat it. Honest. Anyroad,' he continued amid pithy disbelief, 'what time are yeh goin'?'

I looked at an amused Teresa. 'Oh about seven,' she said.

He slipped his greasy cap on the back of his head. 'Right,' he said. 'An' God 'elp them there Children of Mary when I gerr'in among 'em. They won't know what's 'it 'em!'

'Ah go on with yeh,' said Mam. 'You get worse you do, instead of better.'

'Yeah,' he agreed, 'that's what me mam says . . . See yeh.'

*   *   *

At ten to seven Dinny turned up at the bus stop, smart as paint in his Sunday best, and bubbling with anticipation.

'Blimey, you're all dolled up, aren't yeh?' I said, admiring his natty brown suit and matching tie against his white shirt.

'Thought I'd give 'em a treat,' he replied, running his hand across his brilliantined hair, then polishing his finger nails against his lapel. He stared at my uniform. He didn't need to say anything, his look was enough. Teresa knew what he was thinking too.

74

'It feels more comfortable,' I said defensively.

She clucked in annoyance. 'He won't get changed, y'know Din. I keep at him, but he won't. Not settled yet, that's his trouble,' she added glancing up at me accusingly.

I headed her off before he could answer. 'Ah, not t'night, luv. Just let's have a bit 'f fun eh?'

Dinny looked meaningfully at me as he spoke to my sister. 'Take no notice, luv. He won't go back, don't you worry. In fact, I'll lay ten to one on it. How's that?'

The arrival of the bus stopped further speculation, and I was glad of it. A short ride and we were there, and a moment later we were walking under the twin set of steps running up the front of the solid Victorian building.

'Hey,' remarked Dinny, as we walked through the door, 'd'yeh remember us bein' stuck up those lampposts over there when the mayor read the Riot Act out?' I smiled as we turned and looked at the ornamental lampposts across the road. What a day that had been!

'Me mam didn't know that!' said Teresa accusingly. 'You weren't supposed to be there.'

Dinny and I burst out laughing. 'Well, for God's sake don't go tellin' her now, will yeh?' I pleaded in mock fear.

Her eyes twinkled. 'Oh alright then I won't . . . She'll only send you up to bed!'

Safely indoors, we went to our respective cloak-rooms and paid our tuppences. Then, after a short breather for Teresa to gear herself for the climb ahead, we ascended the grand staircase, arms linked, to the ballroom, with just one stop half-way for her to catch her breath and check, yet again, that she had not only taken her pills, but had spare ones with her. Once in the cavernous ballroom itself I felt easier and, in no time, with the consent of the other three helpers, all old neighbours, I settled Teresa down behind the refreshment tables with instructions not to budge, while we got the tables ready. Dinny was already stuck in and having a great time putting out the crockery with the others, amid gales of laughter as they pulled each other's legs unmercifully. In the meantime the hall gradually filled up with eager young dancers.

'Hey Li,' said Dinny as he finished his job, 'there's some right talent 'ere t'night, isn't there?' I followed his twinkling eyes down the hall. He was right. There was. 'Cor!' he added, digging me in the ribs. 'Luk at that one over there!' I followed his pointing finger to a buxom blonde in a bright red dress, with moist, matching lips. 'Ooo,' he added with indrawn breath, 'she's a right cracker that one. I wouldn't mind . . .'

'Hey Dinny!' broke in a high-pitched voice behind us. I turned and grinned. It was Mrs Adams, an elderly neighbour from the old street, who had rollicked us many a time when we were lads. Now there was an amused gleam in her eye. 'You just keep yeh eyes on the cups, Dinny Devlin. Never mind the women!'

'Oh,' he pleaded in a small voice, 'don't tell me mam, will yeh Mrs Adams? She'll kill me!'

She shook her hand at him. 'I might . . . I'm like that, y'know, so just watch it,' she threatened as she turned for the kitchen.

'Hey Teresa!' Dinny called, eyes again on the blonde. 'Any jitterbugging allowed t'night?'

'No there isn't,' came Mrs Adams' voice, as she reappeared with more cups. 'This is a respectable dance this is! . . . Jitterbuggin!' she added disgustedly. 'That's not dancin'. Yeh shoulda seen them last week over at St Malachy's,' she added to Teresa in a lowered voice. 'Disgustin' it was; chuckin' themselves all over the place, they were. Never seen anythin' like it. Skirts flyin', legs showin'. God Almighty, it was terrible. You're never gonna believe this Teresa but,' she continued in an even lower voice, 'there was one'f them, up in the air she was, yeh could even see 'er

76

'Go on,' urged Teresa. 'We'll be alright here . . . Go on.'

In a state of suppressed excitement, I followed him in and out of the strolling dancers until we were in a position to see her clearly. It *was* Antoinette, chattering and laughing with three other girls, and looking lovelier than ever in a graceful, figure-hugging blue dress. I felt numb as my eyes devoured her. Somehow she had changed from the girl I last saw so many years ago. Now she was a woman. The long, luxuriant hair had gone, and the pale oval face was now framed in a neat modern style. But those deep, liquid brown eyes still twinkled wickedly as she laughed with her friends. A heavy nudge in the ribs brought me back to reality.

'Go on then!' snapped Dinny impatiently.

I shook my head. 'She's talkin',' I replied.

He looked at me disgustedly. 'So what?' he asked in amazement. I smiled, remembering his advice about girls when I was about fourteen. 'Gerr'in there mate,' he had said then, 'an' gerr'at it.'

But I knew that wouldn't do. 'I'll try and catch her eye,' I replied.

He snorted disgustedly. 'Please y'self,' he said, 'but while you're catchin' 'er eye mate, I'm gonna catch another cuppa tea before it's all gone, OK?' I nodded absently, without taking my eyes off Antoinette. How long I stood there I have no idea, but I noticed with relief that her left hand was devoid of rings!

Suddenly, with the four girls laughing at some remark, she half turned, glanced in my direction, then carried on laughing. A surge of disappointment swept me, then I realised she had only seen me in uniform a couple of times, the first after basic training, and the second just before I went abroad. Once again she turned momentarily and caught my steady gaze. Her smile receded as her eyes opened wide in surprise. We started towards each other simultaneously.

'Liam!' she said wonderingly. 'But I . . .' I smiled and held out both hands. Words seemed inadequate as she took and held them. As though on cue, the band started up again, and the heartache of years slipped away as we drifted into a dreamy waltz, her friends gazing opened-mouthed at us.

A million words remained stemmed behind the magic of the moment as we moved, oblivious of those around us, in close embrace. If only the music would go on forever! It didn't, of course, and I hesitated uncertainly as it stopped. Would she go straight back to her friends?

With a sigh of relief I found my hand still held. 'I'm with Teresa,' I said. 'Would you like to come and see her?' She smiled with delight and our grip tightened. 'You'll get a surprise when you see her,' I added warningly. 'She's not been at all well.'

'Ah, poor Teresa!' she exclaimed. 'What happened?' In the short walk back to the refreshment tables I told her, but she was still shocked at her appearance. 'Oh dear,' she whispered as we approached, 'she does look ill Li!'

'Yes,' I agreed, 'she does, but there's nothing wrong with her spirit, I'll tell you . . . You'll see.'

Momentarily separated by passing dancers, Teresa saw me first, and gave me a disappointed look. 'Where's Anto —'

She stopped and gasped in delight as she saw her. 'Antoinette! Oh love, fancy see —'

The rest was lost as they hugged each other.

'Where's Din?' I asked as they separated.

Teresa jerked her thumb towards the kitchen. 'In there washing up. Wouldn't let me do it.'

'Right,' said Antoinette with a laugh, 'let's all give a hand, then.'

With one arm round Teresa and the other, unbelievably, around Antoinette, I walked into the kitchen in a state of euphoria.

*   *   *

With my sister in Dinny's safe hands, and a taxi ordered to take them home, Antoinette and I left the hall as though the lost time had never existed. Only the pieces of the jigsaw needed to be put together, and, on the long walk to her new home, they were.

We talked of the letters that had never arrived, of the joint family disasters and moves that had broken the final links, the wrong conclusions we had both drawn in thinking our affections had waned and died.

'Oh Li,' she said sadly, 'what a terrible mix up!'

I gave her hand a squeeze. 'We've been lucky, luv. I wonder how many thousands more were split up and never met again?' I vowed to myself that there was no way I was going to lose her a second time. The welcome I received, when her father opened the door, was akin to the return of the Prodigal Son, and her mother was no less delighted. There was much to talk about, many years to span, but, with the clock already past midnight, Mam and Dad would be worried stiff, even with Teresa's news. So, reluctantly, I had to leave.

The long walk home passed in a tumult of thought, and I found them still waiting up when I got home. They were delighted but, turned one o'clock and with early Mass in the morning, it was too late to talk. Besides, I wanted to be by myself, to think.

'I'll tell you all about it in the mornin',' I said. 'I'm shattered.'

Mam nodded understandingly. 'Cuppa tea?' She enquired.

I shook my head. 'No thanks, I'm going to Communion.' Much as I would have liked and needed a cup, I couldn't break my fast until I had received Communion. I knew I had a sleepness night ahead of me, and Antoinete would loom large in my thoughts.

*   *   *

Bleary-eyed and unenthusiastic, I went through the ritual of Mass the following morning, then dallied fitfully with the equally ritual and unappetising salt fish that was normal breakfast after Mass and Communion.

Mam was absolutely delighted with our reunion. 'You won't be goin' back now, then?' she said, smiling as she put the fish before me. I had dreaded the question, although I was prepared for it. Twenty-four hours before, my mind had been more or less made up to rejoin, but now? Well, things had changed a bit.

I looked at her uncertainly and shrugged. 'Dunno,' I answered. Her smile vanished in disappointment and I felt guilty. 'Sorry Mam,' I added lamely, 'I just don't know what t'do, honest. We've only just met again, y'know. There's a lot to . . .'

'Well,' she replied with a slight edge to her voice 'whatever the hell you are goin' t'do, you'd berra do it soon. Anyroad,' she continued, shifting things about on the table irritably, 'if you're goin', when are yeh goin'?' Dad, sitting on the opposite side of the kitchen, lowered his newspaper and looked at me intently as they both awaited my reply.

'My leave finishes on Friday,' I answered, 'but, to be right, I would have to report Thursday as far as I . . .' Con, straight from Mass, interrupted as he came in half-way through my explanation.

''ello,' said Mam in surprise, 'you're early t'day!'

He grinned as he reached for the teapot she had just put down. 'Yeah, went to eight o'clock Mass this mornin'. I wanted to catch 'im,' he added with a nod at me, 'before he went out.' I raised my eyebrows in surprise. 'Aunt Min tells me you've met up with that Antoinette again,' he continued. I looked at him silently. He had never liked her and I sensed the dislike in his tone. He always reckoned she had a bad influence on me.

Mam was puzzled. 'How the hell did our Minny know that?' She demanded. 'They only met last night!'

Con laughed. 'Search me. You know Aunt Min better than I do.'

'Well I'll be damned,' replied Mam. 'Anyroad, what d'yeh want t'see him for?'

'Tryin' t'gerr'im a job, that's all. Just thought I'd lerr'im know, like, in case one comes up.'

I groaned as Dad lowered his paper and caught my expression. Whenever Con walked in, since I had returned home, there was always the danger of possible trouble. Like everyone else in the house, he was fiery, and his current political dedication was like a powder keg waiting for a match. It wasn't that he didn't like me, or vice versa, because he obviously did, but once started, our tongues tended to run away with us. My reunion with Antoinette, I knew, be a flashpoint. He hated her and blamed her entirely for my attitudes, always had, ever since we had moved next door to her and now Dad provided the match. He told Con I was probably going back in the Army. To listen as my brother hit the roof, no one would believe we had all just been to Mass and Communion. Whatever grace we had obtained went straight up the creek as tempers shot up. Dad, worried at the growing hostility between us, stamped his authority to ensure peace for Mam and Teresa, while Mam, deeply worried about me, and impatient with Con for his continual politics, flew at us both. She gave us a better sermon than the priest, and certainly a damned sight closer to the point. Thank God Teresa was still at Mass.

I tried hard to explain to my brother that I had nothing against the Yard, that all I wanted was to 'Gerr'on a bit'. I might just as well have talked to the wall, because all I did was to reinforce his deep suspicions about 'her' influence, despite the fact that we had only just met again!

83

Perilously close to blowing, I gave up before Mam chucked us both out. 'Look Dad,' I said quietly after he had finally shut us both up, 'I think I'll take meself for a walk, sort things out a bit, like.'

He put his paper on the floor as Con rose. 'I was only tryin' to 'elp him!' he complained irritably.

Mam gave him a withering look. 'Well,' she snapped, 'yeh goin' a bloody funny way about it! Like Docherty went to Dublin . . . Backwards!'

'Alright, alright, that's enough!' broke in Dad, getting up. 'I'll come with yeh Li,' he suggested. Everyone looked at him in surprise. Dad's Sunday was usually sacrosanct and unchangeable. Mass, breakfast, read the paper, then round to the club to meet Uncle Matt. He must have been worried to change that.

'You comin Con?' he asked.

Con gave me a sidelong look and shook his head. 'No thanks, I'll 'ang on till Teresa gets back.'

The last time Dad took me for a walk, I had learned a few home truths. I had the feeling I was going to learn a few more. For an hour or more we strolled round the town and the park, occasionally sitting on a bench or leaning over the railings to watch the ducks, and all the while he worked on my problems, making me think. My enquiry as to why Con was so bolshie when he used to be so quiet before the war, was met with the terse statement that he was running with the wrong crowd, with a prediction that he would wake up sooner or later. He added a rider to the effect that I should keep my mouth shut, and not argue with him.

'I shut him up at 'ome,' he said, 'but you can't do that, so don't get involved.' He added with equal bluntness that I was as bad as Con in the opposite direction, so it was six of one and half-a-dozen of the other. My protestations were brushed aside with equal speed when he said that I couldn't pull his leg, he knew me too damned well, so, 'shurr'up'. Nor did he entirely disagree with Con over my going back. I would have to come out sooner or later, and it wasn't going to get any easier; but it was up to me, it was my life.

He wanted to know where Antoinette fitted in. Was I thinking about her in my plans? Since it was only hours since we had met again, I laughed. He stamped on that. She was a good girl and he reckoned we would marry. Did I want to drag her round in the Army? He advised me to think about it. I did, and I didn't fancy it. For the second time since I came home I was told that I didn't know my arse from my elbow, and that it was about time I did. Finally he suggested that, since I still had until Friday to make my mind up, it might be a good idea to go back before then, just to have a look round and see how I felt without signing anything. Then, if I still wanted to go, well go. They wouldn't try to stop me. All they wanted was for me to be settled and happy wherever I was. I gave my solemn promise to do just that.

'Good,' he said, as we watched an excited little lad land a fish from the park lake. He grinned and nodded at the lad as the fish was unhooked. 'Y'know,' he said thoughtfully, 'you fellers are a damned sight more trouble now than when you were his size.' I laughed. He was nothing if not straight. 'Come on,' he continued, 'we'd berra git before your mother sends a search party out!'

6

Fate Takes a Hand

I seem to have spent the whole of that particular
Sunday walking and talking, first to Dad, then, on a
long, circuitous route back to our house for a family
reunion with Antoinette.

Except for the sheer novelty of being together after a
long absence, it was as though time had stood still. Our
mutual affection was, thank God, as strong as ever. No
need for stumbling words, no need for billing and
cooing to rekindle the flames, nothing. All that had
happened was that we were seven years older, the rest
remained as it was. Despite this, however, there were a
thousand and one questions to be asked and answered:
not the time-consuming questions of love — they were
already answered without the use of words — but
urgent, practical questions.

The first, as to whether I was going back, was
inevitable, and this brought another one: what did she
think of it?

Adroitly she passed it straight back. 'It's up to you, if
that's what you want.' I told her about my leave being
up the following Friday and Dad's advice on it. She
agreed with him, and then, with an amused smile,
added a rider that I should go in civvies. 'Then you
might think like a civilian instead of a soldier, as you
do at present.'

Suddenly we were discussing her plans for going
back to college in September and my lack of enthusiasm for another separation.

Her reaction was immediate. 'Typical!' she said. 'Absolutely typical. I suppose if you go back into the Army we wouldn't be separated? But if I go to college we would! God Li, you haven't changed much, have you?'

'Oh aye, I forgot about that.'

She smiled cynically. 'You would!' We had a good laugh and moved on to less dangerous topics: the difficulties of landing a decent job, and my fears of finishing up in a dead-ender, or getting myself mixed up in politics, of Union arguments if I did. Finally the most important thing — our reunion. I admitted I was completely flummoxed by it, although before the dance I had pretty well got myself sorted out, but now . . . Well?

'What do you mean, flummoxed?' she demanded. 'I've told you I don't mind you going back if that's what you want.'

'Yeah but . . .' I began. Suddenly I was lost for words as we both stopped and looked at each other. 'It's you!'

She gazed at me, puzzled. 'Me! Why?'

Never a romantic, I searched desperately for the right words without sounding too daft. 'Well,' I blurted out, 'I nearly lost you once, an' I'm damned if I want to take the chance again, that's all. Now you know why I'm flummoxed.' She stopped again and unhooked her arm from mine and gazed at me in a mixture of amusement and exasperation. Then she giggled.

'What the hell's so funny?' I demanded edgily.

'You,' she replied merrily. 'Do you know what you have just done?' I shook my head in puzzlement and still the penny didn't drop. 'No, what?'

'Well, is it, or isn't it?' she demanded with a laugh. 'You've said you don't want to be separated again, and we can't live together single, can we? So?'

'Hell's bells!' I gasped involuntarily as she watched in amusement. 'Yes,' I agreed finally, 'put that way, I suppose it is OK then, it's a proposal . . . And now,' I added with a laugh, 'I suppose you're flippin' well goin' to turn me down?'

She cocked her head sideways and pursed her lips. 'Well,' she said with wicked smile, 'you could have been a bit more romantic!'

'That's alright my love,' I replied, ignoring the passersby and kissing her impetuously, 'I'll go down on my knees when we get home, how's that?'

And so the most momentous decision of our lives was accidentally made. We agreed I would go back to camp on Thursday and perhaps take a chance on the only job that looked like giving us peace and security, and hoped that any separations entailed would be minimal. But for the moment we would keep the secret of our understanding to ourselves, until things were more settled, although we doubted it would come as a surprise to anyone.

Our reception as we walked into our house sealed my pleasure. All the family except Con and his wife were there, and Antoinette was swamped, as everyone tried to greet her at once. For the first time in many years, the table had been brought into the centre of the room for everyone to squeeze round and, as they sat chattering like monkeys, I felt, for the first time since I had returned, truly happy in a real family celebration. Tomorrow could take care of itself.

With no mention of our secret, and much to think about, Thursday quickly arrived, and a beautiful hot day it turned out to be. At ten, Antoinette arrived to see me off at the station. At eleven, dressed as she wished, in civvies, I would be gone. Dad hadn't said much when I saw him off to work, just 'Good luck — and think!' But Mam wasn't at all happy. Not that she said much either. She wouldn't try to influence me one way or the other, but I knew that mobile face far too well not to know she was in a turmoil. Aunt Min, straight round to our house from early morning Mass, left me in no doubt how she felt. She was 'agin it!'. So was Bernadette.

By ten thirty it was sweltering, with Mam getting more hot and bothered by the minute. 'Hey Li,' she requested irritably, 'open that front door, will yeh? And stick the iron against it. It's flamin' roastin' in 'ere.'

Automatically I went to the cupboard under the stairs to get the old flat iron, used as a door-stop. I was just jamming it against the door when Bernadette popped her head into the hallway, to tell me Con's wife wanted to see me.

I dropped the iron and dashed back to the kitchen. 'Hello Edie, what's up luv?'

'Con told me to tell yeh 'e's comin' round at dinner time.'

'I'm goin' in a few minutes, Edie.' She looked glum. 'What's it about anyway? Did 'e say?'

She shook her head. 'Dunno really. Somethin' about a job, I think.'

I grimaced 'Never mind, luv. Tell him I went at eleven, OK?' I glanced across at Antionette as Edie left disconsolately. She just raised her eyebrows. I looked at the clock. Twenty to eleven! 'Right,' I said to Antoinette, 'I'll just nip upstairs for the rest of my kit, then we're off.' She nodded as Mam came back into the kitchen, obviously in a mood. I went upstairs without a word and was just opening my bedroom door when I heard the knocker thump.

'Who the hell's that?' I heard Mam say. The next minute there was a howl of anguish. I flew downstairs to see what had happened. It was Mam, right leg twisted under her, elbow jammed against the low step, and white with pain. An itinerant peg-seller looked down at her from the other side of the doorstep.

'Mam!' I cried racing up the hallway and bending over her. 'Are you alright? What happened?'

'Fell over the flamin' iron. Ooh,' she gasped painfully. 'I think it's broke,' she added as everyone crowded forward to look. As I lifted her gently to a sitting position, she cried out again.

89

'Shall I call an ambulance?' asked Antoinette anxiously.

'No,' broke in Aunt Min before I could reply, 'take too long. Bernadette, nip down an' see 'arry, will yeh? He'll run 'er to the 'ospital.'

Good old Harry, I thought. He won't refuse. Mam wouldn't be the first who had been rushed to hospital for minor injuries by the jovial greengrocer from the corner shop. It wouldn't matter if it was the middle of the night to him. He always reacted like a shot, had done for years. He wasn't long this time, either. By the time we'd got Mam comfortably on to a chair near the door, he was there. He'd even covered the front passenger seat with a tablecloth.

Teresa, just coming back from Aunt Sarah's to see me off, went white with shock when she saw Mam propped up in the hall. 'Jesus, Mary and Joseph!' she gasped. 'Whatever's happened? Are you alright, Mam?' she continued, without waiting for a reply, as she leaned over her.

Mam nodded painfully. 'Ow!' she exclaimed as she moved. 'It's all down me leg, y'know, and me elbow. Ooh, God it's sore!' For a few moments it was chaos in the tiny space with everybody trying to help, but, with them all shooed back to give us elbow room, and Mam fixed up with a rough sling on her arm, Harry and I managed to carry her, still on the chair, round to the van. From there it was an easy lift into the passenger seat, and the short journey to the hospital was soon completed. I felt a lot happier once she was in safe and capable hands.

She caught my hand just before they took her into a side room for examination. 'What about your train, Li?' she asked quietly, the grey-blue eyes searching my face.

I grinned and gave her hand a squeeze. My problem was solved. Fate had solved it for me. 'Don't worry Mam, I'm not goin' anywhere. See yeh later.' Pain and worry vanished from her care-worn face as I spoke.

She squeezed my hand in return. 'Thanks be t'God for that!' she said quietly as the porter wheeled her away. I checked with the nurse how long she would be, and was told she would have to stay overnight for observation, but that we could come in the evening to see her.

I got home the same time as Dad and, within minutes, his dinner forgotten, we were on our way back to the hospital. The news was good: no breaks, just a severe sprain in the knee, another small sprain in the ankle and a badly bruised elbow. But she would still have to stay overnight. Back home, Con was waiting impatiently for news and also for me. He was delighted Mam would be OK.

'So,' he said gleefully, 'yeh didn't go after all?'

'Well I could hardly leave Mam lyin' in the flippin' hallway could I?' I answered, as Dad sat down to dinner made by Aunt Min.

'It's a good job you were still 'ome,' said Dad, as I went across to Antoinette.

'Oh that's alright Dad,' I answered, still looking at her. 'I'm not goin' back. I've made my mind up.'

He looked up at me. 'You're sure? You've still got tomorrow, y'know!'

I shook my head.' It's OK Dad, I'm sure.'

Antoinette smiled at me. 'Good,' she said.

'Right!' broke in a beaming Con. 'That makes things easier then. I've got another job for yeh.' He saw the look on my face. 'Oh don't luk like that,' he continued with a grin. 'It's not down the Yard.'

'Where is it, then?' I asked suspiciously. 'And doin' what?'

'Greens, y'know, the fridge people. You know where it is!' I nodded. 'It's a nice little job too, I'll tell yeh: plumber's mate.'

'Plumber's mate!' I gasped. 'Me?' I gave Antoinette a horrified glance.

'Yeah,' he snapped, his good humour vanishing fast.

'What's wrong with that? Luk,' he added, stabbing his finger at me, 'it wasn't easy t'get neither, I'll tell yeh. You ask me Dad.' Dad shook his head in agreement. I hesitated. The very thing I had been trying to avoid had happened. Con got irritable. 'Luk Li,' he continued bluntly. 'Do yeh want it or don't yeh? I've gorra let them know on me way back to work.' I looked at Antoinette. She remained impassive, watching the shortening temper as my brother's short fuse began to burn out. 'Come on!' he snapped, 'Warr'is' it? Yes or No?'

'When does it start?' I countered.

'Monday, eight o'clock.' With my Army lifeline now gone, money running out fast, and a marriage in prospect, I didn't have much elbow room. I capitulated. All Con's aggression vanished in an instant. His face lit up, and so did Dad's. 'You won't regret it,' said Con triumphantly. 'Just keep yeh nose clean an' you'll be well away,' he added, putting his cap on. 'Right then,' he continued contentedly, 'tell me mam I'll be round t'see 'er t'night. What's visitin' time?'

Con was wrong, I did regret it. At times bitterly.

*   *   *

By Sunday night, with Mam back home and everyone except me delighted I was staying in Civvy Street, I made myself even more depressed by taking a quick look at my new place of work. I even kitted myself out with a new pair of overalls for the occasion, on Dad's advice. His other advice during the course of several conversations, seemed to hinge on keeping my temper, keeping my nose clean, or, in Northern parlance, don't stick the damned thing where it wasn't wanted and, most important, keep my mouth shut! All my enquiries as to why this, or why that, were met with enigmatic answers such as 'Well, it's not the same as it used to be', or, 'Watch out for trouble makers', etc, none of which gave me much confidence about what I had let myself in for.

But Antoinette seemed determinedly cheerful. 'It'll be alright Li, you'll see,' she said. 'At least you'll be home.'

'Yes,' I had replied, 'but after September you won't be, will you?'

In fact, about the only cheerful thing that came out of our long talks that weekend was that we tacitly decided, if everything went well, that we would get married at Christmas. If not then, then maybe Easter. Of course the ugly question of cash quickly reared its head, and by Sunday night I was beginning to wish I'd put that damned flat iron in its proper place by the door.

The weather on Monday suited my mood to a 'T' as I gazed out of the kitchen window at the soggy back yard. Dad tried to cheer me up by telling me I'd soon get into the swing again, but Mam wasn't so sure, while Teresa, always concerned for me, chided them for worrying me. Not that Mam took much notice: her concern was that I should listen to Dad's advice, and above all to watch my tongue, all of which I vowed I would do. Dad looked at the clock — a quarter to eight. My heart sank as Teresa handed me my dinner tin and small oval, double-ended brew tin containing tea in one end, and condensed milk and sugar in the other. These items, together with my enamelled brew can with it's lid-cum-cup, had been my pride and joy in the old days, but now I wasn't so sure.

'Come on,' ordered Dad, 'we'd berra gerra move on.'

'Don't forget now,' warned Mam, in a final plea for peace, 'watch yeh tongue!'

I nodded and followed Dad out.

We walked in a desultroy silence until I spotted the familiar jaunty figure of Dinny getting off the bus, diddy bag over his shoulder and a broad grin on his face.

'What did I tell yeh,' he said triumphantly, 'couldn't

keep away, could yeh?' Jovially he fell in step beside us, my misery obvious. 'Cor bloody 'ell Li, what's up with yeh? Honest, you've gorra face like a farmer's arse on a frosty mornin'.'

I just had to laugh. 'Ah — y'know,' I replied enigmatically.

'Are yeh with your Con?'

Dad answered for me. 'No Din, he's at Green's, y'know, the fridge people.'

'Oh great. Who are yeh workin' with?'

'Plumber called Len Williams. D'yeh know 'im?'

He smiled broadly, 'Oh old laughin' boy eh!'

His tone made me scowl. 'What d'yeh mean, laughin' boy?' I demanded irritably.

He winked. 'You've seen Buster Keaton laughin', 'aven't yeh?'

'What are yeh talkin' about? He doesn't laugh,' I retorted.

He winked again. 'Neither does Len, mate,' he said with a grin. I could have kicked him. 'Anyway,' he added to complete my gloom, 'I'll see yeh down the Yard later on; Len's workin' on our ship. Cheers.' With a cheery wave he was gone, and Dad and I turned the corner to my new abode. He left me with a warning and a plea.

'Just remember what your mother said,' he reminded me, 'and if you're asked t'do anything, just do it. No arguin'. Alright?'

I nodded silently and watched him go, then, self-conscious in my new and unfamiliar overalls, turned through the door of my new world.

A dozen or so blokes stood around chatting or reading newspapers. I stopped uncertainly, just inside the door, not quite knowing where to go. Several pairs of eyes turned towards me, weighing me up. Suddenly a short, thick-set bloke about Con's age, with a heavily stubbled chin, and a cigarette dangling from his mouth, came towards me, his cheerful face beaming under his filthy flat cap.

94

'Your name Sullivan?' he enquired, rolling the cigarette expertly from one side of his mouth to the other. 'Con's brother?' he added. I acknowledged it. 'Told me the other night in the pub you were startin',' he continued in a friendly tone. 'You're with Len, aren't yeh?' Again I nodded. 'Norr'in yet,' he announced flatly. 'But that's Len all over. Come on and meet the lads,' he invited with a flick of his thumb towards the watching group. 'Oh,' he added as we moved towards them "ave yeh clocked on yet?' I suggested I would leave it until my mate came. 'Fair enough,' he agreed amicably. 'Come on then, I'll introduce yeh.'

They were a lively crew and no mistake, good naturedly pulling my leg about the new overalls; just coming back into Civvy Street; my new mate, and a dozen other things. Then, on the stroke of eight, Joe, my new-found friend who had introduced me, nudged me and flicked his head towards the door.

'There's yeh mate Li. Yeh cin 'ear 'im a mile off.'

I turned as the group broke away to their work, and saw, cigarette in mouth, and coughing his heart up, a tall, thin, almost emaciated figure strolling, hands in pockets, cap tightly on his head, towards the Time Office.

'Jesus,' opined Joe as he turned to leave, ''e 'ad a few last night by the luk of 'im. You'd berra go an' tell 'im you're 'ere. See yeh.'

'Right,' I replied, 'see yeh.' Len stopped as I walked towards him, and looked at me bleary eyed. 'Hi yeh,' I said as I approached with hand extended. 'I'm your new mate. Sullivan.'

He took a long drag at his cigarette, exhaling the smoke through his nostrils like a medieval dragon and slowly extended his hand as he eyed me up and down. 'Hi,' he replied non-committally, as our hands met. The brief greeting over, he nodded towards the office, and shuffled forward. 'Come on,' he said without enthusiasm, 'we'll get your card.'

With our time cards punched in the machine hanging outside the office, I embarked on a day that I shall always remember for its mind-boggling boredom and frustration. The mental turmoil of performing the most menial of tasks, of having little or no part in the work in progress other than putting a tool into, or taking one out of the bag, to pick the bag up, or put the damned thing down; take it there, or bring it here! By five o'clock I hated that tool bag with a deep, near homicidal hatred, and this was only the first day! God, how I longed for the barrack square.

Once again, as Dinny had forecast, I found myself in the Yard aboard a refrigeration ship and not, as I had hoped, out on some private work. Around us, as my mate worked in his soon-to-be-familiar slow and methodical way, the cacophony of the Yard bellowed at us. What little conversation we had was monosyllabic and shouted. By the time the lunch buzzer brought relief, I was in a mood to throw both Len and his bag of bloody tools over the side. However, with my feelings firmly battened down, I gratefully climbed the ladder to the sunlit deck. But my task was not finished yet: I found out that I was also expected to be a servant, as Len gave me his can to brew.

The conversation that followed, as men sprawled out on the deck eating their sandwiches, revolved round just one subject, the 'screwy' problem between the sheetmetal workers and the joiners. I sat in silent disbelief at some of the views expressed. It appeared, from the passions exposed, that the affair was a matter of life or death to most of them, and talk of strike flowed freely from the militants present. Len, far from lethargic, waxed eloquent on the subject.

It wasn't until after lunch that I finally put my foot in it as we settled into the job below decks. Len asked me what I thought about the argument as I was getting the tools out.

Without thinking I answered bluntly. 'Sounds like a

lot'f codswallop to me,' I confessed airily. 'Some-body's got to drill the bloody holes, so why the hell don't they just gerr'on with it?'

He reacted as though he had been stung. 'Y'what?' he demanded. I repeated it and opened the floodgates of his fervour. I cursed myself for the off-the-cuff remark. I'd done the very thing Mam had asked me not to do. Oh hell!

At half past six I was washed, changed, and ready to collect Antoinette, when a furious Con walked in, still in his working clothes. Len had obviously passed my views on. I sensed trouble, and so did Mam and Dad, but I'd had enough for one day.

'See yeh,' I said, heading for the door. 'Got to meet Antoinette, I'm late already.' I looked at Mam as I left. Without moving her lips I could almost hear her saying, 'I warned you, didn't I?'

7

Walking on Eggshells

For two weeks things went reasonably well as, mindful
of Dad's warnings and Len's reaction to my off-the-cuff
remark on my first day, I walked warily, making
tentative friendships, relearning the ropes of this new
industrial and political jungle.

Each day I baulked at the hours of boredom before
me, but, circumstances being as they were, there was
little I could do about it. But it was difficult. Much had
changed in working attitudes, although the native
goodness, friendliness, and the lightning, often devastating wit, and the spontaneous generosity of indi-
viduals as people, were all still there in abundance.
Yet things had changed dramatically. Once within the
gates, whether it be the Yard, or the shop we worked
from, there seemed a subtle and permanent under-
current of discontent. Fiery and independent, I found
it difficult to adjust. It was like walking on eggshells,
but adjust I must. However, despite all my efforts, I
dropped another clanger on the day our particular job
finished in the Yard.

It was all so stupid, so frighteningly simple. It
happened at the end of what had been one of the few
relatively happy days I had had since starting when,
with the job finished well before the expected time, I
thought I would get a bit of firewood for Mam.

'What time is it Len?' I asked as he sat drinking the
last of his tea, and with the tools already for leaving.

He checked his watch. 'Four o'clock,' he replied.

'Why?' I explained about the wood and he was all for it, even rummaging in the bag for a piece of string to tie it up. 'You'll find loads of it up in the tween decks,' he suggested. 'Plenty of chippies workin' up there. Oh,' he added, 'there's no rush, bags of time.' I thanked him and minutes later stood on the tween deck just one deck down from the main deck. He was right, there were bits and pieces all over the place. I started gathering some.

'Gerrin a birra cock wood, mate?' asked one of several workmen nearby.

'Yeah,' I replied. 'Come in 'andy.' With a decent bundle collected, I spotted another piece just a little too big to fit into the bundle. Luckily there was a saw lying nearby. 'D'yeh mind if I use this for a minute, mate?' I called across to a bloke I thought was a carpenter.

'No, norr'at all wack, 'elp y'self,' he replied with a grin. I thanked him, picked it up and began to saw. Half-way through I felt a presence behind me. I half turned, winked at the bloke watching me and carried on sawing.

'What d'yeh reckon you're doin' then?' he demanded gruffly. I stopped, and straightened up. He was about my size and stocky, wearing a chippy's apron and heavy scowl. 'Guess!' I said jocularly.

His scowl deepened. 'You a chippy?' he snapped.

'No. Why? He said I could use it,' I added, nodding at the bloke I had asked.

'Just purr' it down mate!' he·snapped agressively. 'Only chippies use saws, an' you bloody know it!'

I bridled at his tone. 'Don't talk so flamin' daft!' I snapped back, continuing to saw. 'It's only a birra firewood.'

'Purr' it down,' he ordered angrily.

I stopped and glared at him. I knew in my heart that I should put it down, but his attitude brought every ounce of stubbornness to the surface. Nobody was going to talk to me like that and get away with it. All he had to do was to ask properly. My solemn promises to Dad vanished as I faced him, offending saw in hand.

'Get stuffed,' I snapped and turned to begin again as a new voice joined in.

'It's only a birra cock wood, Bert for Christ's sake!' somebody shouted across, as interested workers, sensing trouble, stopped to watch.

'You know the rules!' Bert shouted back. 'An' 'e's no bloody chippy!'

One of the workmen recognised me. 'Hey Bert,' he said, 'that's Con's brother, y'know Con Sullivan. He's workin' up the bow end now.'

'I don't give a bugger 'oo 'e is,' he replied, glaring at me.

For the sake of peace I should have compiled, but there was no way I could back down with his attitude, I just couldn't. Nature wouldn't allow it.

Bert turned to a fellow chippy. 'Hey Frank,' he said, 'go an' fetch 'arry will yeh?' Frank vanished up top, as I stood, saw and wood in my hands at the centre of a silent tableau. All he had to do to resolve the situation was to ask me to put it down, not demand it. Moments later another chippy arrived. I guessed who he was: the shop steward.

'What's all this then, Bert?' he asked my infuriated adversary.

Bert snorted. 'Gorra bloody comedian 'ere 'arry. You tell 'im!' Harry appraised me of the rules again then repeated the demand. If he had asked, OK, but he didn't.

'Ask me,' I invited.

He grimaced in sudden anger. 'I'm not askin', mate, I'm tellin' yeh! Put the bloody thing down or there'll be trouble.' As far as I was concerned he was wasting his time.

Suddenly I heard Con's voice as he edged his way through the onlookers, then stood looking daggers at me. 'What the bloody 'ell's up with yeh now?' he demanded angrily.

'Nothin',' I replied, 'just sawin' a birra wood for me mam, that's all.'

'Y'know damned well you're not supposed t'use the tools, don't yeh?'

I shrugged. 'I didn't know till they said so,' I replied, nodding at Bert and Harry.

Con came forward with an anxious look in his eyes. He knew I was being mulish and why. 'Li,' he pleaded quietly, 'for Christ's sake knock it off, will yeh? You'll 'ave the whole bloody ship at a standstill if you keep this up!'

I felt sorry for him, but I was damned if I was going to be threatened. 'If he wants me to put his bloody saw down, Con, then I want to be asked, that's all, just asked. Nothin' else.'

If looks could have killed I'd have dropped dead on the spot. Con's eyes flickered to Harry, then Bert. Neither spoke as he finally turned to me and said quietly, 'Give it to me Li. Please.'

I smiled, gave him a wink and handed it over. 'You've just said the magic word, Con. A pity they don't know it!'

My brother stuck his angry face close to mine. 'I'll see you later,' he hissed.

*   *   *

Len held his head in his hands when I got back and told him what had happened. 'Bloody 'ell,' he said, 'thank God we've finished 'ere t'day.'

I was in and out of the house in a flash that night. I had had a bellyfull and, knowing Con would be round, didn't want any inquests. It would be bad enough when Dad got to know.

Antoinette knew something was wrong the moment she saw me. 'More trouble?' she asked, before I was half-way through the door.

101

I kissed her and grinned. 'Oh, the usual, luv.'

She gave me a quizzical look and shook her head. 'I don't know,' she said resignedly. 'There's always something down there Li. I wish to goodness you could get something else.' She seemed fed up.

'You worry too much,' I said lightly. 'I'll settle, you'll see.'

She didn't seem convinced, as we walked into the kitchen. Both her parents expressed surprise at my early arrival. I didn't enlighten them, but they knew I hated the job. Her father asked if I had settled yet.

'You'll never settle in that job,' broke in her mother before I could reply, 'you're too independent.'

'To tell you the truth,' I replied with a laugh, 'I wouldn't mind going to college with Antoinette, and that's a fact.' For a few minutes I managed to steer the conversation away from my job and its problems, then suddenly her father asked an unexpected question. He wanted to know if I'd done any teaching in the Army.

'Oh yes. Part of the job really. Not the kind of teaching Antoinette's goin' t'do, but yes, it was teaching. As a matter of fact,' I added, blowing on my fingernails and polishing them on my lapel, 'I'm a *bona fide* PT Walla.'

Antoinette looked at me in surprise. 'You never told me that,' she said. 'That could come in useful.'

I shook my head in amusement. 'In Civvy Street! How d'yeh make that out?'

'Oh I don't know, but it might. It's a qualification, isn't it? Still,' she continued, 'at least you've got a job, that's something. It's not . . .'

I held my hands up in supplication. 'Oh I'm tryin' luv, believe me I'm tryin', and for a very good reason.'

She took my meaning, lowered her eyes and smiled. Her parents caught the expression, put two and two together and came up with four. Her father's next question confirmed it.

'What are your plans, Li . . . Or shouldn't I ask yet?'

I glanced at Antoinette, she smiled and gave an imperceptible nod. Oh the hell with it I thought, and dived straight in. 'We want to get married,' I said bluntly. Their spontaneous delight surprised and heartened me, as her mother rose to plant a kiss on Antoinette's cheek and her father vanished for a moment to return with a bottle.

'Just a bit left over from Christmas,' he explained, as he poured. With good wishes drunk, it suddenly became all business. Had we told my parents? No. Well, I had to tell them tonight, it was only fair. With this last remark came another problem. If I knew my brother, Dad would have been appraised of all the grisly details of the recent fracas, and my name would be mud, especially after promising to keep out of trouble. I wanted Antoinette to share our news with me, but first I needed 'sea room' for manoeuvre.

I told a black lie. 'Oh no, not tonight, Mrs Kavanagh. Me Dad won't be in till late. Tomorrow eh?' They agreed, and the next moment I found myself being hauled into the parlour for a quiet chat with her Dad, while mother and daughter were swept away on a flood of questions and answers.

* * *

I had my talk the following evening, but it wasn't about getting married. In fact, with one thing and another I barely got round to seeing Antoinette. I knew something was wrong, the moment Mam had finished clearing up, and announced that she and Teresa were going round to see Aunt Min, because she rarely, if ever, went out in the evening, except on a Saturday with Dad to the pictures. But I passed no comment. It wasn't until Con arrived, looking more serious than usual, that I got the message. It had all the earmarks of a 'session' with Dad, with Con in close support. I wasn't kept waiting long. Almost before the door had closed behind them, Dad fixed me with one of his looks.

'What's up?' I asked innocently, as Con went into the back kitchen to put the kettle on.

'What's all this I 'ear?' he demanded.

'Oh, y'mean about the chippy?' I queried as my brother returned and sat down grimly, irritated by my amused expression.

'It's not funny!' he growled, turning to Dad. 'You know what they're like down there, Dad. Tell 'im'

'Just a minute, you!' snapped back Dad irritably. 'Leave this t'me, will yeh?'

'All I did was to get a birra wood, Dad. What's wrong with that?' I complained.

'Nowt,' he growled. 'Its how yeh gorrit that's important. From what I 'ear, you bloody near caused a walk-out! Is that right?'

Before I could answer Con cut loose. 'Yeah,' he snapped, 'an' if I 'adn't got wind of it he wou . . .'

Dad rounded on him. 'Now you shurrup a minute,' he warned. 'As far as I cin see, it's six of one an' 'alf a dozen of the other. Let's 'ear his side of it eh? There's two sides to every story, y'know.'

I explained in detail all that had happened and admitted that I'd been bolshie once the bloke started threatening me. I told him that all I wanted was to be asked, not ordered.

'Look Dad,' I began, but he shut me up.

'No, you luk. An' for Christ's sake listen for once. It might save a lot of flamin' trouble!' He gave me the length of his tongue for minutes on end. It wasn't as though he hadn't warned me, he said, but no, I was too damned pig-headed by half. 'Oh it's no use you tellin' me you don't know the ropes, my lad,' he ended, 'because you damned well do. Oh, I know it's changed a lot, but you know bloody well that yeh don't 'andle tradesmen's tools!' I explained again that I had asked to use the saw. He swept it aside with the terse statement that whoever said I could wanted his 'bloody bumps' read. Then he turned to the effects on Mam and Teresa of the constant arguments between Con and me. They were sick and tired of it, and it would stop now. If anyone was going to cause trouble from now on it would be him, not Con or me. Con made to protest, but got chopped off just as quickly as I had.

I had never seen him so riled; as far as stubbornness was concerned, Con and I were only learners. Nothing was going to stop him that night, and nothing did; he roasted both of us. Then, a little calmer, as his immediate temper waned, he patiently outlined the reasons for the attitudes that I found so frustrating at work. He revealed, much to Con's militant annoyance, that he found some of the things going on just as daft as I did. But reasons there were, good solid reasons, from the memory of tradesmen walking the streets in the hard times, when anyone handy would pick the tools up.

'Aye,' broke in Con at that stage, 'as soon as I'd finished my apprenticeship, they chucked me straight on to the street. You don't know anythin' you don't,' he snorted angrily.

'Alright!' warned Dad irritably, 'that's enough of that! I'll purr'im right, don't worry, so you just shur-rup!' Con subsided.

'Yeah,' I said while I had the chance, 'that's all very well, Dad, but warrabout this other stuff. Y'know — unions an' that? I wasn't there a flamin' week an' I was told three or four times about joinin'. Surely t'God it's up to me whether I wanna join or not, isn't it?'

This touched Con on a raw spot. 'Well 'e shoulda joined by now.'

Dad glared at him ferociously. 'Alright, alright!' he snapped. 'Keep yeh flamin' shirt on. He only asked a question, that's all.' I looked at the clock as he spoke and groaned inwardly. I should have been at Antoin-ette's half an hour ago, but I daren't just walk out, not until Dad had finished, and he certainly hadn't finished yet. I looked at my seething brother. I just couldn't make him out at all. Before the war he had been the exact opposite, and hated trouble, but now, blimey, he was so far left it was unbelievable. It worried the life out of Mam, and I couldn't forgive him for that, and he sure wasn't going to convert me with that attitude.

'Of course it's up to you whether you join or not,' said Dad answering my question. 'But, and I would think about this if I were you, lad, if you don't, then you can expect a rough ride if anythin' blows up, and don't kid yourself otherwise. After all, that's what the unions are all about: solidarity.' Con nodded in approval, then glowered as Dad continued. 'That's not to say that I agree with all that's goin' on, because I don't but, as I say, think about it. It's up to you and . . .' The door bell interrupted him. 'That'll be your mother,' he ended. 'Go an' open the door.'

I went. It wasn't Mam, it was Dinny. I was delighted to see him. 'Just thought I'd pop round an' see how you were doin' like,' he said. I rolled my eyes. 'D'yeh fancy a jar? I've got somethin' t'tell yeh,' he invited.

'No thank's Din, I'm havin' a natter with me Dad an' our Con. Come in, have a cuppa.'

He smiled at me, amused. 'What are they on about, as if I didn't know?' he asked, as we walked in to the kitchen. I checked the clock again as he greeted them. Half past eight! Hell, she would wonder what had happened to me. Disgruntled, I turned to see Dinny grinning broadly as he spoke to Dad.

'I see he managed to put his foot in it again,' he said with a laugh. God, I thought, news sure gets round fast down there.

'Yes,' replied Dad wearily, 'we've just been talkin'. He'll learn.' He stopped as he looked at the clock. 'Hey Con,' he added, 'I thought you said you were pickin' Edie up at eight . . . 'Ave yeh seen the time?'

Con checked the clock and gasped. 'Oh hell,' he said irritably, 'I'd berra get. Y'know what Edie's like for worryin'.' I felt a sense of relief as he donned his coat, even though he did turn at the door with a parting shot. 'Now you just watch it, OK?' I nodded silently and sighed anew as the door closed behind him. I apologised to Dad for all the trouble.

He shook his head wearily. 'Oh I know what it's like,' he said, 'but as I told yeh before Dinny came, think about joinin' the Union. It might save you a lot'f trouble. But if you can't or won't fall into line, then the only advice I can give you is to get t'hell out of it altogether.'

'That's good advice Li,' broke in Dinny. 'I'd think about it if I were you. Like y'Dad says, it can get rough.'

I smiled wryly, then looked at Dinny's suddenly beaming face. 'What are you lookin' so pleased about?' I demanded.

He held his hands up. 'You're never gonna believe this, mate,' he announced, 'but d'yeh know who I've just seen?'

I grimaced. 'Who?'

His smile broadened. 'Father Fielding!'

For a split second the name meant nothing, then it dawned. 'Henry! Our Henry?' I was absolutely delighted.

'Yeah, couldn't believe it. Been t'see his mam, she lives up near us. Cor, he looks great!'

'Well why didn't you bring . . .'

He cut me short, explaining that he had only seen him for a few minutes by pure accident as he passed a bus stop, with Henry about to board for the station. The years suddenly fell away as I tried to picture the small, slight figure on the day he left to start his training. It didn't seem possible that so much time had passed. God, I wished I could have seen him. Dinny explained that Henry had been on Church business to St Malachy's from his parish in Shrewsbury, and had taken the opportunity to nip home and see his mother. Dinny had told him I was back home and he sent his regards but couldn't come because of his train. What a pity! Of all the gang, Henry — quiet gentle Henry — had been the universal favourite. But at least I knew he was well. Maybe we would see each other again sometime. I know Dinny felt the same way. His news, after the trauma of the evening, had been like a burst of sunshine.

For a moment I had completely forgotten about Antoinette. Suddenly I remembered. 'Oh hell!' I exclaimed 'Antoinette. Luk Din I've got t'go, honest.'

'Blimey,' he said, 'you're keen. Don't tell me yeh serious then?'

'What d'yeh mean, courtin'? Of course I am. Only for the war we . . .'

He burst out laughing. 'You're never gonna get married are yeh?'

'Of course we are . . . Christmas if possible. If not, then . . .'

Dad's gasp, and the rattle of the key in the door were almost simultaneous. He was still staring at me, flabbergasted, as Mam and Teresa walked in. 'He's gerrin' married!' he announced to a disbelieving Mam. She didn't even notice Dinny in her surprise, while Teresa, ever emotional, squealed in delight.

'You're not!' said Mam, hand to her lips. I nodded and a smile swept her face. Hell I thought, this is not what I intended. All my plans for the evening had gone haywire with a vengeance, but still, everyone seemed delighted! I looked at the clock again. A quarter past nine!

'Look Mam,' I broke in as they chattered excitedly, 'I'd better go round to Antoinette's before it's too late. I should 'ave been there at seven!'

'Are you bringing her back?'

'No, it'll be too late. I'll tell her you all know, though. That'll please 'er. Come on Din, let's move it, eh?'

Minutes later we were ready and left the house amid a chatter of speculation. At the street corner we parted, as we had done so many times in the old days, under the street lamp. If only Henry could have come, it would have been like the old days.

'Good luck, Li. Give my regards to Antoinette, won't yeh? Oh yeah,' he added, 'do me a favour, will yeh?'

'What's that, then?'

'Just watch yeh step down the Yard, Li. There's some rum uns about nowadays just itchin' for trouble, so . . .' I glared at him. He laughed. 'Oh I know you cin take care of y'self Li, but this is different. If yeh do run inter trouble, it might not be one to one against yeh.' I nodded my understanding. 'If you get any problems,' he added seriously, 'don't go off half-cocked, mate, like you always used to. Just 'ave a word first, will yeh?'

I reassured him. 'OK Din, I'll remember.' A sudden thought struck me as he turned to go. 'Hey Din!' I called. 'Warrabout bein' my best man, eh?'

He smiled broadly. 'Thought you'd never ask!' he replied, sticking his thumb up.

8

A Slight Squall

With less than a month to go before Antoinette left for college to complete her training, and just four months to the great day itself, I found myself caught up in an irresistible whirl of activity. Unlike Mr Micawber, who constantly waited for something to turn up, only to be disappointed, I was praying to God that nothing would turn up! But it did, mostly problems, and in shoals.

At work, of course, there were always problems, but these I had learned to put up with, while at home and at Antoinette's the wedding and the arrangements seemed to consume them: talk and more talk, and plans with more detail than a military operation, all of which made elopement seem an alluring alternative. Amidst it all, I alone, to my eternal shame, seemed the only one worried and miserable, but with good reason. I was broke. With seemingly a million new problems to face, I felt trapped, helpless. Where would we live? I had the chilling vision of a couple of grotty rooms furnished with orange boxes, with jam butties for Sunday dinner. I went through moments of near desperation, with treasonable thoughts of backing out flickering through my mind. In fact, though I would have died rather than admit it, I had the 'shakes'! The trouble was, I couldn't tell anyone, least of all Antoinette.

Only one thing pleased me at this traumatic time, and this was the transformation in Teresa. She seemed to have taken on a new lease of life and just bubbled with happiness, and for that, a journey to hell and back would been worthwhile. After the first few hectic days I took Dad's advice to leave 'em to it, and set about the more important and urgent problem of trying to penetrate the formidable shadows of the future. I had an abiding fear of being stuck in a job in which I felt bound, gagged, and completely stifled. I hated it but, with little money, depended on it absolutely and so, in the general happiness around me, I alone remained in the depths of despondency.

The most pressing problem was money, with an even bigger problem of how the hell to get some! Short of robbing a bank there was only one way: work, as much overtime and odd jobs as I could get. Therefore I was pleased when my cousin Alf appeared on the scene with a gleam in his eye, just as I was finishing my dinner three or four weeks after our announcement.

He beamed as he sat down. 'How's it goin' then? All set to get spliced?'

I nodded non-committally as Dad glanced up from his paper and grinned. 'Got another job on then eh, Alf?' he queried.

'Yeah,' replied Alf, 'birr'of a paintin' job, like. Thought he'd like to earn a few bob,' he added with a jerk of his head at me.

I looked at him suspiciously. 'Oh,' I said, 'what is it this time — another favour?'

He looked hurt, then brightened. 'No mate, a doddle this one, right up your street, honest.'

I grimaced. I knew Alf too well to be enthusiastic. 'Well if it's anythin' like the cellar job Alf, y'know what you can do with it, don't yeh?' Dad looked over his glasses and smiled broadly as Alf laughed, then went into a coughing spasm.

'Na, nothin' like that Li,' he gasped, when he got his breath back. 'Piece of cake this one. Straight up. I wouldn't kid yeh, yeh know that.'

I wasn't so sure. I needed the money badly, but my

111

cousin had about as much business sense as a ruptured cuckoo. Like a fool, I had done one or two jobs with him since I came home, with the last one less than a week ago. That too was a 'piece of cake', but the customer wasn't all that pleased when he leaned on the shelves that Alf swore he had screwed up, and they collapsed under the weight. The few bob it had fetched never even covered the time we'd spent. Still, it wouldn't cost me anything to ask.

'OK,' I invited, 'let's have it, then. What is it? Where is it, and how much?' The first question he answered vaguely, the second that it was at the North end of the town, and the third that it would fetch five or six quid each.

Not bad I thought. 'How long will it take d'yeh reckon?'

He blew through his lips. 'Oh two or three evenin's maybe. I tell yeh Li, it's money for old rope, mate.'

It sounded tempting, but knowing him I wanted to see it first, and with Antoinette coming at seven I was in a bit of a dilemma. I tried to get a few more details but without success, so I made up my mind to have a look. 'OK Alf, we'll go an' have a shufty. No promises mind, but if it's anything like, well, we'll see.'

With glowing phrases, he extolled the virtues of the fortune about to fall into our laps as I finished my dinner, but I remained cynical. He slid round all my enquiries regarding the extent of the job, who was supplying the paint and so on, with a series of nods, winks, and mono-syllabic answers leaving me distinctly uneasy as we headed for the bus stop.

Within half an hour all my worst fears were confirmed. It was a Lulu. As it turned out, he didn't even know the woman. She was a friend of Aunt Sarah's. My heart sank as we walked round. It would have taken two tradesmen painters a fortnight or more to do it. An old, high-ceilinged Victorian house with a main bedroom the size of a small football pitch to be done, and a hallway and landing with more doors than we had altogether in our house, and every one of them blistered. Alf watched me in growing disappointment as I scowled.

The customer, an old lady nearer a hundred than seventy, was as deaf as a post and chattered constantly as she followed us about like a noisy ghost. 'You'll be sure the grainin's done proper won't yeh?' she shouted as I ran my hand over the cracked doors.

I looked at Alf, amazed. Graining? 'She must be kiddin',' I said. 'Look at it!'

He did and shrugged. It hadn't been touched for years. 'Well I didn't know, did I?' he said despondently as the old lady chattered away.

'You shoulda flippin' well found out, shouldn't yeh?' I snapped as she pulled at my sleeve. 'What d'yeh want dear?' I shouted, without any effect.

She cupped her thin, claw-like hand over her ear. 'Y'what?' she screeched.

I glared at Alf, standing dejectedly beside us. 'I said, what d'yeh want dear?' I repeated.

'Yes,' she replied, 'an' two coats, mind yeh. I want no skimpin', neither!'

'Y'what?' I asked desperately, as Alf started to titter.

'Oh aye,' she continued, as though I hadn't spoken, 'and another thing. I want them there ceilin's washed first, y'know. Oh yes.' Alf, unable to contain himself, turned away as I gazed dumbly at her.

'Hey Alf!' I snapped irritably. 'Come an' give us a flippin' 'and 'ere, will yeh. It's your job, not mine. You talk to 'er.'

Alarm crossed his now serious face and his eyebrows shot up. 'Me! Oh no,' he protested. 'You do it, yeh doin' great Li, honest.'

I gave him a homicidal look as I felt another tug at my sleeve. I looked down into the watery blue eyes. 'Yes dear. Warrisit now?' I queried exasperatedly.

'Brown,' she said, nodding her head decisively and pointing a bony finger at a door. 'I like brown . . .'

I gave up. 'Come on mate, you have a go, I'm fed up. It's like talkin' to a flippin' wall.'

She looked at Alf, then pointed an accusing finger at me as he tried to speak. ''E won't answer me!' she complained. 'What's up with 'im?'

'That's alright Mrs Thompson!' he shouted.

'I thought you said you didn't know 'er,' I snapped accusingly.

'I don't . . . Just 'ang on a minute luv, will yeh?' he pleaded as she tugged at his arm. 'I'm just gonna talk to . . . Oh t'hell with it!' he ended in exasperation. 'She can't 'ear a dicky bird, Li.'

'I know that,' I snapped, 'but you said you didn't know 'er.'

'I don't. Just 'er name, that's all.'

For a few constantly interrupted minutes we discussed what to do. We didn't want to hurt her feelings, but there was just no way we could undertake the job and be fair. It needed proper painters, not odd job men. I told him so. He expressed alarm. He had promised Aunt Sarah, as a favour. I suggested that if she was that keen she could come and do it. To mollify him I agreed to go up and have a look at the bedrooms. I wished I hadn't. She followed us all the way, demanding this, ordering that.

I gave up. 'Come on Alf, let's go down. There's no way we can do this, especially not for six quid. I'd sooner get some overtime in at work, mate.'

The next problem was to tell her. With her hand cupped over her ear she listened to no avail, then wagged her finger admonishingly at me while Alf, hands in pockets, whistled gently, exonerating himself from the proceedings.

I finally lost patience. 'Hey Alf,' I snapped, 'don't stand there flippin' whistlin', mate. Give us a 'and will yeh? 'Ave yeh gorra birra paper on yeh?' He rummaged in his pockets and came up with an old envelope and a pencil stub. 'We can't do it Luv,' I wrote in large letters and handed it to her.

She didn't have her right glasses, she announced shrilly. It took us another valuable fifteen minutes to find the damned things and she burst forth anew when she understood. We apologised all the way to her front gate, at the top of our voices.

'Hey Alf,' I pleaded as we walked to the bus stop, 'next time you gerra buckshee job, for Christ's sake look at it first, will yeh, and price it!'

'Yeah,' he agreed. 'Still,' he added with a grin as we boarded the bus, 'nice old soul, wasn't she?' I passed no comment. I felt choked at the loss of good money, but it just wouldn't have been fair to the old dear.

I tried to explain this to Antoinette when I got home and hived her off from yet another discussion into the quiet of the parlour. I felt irritable and edgy as we sat down.

'Never mind, love,' she said encouragingly, 'everything will turn out alright, you'll see. Rome wasn't built in a day.'

I was in no mood for comforting words. The problems to me seemed endless, and on top of that I found all the fuss irritating. Every time I walked through the door they seemed to be discussing something to do with the wedding. She was lucky, an only child with, as far as I knew, very few relatives, except her Uncle John, a steward on the Mauretania, an aunt with a boarding house in Morecambe, and another aunt in Stockport. But me, I had legions of them and all, in one way or another, seemed involved.

'You're quiet,' she said with a little squeeze on my arm.

'Oh, just thinkin',' I replied with a sigh.

She laughed. 'You worry too much love. It's good fun. For goodness sake cheer up a bit, will you?'

Suddenly I felt fed up with the whole damned thing, and snapped her head off. 'It might be fun to you,' I growled, 'but as far as I'm concerned, I'm sick to death of listenin' to weddin' plans. There's other things besides that, y'know!'

All her good humour vanished. Lips pursed she sat bolt upright. 'Well,' she snapped back, eyes glinting, 'if that's the way you feel, then perhaps it would be best if we don't get married!'

I looked at her startled. 'Oh don't be so damned daft, woman!' I felt her tense as she drew away.

'I suppose you'd feel better if everyone went round with long faces,' she said furiously. 'Then you'd complain that nobody gave a tinker's damn . . . Men!'

I came within a fraction of blowing my top, but Teresa's cheerful voice saved the situation. 'Come on you two,' she shouted through the door, 'supper's ready.'

We rose in hostile silence and opened the door. Teresa spotted the tension in a second.

'Hello, what's up?' she enquired bluntly. 'Had a row?' I shrugged silently as I went into the kitchen.

Mam took one experienced look at me. 'And what's up with you, then?'

Antoinette answered for me. 'Oh he worries too much,' she said exasperatedly.

Mam laughed. 'Huh,' she snorted, 'take no notice of him, luv. He's the other end of his father. Sit y'selves down.'

I cursed silently to myself but said nothing. It was alright for them. All they were thinking about was the wedding, but I was the one who would have to figure out what would happen after it. Women!

The walk home was long and silent. I didn't even go in when we got there. We looked at each other in solemn antagonism in the light of the street lamp, assailed by a thousand and one intangible, unexplainable doubts. I wanted to embrace her but perversely held back. I wanted to say sorry, but was too damned pig-headed to do so. After all, I thought, self-righteously, my worries were real worries – a decent job, somewhere to live, bills to be paid, and God knows what all, so what the hell was she so peeved about?

Honest, it would make you spit! I looked at her solemn face and gave up, then, with a quick peck on an unresponsive cheek, I left.

'See yeh tomorrow,' I grunted as I turned on my heel.

* * *

After a restless night I was still grumpy when I got to the works the following morning. Len wasn't feeling too rosy either, after a night on the beer.

'What are we on this morning, then?' I asked without enthusiasm.

'Nuthin' much, coupla little jobs down the Yard t'check up on, then back 'ere.'

The jobs turned out to be on the new fridge boat, fitting out in the basin. With nothing particular to do in the huge hold as Len worked methodically in a corner, I gazed interestedly about me. In the centre of the deck lay a pile of hooks and pulleys ready for fitting, and near them three or four labourers like myself, waiting for their mates, the fitters. Ever curious, my eyes wandered round the hold, then up to the deck head where line after line of steel piping awaited the fitting of the hooks and pulleys. Picking up one of the hook sets to examine it more closely I fiddled in silence for a moment or two then, having satisfied myself how they worked, thought I would take it a stage further and hook it on to the over-head piping to see the effect. Completely forgetting the incident with the chippy, I moved a convenient box over to stand on, in order to reach the pipes. The labourers watched me interestedly. One of them, smiling broadly, sauntered across and looked up at me.

'What yeh doin' there then?' he asked pleasantly.

'Oh, just fiddlin' y'know. Thought I'd see how it worked like.'

He grinned. 'I don't think I'd bother if I were you, mate. That's a fitter's job!'

I cursed myself for my stupidity as I got down. 'Oh yeah,' I said with a laugh, 'never thought of that.' I felt irritable with myself as I sauntered away. That's just what I didn't need at the moment, more arguments at work, especially after falling out with Antoinette.

At half past eleven Len expressed himself satisfied with what he was doing.

'Right, that's it then,' he announced, handing me a spanner to put away. 'Luk,' he added, 'we've gorra birra time t'spare, so I'm just gonna nip ashore t' see a mate of mine.'

'What d'yeh want me t'do?'

He shrugged. 'Please y'self. Stay aboard if yeh want. I'll be back when the buzzer goes.'

'Oh right, I'll see if I can find Dinny. Y'know, Dinny Devlin?'

He laughed, 'Everyone knows Dinny. Anyroad, t'save yeh feet, 'e's workin' midships on the main deck. See yeh later.'

It was the first chance I had had since I came back into the Yard to have a quiet look round, so, with the bag over my shoulder I strolled along the cool sunlit deck, watching the various jobs in progress on my way midships. A shrill whistle brought me up sharp. It was Dinny, goggles tipped back over his cap, welding gear in his hands and a broad grin on his face.

'What the hell are you lookin' so worried about?' he asked jokingly.

'Nothin'. Just thinkin', that's all. Lukin' for you really.'

'Well, you've found me. Just 'ang on a minute, will yeh? I'll be finished in a tick. Luk,' he added, 'knock a coupla brews up, will yeh?' He flicked his thumb portside. 'You'll get some 'ot water over there.'

With the tea made and the buzzer blasting out, we settled ourselves starboard, overlooking the sunlit basin for a quiet chat. He pulled my leg as usual about the wedding.

'Yeah,' I retorted, 'it's about time you thought about it too, isn't it?'

'Oh no mate, not me. Luv 'em an' leave 'em, that's my motto, you know that.' For a while it was quite like old times, then inevitably the subject got round to jobs and money.

I signed heavily. 'Blimey, don't talk t'me about money, Din. There seems no end to the stuff we've got to get. Honest t'God, I never realised what was involved. We'll be flamin' lucky to gerr'away even for a few days, the way things are goin'. Even with overtime it's slow comin' in.'

He looked at me sympathetically. 'I can imagine,' he replied, then fell silent for a moment or two. 'How d'yeh fancy doin' a few foreigners with me?' he asked out of the blue.

'Foreigners? I didn't know you did any private work, Din.'

'Course I do. There's always somebody wants a birra plumbin' done and, if the price is right, I do it. It's always 'andy to get a bit stashed away if yeh can. Certainly come in 'andy for you right now, wouldn't it? What d'yeh reckon?'

I was delighted. The few jobs I did with Alf were helpful, but he was a shocker at getting the right price. Half the time it was favours, with little return. 'You're on mate,' I said gratefully. 'The more the merrier at the moment.' It was a huge relief. If Dinny took a job there would be no favours about it. He was nobody's fool. But I was a bit puzzled. 'I thought you were all fired keen on this Union stuff, y'know, meetin's and God knows what all? Like that night in the pub over this 'holes' thing.'

He raised his eyebrows cynically. 'Oh I am, but it's not the be all and end all, I cin tell yeh. I know what I'm doin'. Gorr'it all worked out, mate.'

He proceeded to explain just what it was he had worked out, and it shook me a bit. Like me, he revealed

119

unexpectedly, he too was ambitious but, unlike me, he knew exactly what he wanted and, more important, just how he was going to achieve it. I was fascinated. He wasn't shop steward for nothing, it turned out. That was a mere rung on the Union ladder. He was aiming for the top, as a full time union official. He even had it worked out on a time scale to haul himself through the heirarchy to area representative, or even higher. In ten years of good conscientious work he reckoned he would be home and dry on a nice, clean-hands job.

'You crafty sod,' I said admiringly. 'Trust you!'

'Why not?' he demanded. 'Now you know the reason why I don't wanna get married, at least not yet. If I did, we wouldn't see a helluva lot of each other, would we? That's no kind of marriage Li, is it? No, as I say, for the moment I'll just play the field and see how things go. Oh, by the way,' he added, rummaging in his pocket, 'how about buyin' a coupla draw tickets?'

I groaned. 'Blimey Din,' I said half heartedly, 'I'm tryin' t'save money, not spend it.'

'Oh come on, yeh miserable sod. It's for the Union benevolent fund. Threepence each, that's all. Come on, don't be so flamin' mean.'

'Oh alright then, give us two. That'll be another tanner up the creek!'

'Ah shurrup,' he replied with a grin as he handed me the tickets.

It was one of the happiest hours since I returned as we laughed and joked, reminisced about the old gang, and Henry in particular, recalling the fun we had had, until the one o'clock buzzer called us back to reality. I felt relaxed, as though I had been on a short holiday, and the worries of the past week about money eased considerably. If I knew my Dinny, there would be no shortage of 'foreigners' now that he knew that the cash would be handy for me. And with Alf's erratic, sometimes unpredictable contributions and hair-brained 'favours', my outlook considerably brightened. It wasn't until Len whistled for me to join him on the portside that Dinny had second thoughts.

'Hey Li,' he said as I turned to go, 'don't forget, you never 'eard what I said about what I'm after in the Union! That's just between you, me and the gate post, right? And especially don't mention it to your Con. Y'know what he's like!'

I grinned and banged my ear. 'Y'what Din? Y'know that's funny, I can't 'ear a damned thing.'

He laughed. 'Good. Let's 'ope yeh memory's just as bad.'

9

Future Planning

Suddenly, as though time had slipped into top gear, it was the thirty-first of August. Antoinette would be on her way to college, and I was not looking forward to it one little bit. I felt edgy and uneasy by the number of rows we had had over the past fortnight, with both of us seemingly working in opposite directions, the worst one being barely a week ago as we had strolled through the park.

Brooding as I had been over, to me at least, enormous problems, and not a little irritated with her over her delight in what to me, were relatively unimportant preparations, I just happened to mention yet again the difficulties of accommodation. Quite reasonably, she told me that I was worrying unnecessarily, something would turn up.

'It's alright for you!' I had snapped. 'It's me that seems to have t'do the worryin'.'

She reacted as though she had been stung. 'What?' she demanded, whipping her arm from under mine. 'Anyone would think you were doing all the work. Well let me tell you, you're not! We,' she continued, tapping herself on the chest, 'your mother, my mother, Teresa and everybody's working hard. The only who isn't helping is you!' Ignoring the glances of the curious passersby I glared back at her furiously. Well, I thought, of all the bloody cheek! Here's me, working all the hours God sends to get a few bob together, getting segs on my eyes looking for a place to live, worrying about this, that and the flamin' other, and she says a thing like that! Oh no, that wasn't fair by a long shot.

'Whaddy yeh mean?' I demanded, reciting all the things that were worrying me.

'Yes!' she hurled at me, 'and that's all you're damned well doing, worrying. That's not helping, is it?'

I nearly took her head off in righteous indignation. 'Right,' I snarled, 'if that's the way you feel about it, you can call the whole flamin' thing off!'

Face tense, eyes flashing angrily, she glared back defiantly. 'Alright,' she hissed, 'if that's the way you want it, then I'm going, and,' she flung back at me as she turned on her heel, 'I don't want to see you again . . . Ever!'

In a turmoil of astonishment, anger and remorse I watched her go, back ram-rod straight, head up, and with a defiant swing of her arms as she marched out of sight round a bend in the pathway. I felt numb, and momentarily panic-stricken as I realised what I had done. Every nerve urged me to run after her, to explain it was all a mistake, to take her in my arms and hug her tight, but pride held me prisoner. Instead, I leaned despairingly over the railings, watching the ducks and envying them their serenity. I felt hurt, angry and confused all at the same time.

It was true I wasn't doing anything in the actual preparation. That was women's work; I had to think ahead. Of course I was doing something. At the same time, deep in the back of my mind, was a persistent nagging worry about Teresa, despite her present happiness. No, I thought, angrily scuffing the ground with my foot, I did have things to do: to me, damned important things. She just wasn't being fair.

I took a long, lonely and argumenative walk, chunnering to myself every foot of the way. How the hell could I tell them at home that everything was off? How would Teresa react? The thought appalled me. I just couldn't tell them, and anyway, the very last thing I wanted was to call it off. Disconsolate and angry with myself for that momentary flash of temper, I walked towards the park gates on my way home, a thousand excuses tumbling through my mind to explain Antoinette's absence when I got there, but, thank God, I didn't need them. Sitting on a bench near the gates, head down, staring at the ground in front of her was my dear love. My heart went out to her. I wanted to run the last few paces, but didn't. Instead I walked quietly and sat down beside her. As she raised her head the tears were streaming down her cheeks.

'I'm sorry luv,' I said, but words were not needed as we embraced. The storm had passed.

* * *

Now, with an hour off to see her to the station, we walked the last few paces to the train. I would feel lost without her.

'Come on Li, cheer up. It's not the end of the world, you know.'

'I just wish you were coming instead of going, that's all luv.'

'Well, it won't be long before Christmas. It'll soon pass, then we'll have a couple of weeks to ourselves, won't we? Oh yes, I forgot to tell you, Uncle John's sailing again next week.'

'Oh aye . . . Same run?' I had only met her father's brother once. He was a nice, homely sort of bloke.

She nodded. 'And you know what?' she said, as we made our way down the steps to the crowded Underground platform. I shook my head. 'He's bringing the material so mother can make my dress.'

For the first time that morning I felt more cheerful. 'Oh great!' I replied, and was even more delighted when she added that for the next few trips he was also

124

going to bring food back for the reception as well. It was to be his wedding present to us. It was the first bit of really good news I had had for some while because, with rationing still on, food, I knew, had been one of the greatest problems. In one stroke a big question mark for the women had been removed, and the Mauretania, having at least three more trips to make before Christmas, it promised well.

'Now do you feel any better?' she asked with a laugh. There was a sudden surge in the surrounding passengers as I assured her I did, then my heart sank at the sound of the approaching train.

In a few minutes she would be gone. I put my overalled arm about her waist, reluctant to let her go. Still holding her, we were nearly bowled over as the train stopped and the rush began. She said something that I couldn't hear in the noise about us. The whistle blew. She shouted again as she was carried through the door. Just before it closed, I made out that her father wanted to see me. My question why was lost as the automatic doors closed on the packed occupants. I swore to myself. I hadn't even got a parting kiss.

Upset and irritable, I made my way into the busy street and headed for the Yard, where we were still working. The prospect of Len's company all day depressed me further. Still, I thought, cheering myself up, I could always have a natter with Dinny when the buzzer went. He was always good for a laugh.

* * *

With Antoinette away it was a golden opportunity to get extra overtime and a few jobs with Dinny, and it was almost a week before I finally got round to Antoinette's to see her dad. Even then I barely got a word in edgeways as her mother, brimming with enthusiasm, dominated the conversation. I explained in reply to her remark that the 'wanderer' had

125

returned, that I had been working late, and also, in response to a further question, that I knew all about Uncle John and what he was going to do, for which we were grateful. But her next query caught me unawares.

'Have you thought anything about where you're going to live?'

I groaned inwardly. I hadn't a clue. We were still looking, but nothing had turned up so far. I said so and added that Mam had said we could always stay there until we found something. But our house was too small and I knew it it.

Mrs Kavanagh agreed. 'Well,' she said, nodding at her husband, 'we've talked it over and you know you're more than welcome here until you sort your-selves out.' I stayed silent for a moment. The grapevine seemed to be in general agreement that in-law's were a dodgy proposition, even though they were nice. She guessed my thoughts. 'Oh don't worry,' she said with a laugh, 'nobody'll bother you. There's plenty of room here.' I looked at Mr Kavanagh, who smiled in assent.

'That's right, Li. As she says, you're very welcome. There's a couple of rooms upstairs and they're yours if you want them. Think about it. It'll save a lot of problems till you get settled.'

'It's up to you and Antoinette,' interrupted his wife. 'I shan't mention it again. Just so long as you know you're welcome.'

'Have you mentioned this to Antoinette?' I queried.

'No, not yet, but she knows you're welcome anyway, let's know what you both decide.'

It was a good offer and kindly meant and, as she said, they did have loads of room. It sure would solve a lot of problems, in spite of the talk of in-laws, and Mam wouldn't mind. She wasn't daft. She knew our house was too small. Not that they wouldn't squeeze up if necessary.

'Hey,' broke in Mr Kavanagh with a sidelong look at his wife, 'I want a word with him too remember.'

'Oh yeah, so Antoinette told me before she went,' I said. 'Just been too busy to come round, that's all. What was it then? Something good, I hope?'

He shrugged. 'Well I don't know really, just something I heard in the office.' He went on to describe a piece of news that had come into the Gas Board office where he worked. It appeared the Coal Board, due to a shortage of men for the mines, was going to hire some of the displaced people from the camps in Europe. The problem was, apparently, that they would have to be taught some English first, otherwise they would be a danger below, if they couldn't understand the notices and instructions. He thought I would be interested. I laughed. How could a thing like that affect me? I knew nothing about mines and said so.

'Hang on a minute,' he retorted, 'I haven't finished yet. You'll see if you listen.' I did, closely. 'They want instructors,' he continued.

'Look Mr Kavanagh,' I interrupted, 'I couldn't teach English! According to Antoinette, when we first moved next door to you, I could hardly speak it myself!'

They burst out laughing. 'Yes, and don't we know it . . . The little madam,' said her mother.

Her husband was adamant. 'Look Li, it's worth an enquiry isn't it? I know you're keen to get on a bit, so you've nothing to lose, have you?'

'Fair enough. As you say, there's nothing to lose. Any idea where they are going to do this job? Y'know, schools, colleges or what?

He shook his head. 'Don't know really. Probably one of those empty Army camps or something, God knows, there's plenty of them. Anyway I'll snoop around, see what I can find out, OK?'

'Why not?' I agreed. Before I could continue, his wife broke in again impatiently.

'Now,' she asked in a business-like tone, 'has Antoinette mentioned the honeymoon?' Cor blimey I

127

thought, she would mention that! It was one of the many problems I was trying to cope with. True, with Dinny's 'foreigners' providing extra cash, I wasn't doing too badly, but if we managed a few days at a hotel we would be doing well.

I shook my head. 'No,' I answered, 'she's never said a word. Why?'

She clucked heavily. 'Typical,' she snorted. 'I told her all about it while she was packing. Anyway, if you agree, my sister Louise says you can stay in her guest house for a week or two. It's up to you.' I looked at her in amazed delight. Another problem off my back.

'Won't cost you a sausage, y'know,' interrupted her husband, grinning. Flippin' heck! It was as good as a win on the Pools. However, I answered cautiously that Antoinette might have something else in mind.

Her mother laughed at the idea. 'Oh don't worry, she'll go if you will. She loves her Aunty Louise. There's only one snag, though,' she added. I groaned inwardly. There would be I thought.

'Oh, what's that?' I asked.

'Well, there'll be another couple there as well. Been booked a long time, she tells me. Anyway, let me know when Antoinette comes home again, so I can tell Louise.'

I suddenly felt as though I was floating on air. Weeks of turmoil slipped away as two of my greatest worries miraculously vanished. I could have danced all the way home. A little of my enthusiasm vanished, however, as I walked in. Alf was waiting for me. He only came when he wanted a hand with something. My good news for Mam would have to wait.

I greeted him suspiciously. 'What yeh cookin' up now, Alf?'

He grinned amiably as Mam answered for him. 'Wants you to give him a hand to move old Fanny Wilkinson, y'know, lives round by your Aunty Sarah's.' Oh flippin' 'eck! I thought, there goes the quiet weekend I had looked forward to, with no overtime to do, nor any job with Dinny. 'Well she can't move herself can she?' demanded Mam, as I hesitated. 'She's only got herself y'know!' There was no need to tell me about eighty-year-old Fanny who, with no relatives, had always been taken care of by the neighbours. Mam was right. She couldn't move herself.

'OK then,' I said resignedly. 'Where's she movin' to?' I queried, thinking of the handcart that had to be pushed.

Alf beamed. 'Oh not far Li, about a mile I reckon. One'f them there new prefabs up the Dock road, y'know, on the bomb site.' I knew just where they were erecting the temporary prefab bungalows. It was only one of the many bomb sites around the town. It could have been further, but with Alf on the job, it was plenty far enough!

We agreed that he would hire the handcart from the local yard that had supplied them for years as low cost transport for many a 'moonlight flit' in the old days.

But I warned him as he turned to go. 'Now luk Alf, get a good'un, will yeh? No sides on it, just a nice flat top, OK? Book it from after dinner time Saturday till Monday morning. Then we'll have a birra time without bustin' a gut.'

He stuck his thumb up as he left. 'You're on mate,' he said.

I should have known what would happen. I nearly had a fit when I saw it parked outside Fanny's about one o'clock on the Saturday. The twit! He'd picked a flat top alright but instead of having two handles to pull with, this one had a single central shaft, with a 'T' piece at the end so two could pull. As an aid to getting a double hernia it was great. For removal purposes it was murder. It had to be held while it was loaded and God help you if you didn't balance the load. Too much on the front and you'd finish up with bow legs, too much on the back and up in the air you'd go as the load slipped.

'Cor hell, Alf,' I said disgustedly, 'they must 'ave seen you comin', mate. What did yeh pay for that?'

'Coupla bob. Not bad eh?' I looked at it critically. Noticing one wheel buckled, I pointed it out to him.

He shrugged my complaint aside. 'Ah,' he answered airily, 'you worry too much. It was OK comin' 'ere.'

'It wasn't flippin' loaded then, was it?' I snorted. 'Anyway,' I added, 'you can't pull that, it's too awkward. Warrabout your ticker?' I asked as I looked at the slight figure.

'Ah come off it, Li, for Christ's sake. Honest, anyone'd think I was gonna drop dead or sommat.'

'Yeah,' I replied seriously, 'with that heap loaded you could be right mate. Y'know what the doctor told yeh about liftin' an' pullin'?'

He snorted disgustedly. 'Oh bugger the doctor!' he snapped. 'If I listened to him, mate, I wouldn't even pick me nose!'

I gave in. 'Alright then, I'll pull, you push, then you can keep your eye on the stuff like, so it doesn't slip.' Mollified, he agreed, and with a further precaution of a piece of wood just long enough for him to jam under the back end to take the weight in case I couldn't hold it up front, we were in business.

We were at it until Benediction on Sunday evening, stripping Fanny's bits and pieces that had stood on the same spot for forty or fifty years. Everything seemed to have come out of the Ark, brass bedsteads, the lot. It was pure murder pulling on the single shaft, while Alf, stick in hand in case of emergency, puffed and joked his way at the back. Loading and unloading constantly threatened disaster, with ribald comments from friends and neighbours at both ends of the journey adding to the general hilarity, and all the while Fanny, anxious for the safety of her precious pieces, hovered like a demented mother hen in the background. But, despite the leg pulling, the laughing, cursing and swearing as we struggled through each crisis, we only had two real mishaps, when, badly loaded and Alf busy talking to someone while we waited at the traffic lights, I finished up in the air as the tumbling load caused a traffic snarl up. Even the policeman who helped was in fits as we reloaded and secured it. However, the second was fatal. We broke a prized possession! The object, small and of vital importance to Fanny, had been a bit of a problem from the moment we had loaded.

'Hey Li,' said Alf as he came round to the front of the cart, holding up a tastefully decorated jerry as I tried to keep the cart level, 'where should I stick this?'

I clucked disgustedly as neighbours offered various unsuitable suggestions. 'Oh jam it somewhere, it'll be alright.' He shrugged as an anxious Fanny came over to ask him to be careful.

''Cos it was me mother's.'

He was nonchalantly dismissive. 'Ah, yeh alright luv,' he answered airily, 'we'll luk after it.'

It wasn't until we were half-way on the journey that I knew something was going wrong.

'Hey Li,' came Alf's anxious voice from behind the high load, ''ang on a minute will yeh, I think the jerry's slippin''

'Oh hell!' I thought, struggling to keep the shaft down. 'Luk, just jam the stick under there will yeh, t'take the weight off me,' I pleaded.

Unfortunately he didn't hear me properly and came round to the front. 'Y'what?' he queried, then everything seemed to happen at once, as I turned to speak to him. The shaft tilted upwards and the load began to slip.

'Jesus!' I heard him exclaim as he dashed back. Next moment there was a crash of crockery. 'Hey Li,' he called unnecessarily, 'the whatsit's broke!'

With the load in imminent danger of following the jerry, I snapped his head off.

'Never mind the flamin' jerry, mate!' I shouted exasperatedly, 'just jam that there bloody stick under, quick!' He did, and in quieter mood we examined the

131

family heirloom. There were painted cherubs all over the place as we collapsed in fits of laughter.

'Ah well, never mind Li,' Alf said philosophically as he held the decorated handle, 'she won't need it now anyway will she? There's a lavvy inside in the new place, isn't there?'

*　　*　　*

It was a long and busy time before I saw Antoinette again, and when I did I was quite shocked. She looked shattered. Her normally pale face seemed even paler. With a protective arm around her as we left the station I enquired anxiously if she was alright. She brushed my anxiety aside and explained that there was a great deal to do at college and the hours very long. What she was more interested in was what had been happening at home. We had a good laugh about the removal job as we got on the bus. She was delighted when I told her of my arrangement with Dinny, the overtime I had been getting, and especially that we should now be alright for money.

'By the way,' I said, 'your mum was telling me about Aunt Louise.'

She looked puzzled. 'Oh, is she alright?'

I laughed 'Of course she's alright. I'm talkin' about going there for our honeymoon.'

A broad smile creased her face. 'Oh, so that's what Mother was on about while I was packing, was it? Honestly, she was talking about so many things, I just wasn't listening.' After asking and being told how I felt about it, she went on to describe her aunt. Apparently she was the exact opposite to her very practical mother. She was dreamy, sentimental, and passionately fond of animals. Oh yes, Antoinette looked forward to seeing her again. I warned her that there would be another couple there as well. She brushed that aside as of no consequence. She asked me how I felt about her parents' offer of the rooms, and again, much to her relief, I agreed with it wholeheartedly. As she pointed out, it really wouldn't be worth our while to get anywhere permanent until she came out of college. All in all, short though the bus journey was, it was one of the happiest I ever made. All the things that had bugged me for so long seemed in an almost casual way to have been solved, and all we had to do now was to keep our fingers crossed and wait for the great day. Everything seemed set for a perfect weekend . . . But . . .

*   *   *

With Antoinette beavering away at home with her college work, to try to give us some free time during the afternoon, I walked into the workshop on the Saturday morning as pleased as Punch. Just four hours to knocking off time and we would be together again! At ten o'clock, working on a relatively simple job down the Yard, Len vanished for a short time then returned, with a broad grin on his face, to deliver some devastatating news.

'We're on overtime this afternoon,' he announced bluntly. I looked at him, horrified. Normally I would have jumped at the chance of the extra money but, with Antoinette home for the first time in weeks, and a thousand things to talk about, I wasn't very pleased, especially at the short notice.

I bridled. 'Oh no, I'm not Len.' He looked at me belligerently. I explained what I had planned for the afternoon, and that Antoinette couldn't get home all that often. It bounced off him like water off a duck's back.

'Tough luck,' he said. 'But if I'm workin', so are you!' He'd just said the wrong thing, in the wrong way.

I blew. 'Oh no I'm bloody well not, Len!' I snapped back. 'I've just told you why!'

133

'Oh yes you bloody well are,' he growled. 'I've just worked this nicely, an' if I work, you work. Right?'

Even if she hadn't been at home I wouldn't have worked, with that attitude.

I stepped closer and glared at him. 'When that buzzer goes, Len,' I said as calmly as I could, 'then I'm goin', an' if yeh don't like it mate, then you can bloody-well lump it!'

'Luk 'ere . . .' he began.

I stopped him. In my present mood it was touch and go whether I told him to stick the whole job up his jacksie. I refrained. Just! Instead I said quietly, 'Now luk, Len, you know I'm keen to get overtime normally. I've told you why I can't work t'day, an' I'm also tellin' yeh I don't want it dropped on my head out of the blue, like a flamin' ton of bricks.'

'It's only just come up,' he protested.

I laughed sardonically. 'Come off it, Len. You said a minute ago you'd just worked it nicely, so how the hell has it just "come up"?'

For a few minutes he tried to bully me into changing my mind. Not for all the tea in China, I told him, not today. He called me a bolshie sod and I agreed with him. I pointed out that I was more than willing to work all night every night when Antoinette wasn't home, but today she was, and that was that. He mentioned that Con wouldn't be very pleased, turning down good overtime. I retorted that it was none of my brother's flaming business. But he was right. Con wasn't pleased that I'd upset his mate. Fortunately I had left for Antoinette's by the time he arrived looking for me. It didn't augur well for Monday!

10

Windfalls

After receiving a cold reception from Con after Mass on Sunday, and geared up for possible trouble with Len when I went in on Monday following the Saturday fracas, I was pleasantly surprised to find him in a good mood and, except for one or two oblique remarks about there being some funny blokes about, the day, and the two following, passed without further hiccups. At home it was different. Mam found a dozen and one jobs to keep me busy, so it was Wednesday before I got the chance to pop up to Antoinette's with, as usual, a string of messages to deliver from Mam.

Mr Kavanagh's face beamed as he opened the door. 'Ah,' he said, 'you're just the man I want to see.'

I held my hand up in protest. 'Just hang on a minute, will you? If I don't deliver these messages, I'll forget the damned lot.' He sat down opposite Mrs Kavanagh with a grin, as I passed on the never-ending pieces of information flowing between the families.

'Anything else?' asked Mrs Kavanagh as I finished.

I shook my head. 'Nope, that's the lot.' But it wasn't. There was one more. 'Oh yeah,' I added, 'she told me to tell you our Seamus is gonna be the altar boy.'

'Ah,' she said delightedly, 'that'll be nice. One of your own on the altar.'

I wasn't so sure. Seamus was a giggler. Once started, he was hard to shut up, and with Dinny there anything could happen.

'Now,' Mr Kavanagh interrupted, as she made to

135

speak again, 'you remember that job I was telling you about, y'know, the Coal Board?' I nodded, surprised to hear anything so soon. He told me they were bringing foreign workers over from Europe and they would be teaching them basic English. 'But,' he continued, as pleased as Punch, 'the thing that interests me, and you I hope, is that they are looking for ex-service-men if possible.'

'But surely,' I pointed out, 'there must be loads of proper teachers that they could get?'

He shrugged. 'Maybe, but that's what I've heard. Perhaps they want them for some other reason, recreation maybe — even discipline. After all, Li, there's bound to be some rum uns among them, aren't there, especially from refugee camps?'

I agreed, I'd seen some of the camps myself and they were rough. He could be right. 'Of course,' I said, 'I have got my PT qualifications, so that's no problem.'

They were both delighted. 'Well, what are you waiting for then?' Mr Kavanagh exclaimed. 'It might be right up your street. What d'you think, May?'

'Why not?' she answered. 'You hate what you're doing now, and you've got no ties. I mean, even after you're married, Antoinette will still be at college, won't she, for a while at least?' I nodded. That was true.

'Worth a chance, isn't it?' her husband said persuasively. 'As May says, you don't like what you're doing, so you've got nothin to lose, lad.'

I didn't know what to do really. I had to think of Antoinette. 'Maybe you're right. I'll have a talk when she gets home.'

He didn't agree with that at all. 'Why waste time?' he asked. 'You might just as well get a letter off now, if you fancy it. Tell her later and, if you change your mind, well, all you've lost is a tuppenny stamp.' It made sense, but I wasn't sure. He was quick on my hesitation. 'You won't be the only one applying, y'know Li. There's plenty like you coming out, don't forget . . . It's up to you of course, but if it was me, I'd be writing pretty quick.' I agreed with him. Why not? A look of concern suddenly crossed his face. 'Oh, I forgot to tell you: the bloke I got all this from told me it was just a short term job. Six months, maybe a year. He wasn't sure.' I snorted disgustedly. I knew there had to be a snag somewhere!

'Oh that's alright,' broke in his wife airily, 'Antoinette will still be away, so it won't make much difference will it? And if it does close down, well, you're no worse off are you?'

'Right then. As me mam says, "No sooner the word than the blow". Where's the writing paper?' Ten minutes later, with the letter ready to post on the way home, I took my leave. Within a day or so I had forgotten it, as more urgent things crowded in and I waited impatiently for Antoinette's next visit at the weekend which, as usual, came and went in a frantic blur.

She was delighted I had sent the letter off, but I warned her not to expect too much, emphasising that even if it came off it would probably only be for a short while. It didn't bother her a bit.

'That's alright,' she said. 'At least it would get you out of there.' I had been relieved. At least we seemed to think alike on the subject.

Fortunately I didn't get much time to brood on anything once she had gone, because Alf and I had been roped in to paper Aunt Min's front room, and working with him always encompassed an air of fraught comedy. This job was no exception. Coupled with Aunt Min's offerings of impromptu and pithy advice, it became hilarious, with the result that, with only sufficient paper to cover the room, one piece finished up upside down in a corner. We spotted it as we stood back to admire our work. But Aunt Min, philosophical as always, brushed the error aside.

'Oh forget it Li,' she said when I apologised. 'Yeh can't notice it over there. Don't worry y'self about it.'

Alf laughed. 'Aunt Sarah will,'

He said authoritively.

She snorted. 'Well if she does, I'll tell 'er t'mind 'er own bloody business!' She would, too.

* * *

By the last week in November, with the letter having faded from my mind under the growing onslaught of Christmas and other preparations, Mam's words came as a shock when I came home from work.

'There's a letter there for yeh,' she said as she laid my dinner on the table.

'Oh great,' I replied. 'She's keen, I'll give her that. I had one only yesterday.'

'It's not from Antoinette,' she said as she went to the back kitchen. 'It's from that there Coal Board place.'

I rocketed across the kitchen, took it from the sideboard and tore it open excitedly. It was short and sweet, just a couple of lines inviting me to an interview in London the following Wednesday. I could scarcely believe it, as I read and reread it, with Mam standing in the doorway waiting to hear what it said.

'Well? What does it say?' she asked.

I looked up with a broad grin. 'I've gorr'an interview! Next Wednesday. In London.'

Her face lit up delightedly. 'Well I'll be blessed!' she exclaimed. 'Thanks be t'God for that.'

'Look,' I said, beside myself with pleasure, 'I'd better nip up to Antoinette's to let them know. They'll be . . .'

She pointed to the table. 'Get y'dinner first lad, an' calm y'self down a bit. Go on,' she insisted, as I read it yet again, 'get yeh dinner. Your father'll be in, in a minute.'

He came through the backyard door as I sat down. I rose immediately and went to meet him, waving the letter.

'Holy sailor!' he exclaimed as he read it. 'An' good luck to yeh,' he added, as we walked back in.

A sudden thought struck me as I sat down to my cooling meal. 'Hey,' I said, 'don't mention this to anyone, will yeh?'

'Why not?' asked Dad, as Mam looked at me, puzzled.

'Well,' I replied, 'y'know what they're like down there, don't yeh? It's only an interview, and if I get it, which I probably won't, then I don't want any sarky remarks.'

He nodded understandingly. 'I know what yeh mean, but what about Teresa?'

I laughed. 'Oh I'll tell her myself, but don't mention it to Con OK? I'll tell him after I've been. It might save a lot'f trouble.'

They agreed, knowing only too well what I meant. If my brother got wind of my trying to leave, he'd be as mad as a hatter. He still wasn't very chuffed over my argument with Len. All in all it was safer to keep it quiet for the moment.

Within twenty minutes, regardless of my digestion, I had completed the meal, washed and changed and was on my way to Antoinette's. They, too, were delighted, especially her Dad, who expressed absolute confidence that I would land it.

With Antoinette unable to get home again so soon after her last weekend, the time, but for Dinny's unexpected arrival, would have dragged. Instead, early on the Saturday evening, he walked through the back door, grinning from ear to ear.

'Hello,' I said, as he plonked himself down beside Teresa on the sofa, with Mam and Dad just getting their coats on for their usual Saturday night out at the theatre. 'What are you lookin' so pleased with yourself about?'

His grin grew even broader as he fumbled in his inside pocket. 'Remember that raffle?' he asked, pulling an envelope out. 'The Union one, y'know?' he explained, as my brow furrowed.

139

I recalled the tickets I had bought on the ship. 'Oh aye,' I replied with a laugh. 'Don't tell me you've won the damned thing?'

'No,' he said as Mam and Dad, ready to go, stood waiting for his answer, 'but you did, mate!' he added, spreading fifteen one pounds notes on the table. There were gasps all round.

'Me? Hell's bells. Fifteen quid!'

Teresa was beside herself with excitement. 'Oh Li!' she exclaimed. 'Couldn't have come at a better time, could it?'

I looked at the money spreadeagled before me. A windfall! Then I looked at the delighted expressions around me. What a golden opportunity to bring even more delight. With overtime and odd jobs, I had more than enough for the wedding. So, at last, I could give.

'Here y'are, Dad,' I said, holding two of the notes out. 'It's on me t'night.'

He recoiled in horror. 'No, no,' he objected, 'don't be so damned daft, you'll need that.' Mam supported him, but I was in no mood for objections.

'I'll be upset if yeh don't Dad, honest I will. So come on,' I insisted.

He and Mam looked at each other, then gave in. 'Oh alright,' he said, taking the notes, 'but I still say you're daft.'

I laughed happily, 'OK then, I'm daft,' I admitted, taking another note and handing it to Teresa.

'Oh no, Li,' she protested, 'what about Antoinette?' She held back.

'Take it,' I demanded, 'there's enough and more, luv. Now come on, otherwise you'll take all the pleasure out of it.' She looked at Dinny, still grinning away as he watched. 'An' it's no good lookin' at him,' I scolded, 'because there's one for him too,' I continued, handing him one, as Teresa took hers.

'Yeh crackers,' he said. 'Y'won't have any left.' I pointed out that even if there was only one left, I would

140

still be better off than when he came. 'Right,' he said, stuffing the note in his pocket, 'I'm not arguin' with that. Now,' he continued as Mam and Dad left, 'warrabout comin' round to the club for an hour?'

I gave him a friendly nudge. 'You're on. Just let me put this lot away,' I added, picking up the money.

What a week it had been, and no mistake. A relatively happy one at work after gearing myself up for a shindig with Len and Con, the surprise letter from the Coal Board and the prospects it held out, and now, this sudden deluge of money out of the blue. It was this that suddenly made me remember an old promise I had made to myself just one week before the war broke out on the occasion of a memorable night out with Antoinette in Liverpool. I had vowed then that I would give Mam and Dad a similar night out the following week, so that they could actually go through the Tunnel for the very first time. The war had stopped that, and the promise had faded from my memory, but now, with a buckshee tenner to cover it, if Antoinette agreed, it was possible. Why the hell not? I had enough for what I wanted, and it would be a nice appreciation for all that they were doing for us. Then, with a bit of luck, the same for Antoinette's parents after the wedding, for the same reason. Yes, that's what I'd do: have a natter as soon as she came home, get it all arranged, then spring it on Mam and Dad! I couldn't wait to see their faces.

*   *   *

It was an anxious few days to Wednesday, even though Dinny, when I told him, with a warning to keep his mouth shut, was convinced that I would get the job. The arguments I had with myself during those few days were interminable. Would I get it or wouldn't I? What if this, or what if that? I argued until I felt as tense as a drum. As Dad said, when he caught me lying on

141

the sofa, staring vacantly at the ceiling on Tuesday night.

'Yeh wastin' yeh time worryin' your guts out Li. What's t'be will be. You've got to learn to take things as they come. If you're good enough, they'll have yeh, if yeh not they won't. Like Asquith said, "Wait and see!"'

I gave in. 'Yeah, you're right, Dad. I think I'll have an early night and a good read, that'll take my mind off it.' So, with a book under my arm, a full mug of tea, and a little calmer in mind, I went upstairs.

* * *

The interview at the Coal Board headquarters was an anticlimax. I didn't even feel as nervous as I had expected, as I faced the rather plump, near-bald, Pickwickian figure on the other side of the desk.

'As a sergeant, you know how to handle men of course?' He smiled benignly as I answered in the afirmative. 'But,' he added, with a more serious expression, 'these are foreigners! That could, er, well it could make a difference.'

'Oh that's no problem, sir,' I replied confidently, 'I've served abroad and I've handled many . . .'

'Ah yes,' he interrupted with a cherub-like smile, 'but how would you communicate? After all, there will be many languages.' Again I felt confident. Obviously he didn't know much about servicemen and their innate ability to communicate with lampposts if necessary.

'Oh quite easy sir. Gestures, y'know?'

The smile on his face broadened as he shuffled some papers about. 'Yes, yes, quite. And er, how do you get along with people?' I looked at him with momentary uncertainty. I could hardly say that I got on great if they left me alone, or that I tended to react like a hand grenade if they didn't. Still I thought, on the whole I didn't do too badly — about average, I supposed.

'Oh quite nicely sir, thank you,' I replied as he gave me a long, thoughtful look.

'Do you have any experience in recreation?'

I was on safe ground here and reached into my pocket for my old Army paybook to pass across. He opened it. 'You'll find the qualifications on the back page, sir,' I suggested helpfully.

After examining it he smiled and handed it back. 'Yes, I see you have. Good . . . Now,' he added thoughfully, 'what about discipline? What I mean is, what are your views on it? Naturally it would be slightly different from what you are used to, if you take my meaning.'

I took his meaning alright. He was saying it would not be as tough as it was in the Services. I steered a middle course, strong as I felt about it. 'That would depend on the rules laid down, sir.' He nodded sagely. 'However, I must be honest; whatever they were, I can assure you that they would be strictly enforced.'

He gave me a quizzical look, but this was one thing I wanted clear for my own sake. I had seen thousands of refugees and knew what they could be like, and I wanted to know exactly where I stood on this question if I got the job.

'You appear to feel strongly about discipline, Mr Sullivan. Am I right?'

'Yes sir, to be honest I do, and for a very simple reason.'

'Oh?' he queried.

'Well sir,' I replied, with a distinct feeling I was putting my foot in it, 'as I see it, without discipline there's no order, and without order there's no progress, so, in my view, it is essential.'

The full lips pursed as his eyebrows rose slightly. I wasn't sure that he liked it, but that's how I felt about it. He gazed at me solemnly for a moment then coughed gently.

'Quite, quite,' he said. His next words confirmed my

143

worry. 'Well Mr Sullivan, I think that's about all, unless you have any questions?' I shook my head, and my heart sank as he continued, 'You understand, of course, I have several applicants to interview yet. The successful candidate will be notified by post, not later than the fourteenth of January ... Thank you for coming.'

I felt deflated.

With the interview at an unsatisfactory end, I rose and extended my hand. His round chubby face beamed as he took it. Despite his limp handshake he seemed a decent old stick. It wasn't his fault he couldn't tell me on the spot. Still, I thought as I made my way to the station, that's life. At least there was one good thing: nobody knew, except close family and Dinny. It might avoid a lot of sarky remarks from certain quarters.

Home again without any good news to tell them, and with January the fourteenth seemingly an eternity away, I came to life in my real world and flung myself into the excitement of coming events. At work, things jogged along without any major hiccups, amid good-natured leg-pulling about my approaching nuptials, which I thoroughly enjoyed. Even Con, still unaware of my interview, and despite his dislike of my snooty choice of wife, joined in the general merriment at my expense, and for this short period I was happier than I had been since the job had started.

At home, too, the tempo of events increased rapidly. Uncle John proved to be a provider extraordinaire, and with one trip still to go, had already produced food and goods, unseen for years in the shops, making eyes pop, and lips drool with anticipation. A whole ham! Even Nicky Benson, our local butcher, was green with envy as he popped it into his fridge for us. Fruit salads, tinned salmon, dried fruit for cake-making, sugar for the sweet-toothed who had been denied so long. Butter — real butter — and tea enough to get blotto on. He provided veritable cornucopia that held friends and neighbours transfixed with envy, while Antoinette was in her seventh heaven over the material he provided for the dress her mother's skillful hands would make.

It was an exciting, happy time. Even Aunt Sarah, our family Cassandra, loosened her stays a bit. I actually saw her laugh a couple of times, as my diminutive niece Patricia practised her bridesmaid's role, wearing an assortment of tea-towels. There was little for either of us to do during Antoinette's latest weekend home, once her college work was out of the way, and we were grateful to be alone for a while, having time to walk and make our secret plans for Mam and Dad's night out.

* * *

Another weekend gone! God, how the time flew. Even Len was cheerful on the Monday as he came out of the time office.

'What are you so cheerful about?' I asked jocularly, as he stood beaming in front of me. 'Had a win on the gee gees?' I added, knowing he liked a flutter.

'No,' he said with a grin, 'but we've gorra nice little job on t'day. Rush job, like. Manchester.'

'Manchester,' I gasped delightedly, 'cor, that'll be a nice trip out.'

'Right then,' he said, with a nod at the bag at my feet, 'grab that an' let's git.'

Minutes later we were on our way to the Underground, to catch the main line train from Lime Street.

'Hey,' he said as we passed a small café, ''ang on a bit. We've got plenty'f time. Let's gerra cuppa.'

I gave him a puzzled look. 'I thought you said it was a rush job?'

'Oh stop worryin' y'self, there's loads of time,' he snapped, walking in. 'Get the tea in, will yeh?'

I held my hand out for the tuppence. I knew my Len.

For fifteen minutes I sat fuming silently as he read the paper in the smoke-filled room. I glanced at the clock. Ten past eight!

'Hey Len,' I queried exasperatedly, 'what time are we supposed t'be goin'?'

He raised his head in surprise. 'What you worryin' about? You're gerrin' paid for it, aren't yeh?'

I repeated his words that it was a rush job. He grinned as he lit another cigarette.

'They said that, not me. Anyroad,' he added with a glance at the clock, 'it's only ten past. It won't take us five minutes t'the station, an' there's loads of trains aren't there?'

I scowled silently. He was the boss, so there wasn't much I could do about it. Instead, I sat and fumed again. After what seemed an eternity he folded his paper, muttering to himself that there was nuthin' in the bloody thing worth readin, and we were finally off. A couple of hours later we were in Manchester in the crisp, wintery sunshine.

'How far is it to where she's berthed?' I asked.

'Oh a couple of miles maybe, dunno really. Anyway, it's a crackin' day. Won't take us long to walk there.'

I pointed at the tools and objected. 'Who d'yeh think I am, Len — Gunga bloody Din?'

He clucked heavily. 'Ah bugger it,' he snapped, 'let's go t'the bus stop then!'

I grinned as he walked along, scowling.

Within the half hour we were alongside and I was gazing at an ageing ship, squatting forlornly in the wet dock. She looked — and was — a tramp, and confusion reigned as we boarded the littered deck and went below to where the job lay. In the half light below decks it was even worse, with tools and equipment in wild confusion everywhere.

'When did you say this was sailin', Len?' I queried.

'Coupla days as far as I know,' he replied unconcernedly.

'Blimey O'Reilly!' I retorted. 'By the look of this lot she'll be lucky t'gerrout on the next forty-day flood!'

For the second time that morning he laughed. 'Oh she'll go out, don't worry. Right,' he continued in business-like tones 'let's gerron with it then.' I sighed with relief for something to do. 'Any idea of the time?' he added.

I checked my watch. 'A quarter past eleven.'

He frowned. 'Luk, I think I'll just check first. If it's gonna be awkward, we'll 'ave an early dinner then work straight through.'

I nodded. It wasn't the first time a job had been spread, but he was the boss. I unpacked the brew cans knowing it would be an early dinner.

At twelve thirty, with dinner over, we were ready to start, when a welder came down the ladder with some equipment. Len glared at him.

'You gonna work down 'ere?' he demanded.

The welder grinned. 'Will be, in a few minutes, mate.'

Len turned to me and nodded. I knew exactly what was going to happen. There was no way he was going to work with welding fumes about. And we didn't. Instead we sat on deck until both welder and his fumes had vanished. Then for an hour all was peace as Len, like the expert plumber he was, quietly chunnered away to himself and I handed or retrieved tools as required. Suddenly he swore.

'What's the matter now?' I queried, fed up to the back teeth.

'Luk at this 'ere bloody flange,' he invited. 'They didn't say nothin' about that.' I craned round the crouching form as he stabbed his finger at an awkwardly placed pipe and flange. Inexperienced, I couldn't see anything wrong and said so. He clucked impatiently. 'There!' he snapped, pointing to the flange. 'That's brass!'

'So?' I queried.

He got to his feet irritably to explain the trouble. According to the rules, apparently, he, a plumber, was only allowed to deal with steel work. This, where the steel pipe connected with the brass flange, was a coppersmith's job, because the flange needed replacement and had to be braised. Oh yes, he told me in response to my enquiry, he was able to do the job OK no problem, but it wasn't his job, so that was that. Used in the Army to just getting the job done, whoever did it, I just gave up.

'D'yeh mean t'tell me that they'll have to send a coppersmith and his mate all the way out 'ere to do that?' I asked exasperatedly.

He grimaced. 'That's their problem. Anyroad,' he added, as though quoting Holy Writ 'it wouldn't 'ave made no difference even if they'd sent a coppersmith this mornin', would it? He couldn't 'ave done our part of the job, could he?'

After a short telephone call from a Dockyard call box, we were on our way home with the job still not completed, with Len firmly convinced that I was crackers for being concerned about the waste of time, and me yet again appalled by the ruthless enforcement of demarcation, however well intentioned. From that moment I knew in my heart that I couldn't, daren't stay in this kind of work, if I wanted a peaceful and productive life. My nature just would not allow it.

We got back at about four thirty, just in time to stow the gear, tidy up a bit and knock off. We had done about a couple of hours' constructive work all day. I was still seething when I got home. Dad spotted it straight away.

"Ello,' he said as I came through the door, 'what's upset you, then?'

'Oh nothin',' I replied unconvincingly.

He gave me a knowing look. I wasn't kidding him, and I knew it. He made to speak, gave a half grin instead, then concentrated on his dinner. We both knew it was more peaceful that way.

148

11

The Great Day

Con, obviously informed by Len of my attitude on the
Manchester job, was not at all pleased, when I met him
on the way home on the last Saturday before Christmas, but I wasn't particularly bothered. Today was a
special day, because today I would fulfil the promise
so long delayed, and I was determined that nothing
would spoil the pleasure of it.

'Look Con,' I said quietly when he stopped me
belligerently, 'you've got your ideas an' I've got mine.
Let's leave it like that eh? Especially today!'

He glared at me irritably. 'An' what's so special
about today?' he demanded.

I explained about the night out we had arranged for
Mam and Dad, and warned him that if he upset
anything I'd never forgive him.

He knew I meant it. 'Fair enough,' he said apologetically. 'Hope they enjoy it, but,' he added in a final dig,
'you've got the unions all wrong, you 'ave, with . . .'

'Aye, maybe,' I interrupted, 'I hope you're right . . .
But time'll tell.'

So the hurdle was crossed and trouble avoided for
this special night, a night of simple pleasure that
stands out like a beacon in the shadows of the past: the
gasps of surprised delight when we sprang it on them
as soon as Antoinette arrived home from college; Mam
and Dad, dressed in their best, chattering animatedly
to Teresa, as we followed them down the path to the
waiting taxi; the exclamations of amazement as they

149

journeyed through the miracle of the Tunnel, near which they had lived so long, yet had never seen; the meal in Liverpool before the brilliant show at the Empire Theatre, then the final journey home. What a beautiful memory! Not for a king's ransome could one moment of it be exchanged. They were so happy I could have wept. The promise had been fulfilled, and I was content.

Our night out proved but a prelude to a frantic approach to the double event, heightened early on Christmas Eve by the delighted gasps of the women-folk, as they inspected Uncle John's latest and final contribution from across the water, for part of it was an item of genuine gold dust to the women — six pairs of nylon stockings! There's little wonder at their delight, when so many of the younger ones had for years been painting black lines down the backs of their legs to simulate stockings. All too soon it was time to gather for the one Mass I rarely enjoyed. It was always too packed and, where I liked to stand — at the back of the church — always too many drunks. But it wouldn't have seemed like Christmas without attending Mid-night Mass. For the first time in many years Antoinette was with me, instead of with her mum and dad, because tomorrow we would be married in her church. But even so, I didn't enjoy it. I was too busy keeping an eye on a young and very merry bloke giving her the once-over in the crowd jammed at the back, and I was gradually getting madder with him. For all the good the Mass did me, I might just as well have stayed at home.

All I could hear was a steady drone from the distant figure on the altar as we were pushed first this way, then the other. Right, I thought, as soon as the impor-tant part of the Mass is over I'm off! With only half an eye on the altar I stuck it out, my hackles rising by the second. A sudden momentary silence informed me that the most sacred part of the ceremony was just about over and, very far from the state of grace I should have been in, I slipped a protective arm round Antoinette's waist and hissed.

'Right luv, let's go before I thump that flamin' bloke!'

She looked at me, startled, but I was in no mood for explanations as I turned her and, giving him a heavy shoulder, pushed our way through the crowd.

'What was all that about?' she asked, when we got outside in the freezing night.

'That flamin' bloke in there, the drunk, y'know? Didn't yeh see him oglin'?'

'To tell you the truth,' she replied with a laugh, 'I could neither see or hear a thing!'

'What a waste of flippin' time,' I answered grumpily. 'Still,' I added with relief, 'we've been to Mass, so we can have a lie-in in the mornin', thank God.'

I was wrong. Everybody was up bright and early, with Teresa insisting I went to nine o'clock Mass with her so that we could go round to see Patricia with her toys immediately afterwards. We met a bug-eyed Dinny on the way out, and he wanted a private word with her. I stood freezing, while they laughed and giggled with an occasional glance at me.

'What was all that about?' I asked, as Dinny gave us the thumbs up and left.

'You mind your own business,' she replied with a smile. 'You'll find out soon enough.'

The rest of the day passed in the usual blur of ritual family visits, interminable cups of tea, and ceaseless leg-pulling over the wedding. We parted for Christmas dinner with our own folks for the last time, then up to my future home for tea. Before we quite realised it, the preparations for the morrow had begun with the arrival of Patricia, loaded with toys and bubbling with excitement, her mum and Teresa, accompanied by Dad, in preparation for the bridesmaids' duties. At nine o'clock I called it a day, and with final advice to Antoinette to have an early night, gave Dad the nod that we should go.

151

We had a nice, quiet and thoughtful walk home on pavements that sparkled with frost, twinkling in the light of the street lamps. Thank goodness Antoinette would get some rest, I thought. She looked bone tired. But for me, there was another ordeal to come.

Stuffed with food, and already well down to the 'plimsoll line', Mam started pouring tea the moment we got through the door.

'Ah no,' I pleaded, 'not for me, Mam. Honest, if I drink any more tea, I swear t'God I'll float out on the next tide!' But it was no use. She warned me that it was a long time until the reception and, with everyone going to Communion the next day, it was either stoke up now or go hungry for the next twelve hours. I gave in and watched in despair as she filled a plate. 'God knows where I'm gonna put it Mam,' I opined.

'Eat it!' she commanded. I did; then, reserve fuel on board and dropping from fatigue, I staggered upstairs.

I had scarcely laid my head on the pillow, it seemed, when Dad knocked on the door and popped his head round.

'Come on lad,' he said cheerfully, 'it's eight o'clock.'

Oh hell, I thought, suddenly awake, two hours to go! My parched mouth cried out for the cup of tea I wasn't allowed. Dinny turned up at nine, even more bug-eyed than the previous day, but smart in a neat blue suit, with his hair slicked back. I asked him what he had been talking to Teresa about, as I handed him the ring.

He gave a tired grin and repeated her answer, 'You'll find out,' he said with a wink to Mam and Dad. I was too tired to argue.

'Oh,' broke in Mam, as I pulled his leg about his appearance, 'don't forget to tell him about the organ pumper!'

'The what?' Dinny asked in a puzzled tone.

I explained that as the church had been bombed and the proper organ damaged, they had kindly dug out an old Victorian hand-pumped one for us. He went off into fits as I added that the old boy doing the pumping expected a backhander for his efforts. 'Don't forget to slip him this on the way out,' I concluded, handing him a pound note.

'Right,' he answered, slipping the money into his pocket and glancing at the clock. 'Come on,' he added, 'we'd berra get our skates on mate, or we're gonna be late.'

*   *   *

Dinny's reaction as we walked into the bomb-wrecked and still-scaffolded church was predictable.

'Bloody 'ell,' he whispered irreverently, 'it's a right wreck in't it? Like bein' down the yard. Reckon we should've come in overalls Li,' he added with a grin. I had to agree with him. It was a wreck. Even the twelve Apostles ranged round the walls in their niches didn't seem to think much of it, either, judging by the expressions on their faces.

'Hey,' he said, with a dig in my ribs as we took our places in the front pew, 'luk at that there pumper feller. Luks liable t'fall over if 'e uses that flippin' 'andle.'

I looked to my left at the small organ, and the tall, elderly and very gaunt pumper standing by for action. 'Yeah,' I agreed, 'he's sure gonna be knocked up by the time he's finished. Don't forget to give 'im that quid, will yeh?'

He nodded. 'He'll 'ave flamin' earned it, mate!'

From the pumper my gaze wandered to the tiny, trim figure of the aged organist, sitting bolt upright as she waited for the bridal party to arrive.

I turned to Dinny. 'Make a nice couple, don't they?'

He grinned as he gazed at them. 'Yeah, they do, but I don't reckon she's much on the boogie woogie, d'you?' I suppressed a laugh, then he nudged me again urgently. ''Eck, 'eck,' he whispered in simulated excitement, 'they're windin' it up!' He was right, the

153

old boy was pumping away like mad and the whole thing creaked in protest. Seconds later, with a seraphic look on her lined face, the organist struck the keys. The result was murderous, again he nudged me, forgetting momentarily where he was. 'Cor, bloody 'ell,' he whispered.

I nearly choked, fighting back the laughter as the priest, resplendent in his white and gold robes, and closely attended by my nephew Seamus, glided silently on to the altar. My eyes opened in amazement as I watched him, then turned to see a broad grin on Dinny's face.

'That looks like . . . No, it can't be!' I began.

With his face beaming with absolute delight, Dinny moved his head slowly. 'It is!' he whispered. 'Our Henry!' Now I knew why he and Teresa had been laughing and giggling outside the church on Christmas morning. They were plotting!

Lost for words, as the organ ground into the Wedding March, I gazed back disbelievingly into those amused blue eyes watching me from the altar steps. What a wonderful surprise, Henry, after all these years! An equally delighted Father Fielding signalled us forward. I turned as I left the pew and stopped as Antoinette came towards me on her father's arm. Numb from one shock I stopped, enthralled, until Dinny gave me an urgent push in the back.

'Come on mate. Shift it!' he hissed as the organ ground remorselessly on. Mutely I took my bride from her father. In that wedding gown, so lovingly created by her mother, she looked radiant. Moments later we stood before Henry. I felt I wanted to shake his hand but couldn't. Instead, he leaned forward solemnly and, with laughter in his eyes, greeted me in the old way. 'Hi yeh!' he whispered softly as Antoinette gazed dumbfounded at this strange priest.

With the long tedious ceremony over, we completed the photographic record for posterity on the church steps, in a temperature ten below zero, then, frozen and starving from the long fast, the multi-coloured procession wended its way to the reception in the church hall. Desperate for a cup of tea and to greet Henry properly, I couldn't get there quick enough. When we did we were amazed. Uncle John and the women had done us proud. It was a magnificient spread, enhanced beyond expectations by Henry's unexpected presence. I still couldn't believe it!

Almost before we realised it, Dinny was reminding us that it was time to go. Another half hour and the four of us were speeding through the Tunnel with Teresa happier than I had seen her for months, whilst Dinny, always at his best in boisterous company, couldn't wait to get back. I also found out just how the plot to get Henry there to marry us was achieved. By all accounts it hadn't been easy, with permissions to be gained here there and everywhere, but apparently Dinny, ably aided and abetted by the family, had been determined to accomplish it. Nothing could have given me greater pleasure.

'Pity you've gorra miss a good do, Li,' said Dinny as we stood on Lime Street station. 'It's gonna be a cracker t'night, I'll tell yeh.'

'Yes,' I answered wearily. 'Maybe you're right Din, but it'll suit me to put my feet up for a bit, I'll tell yeh. I feel knackered, no kiddin'.'

'Oh you'll be alright,' he replied with a laugh. 'You'll be there in a couple of hours, no problem.'

*   *   *

Alone in the subdued light of the carriage, with the click of the wheels beating a soothing rhythm as the world outside faded into total blackness, reaction set in with growing drowsiness as Antoinette recounted the chaos of the previous night. With Patricia over-excited, and Teresa in fits of giggles all night, nothing

155

seemed to have gone right. For more than an hour she continued, laughing and giggling away at one memory after another, while my eyes gradually dropped from so many late nights. Suddenly, nerves tingling in alarm, I sat bolt upright as we sped through a station.

'Hey luv ... We don't go through St Annes to Morecambe do we?'

She looked at me, puzzled. 'Of course not. Why?' I leapt to my feet in apprehension.

'Well we just flippin' well did! Didn't you see it?'

She shook her head. 'No, it couldn't be, Li. You checked the train with the porter at Liverpool.'

'Yes I know,' I agreed, 'still, I could've sworn it said St Annes on Sea.' I checked my watch. Five minutes to six. I relaxed. We had reckoned on two hours. 'Anyway,' I added, 'just keep your eye open for the next station and see what it says.'

Within minutes the train slowed again and a station sign came into view. Blackpool South!

'Oh no!' she gasped, as I grabbed the bags in a flaming temper.

'Of all the screaming twits,' I snarled. 'I asked him if this was the train for Morecambe and he said "Yes mate". God, I wish I had hold of him now!'

'Now it's no good getting in a temper, Li. That won't do any good, will it?' Antoinette snapped as we alighted on the deserted, windswept platform.

'What the hell d'yeh want me t'do?' I snapped back. 'Send 'im a telegram of congratulations?'

She glared at me. 'Oh very funny,' she replied with a sniff. 'Anyway there's a porter. Let's have a word with him.' I looked along the freezing platform as a shadowy figure approached in the misty light. We walked to meet him. 'Now don't lose your temper,' urged my new wife. 'Let me talk to him, please!'

I ignored her as I came face to face with the porter, slamming my bag down. 'That's not the flamin' Morecambe train, is it?' I demanded angrily.

156

He looked at me in surprise then shook his head. 'No it isn't. This is Blackpool.'

'I know damned well it's Blackpool,' I snapped, 'I'm not blind. I cin see that! But your mate in Liverpool said it was the Morecambe train, didn't he?'

He looked at me as though I'd had a few. No doubt he was fed up too, being on duty over Christmas. 'Well,' he snapped back, 'that's not my flippin' fault, is it?'

'Li,' pleaded Antoinette nervously, 'don't make it worse, please.'

But stuck in Blackpool on a freezing night when we should have been snug in the digs with a nice cup of tea, I felt hopping mad, and rounded on him.

'Typical,' I snarled, 'absolutely bloody typical! It's about . . .'

'Just a minute Li,' Antoinette interrupted, as the porter eyed me angrily, 'let's find out what time the next train is.'

The porter shook his head. 'No train to Morecambe t'night lady. You'll 'ave t'go via Preston.'

'Preston!' I exclaimed, horrified. 'D'you mean to . . .'

He shrugged, 'There's no other way, unless you take a taxi.'

'Well I'll go to our flamin' 'ouse,' I snapped.

'How long will it be until the next train?' asked Antoinette quietly.

The porter checked his watch. 'An hour, maybe a bit sooner. If you want to, you can sit . . .'

'An hour!' I exploded before he could finish. 'Honest, it's like Fred Karno's flippin' Army . . . Look,' I added, turning to Antoinette, 'I'll go and try to find a taxi.'

Before she could reply I was off. Calling me back, she gave me a number the porter had given her. I nodded my thanks and turned away for the nearby phone box. Within a minute I was through and, with limited finances, made a cautionary enquiry, then nearly fell off the end of the phone.

'How much is it to Morecambe?' I asked, explaining where I was. 'Five pounds . . . But there's nothing in at the moment. If you can . . .'

'Five quid?' I gasped, without hearing the end of his remarks. I knew it was Christmas, but I was in no mood to be screwed as well as misdirected. 'You must be jokin',' I continued. 'Look, I don't wanna buy the flamin' thing, just go round the bay in it, like!'

'That's the price,' he insisted. 'After all, it is Boxin' day, y'know. Anyway, as I said, there's nothing in at the moment, maybe in twen . . .'

I had had enough, More than enough. 'At that price, mate,' I snarled furiously, 'you can stick your taxi where Paddy stuck 'is ninepence.' I slammed the phone down, storming out of the box. 'D'you know how much they wanted?' I demanded of Antoinette, now sitting in the cold, empty waiting room. She shrugged enquiringly. 'Five pounds!' I growled. 'Five flippin' pounds, just to go round the Bay. It's daylight robbery!'

She looked at me thoughtfully. 'And I suppose you told him what he could do with it, as usual?'

'I sure did.'

She clucked heavily. 'Well, prices are bound to be up a bit, this time of the year.'

'A bit! That's a helluva lot more than a bit, I'll tell you. Anyway,' I added, 'there wasn't one available for half an hour if I'd wanted it, so that's that. A right dump this is, too!' I added, glancing round the dingy room.

'If you'd been a bit more diplomatic,' she snapped, 'we could have been sitting by the fire in the porter's room, instead of here in the cold.'

'What d'yeh mean?' I demanded.

'That's what he was going to say when you interrupted him! Oh, but you wouldn't wait, would you? Oh no . . . Not you. Whoosh! Off you went like a blessed rocket. First you insult the porter, and it wasn't his fault, now you've told the taxi firm what they can do with their taxi! Oh yes,' she added with a flicker of a smile despite herself, 'that's a great help, that is, I'm sure.'

'Well,' I said, sitting down beside her on the uncomfortable seat, 'they make me mad!'

She laughed. 'I had noticed. Anyway,' she added, 'it'll take us about an hour and a quarter to . . .'

I sighed with relief. 'An hour and a quarter? Well that's not bad. We shou . . .'

'That,' she said slowly, 'is to Preston. We change there for . . .'

'To Preston? Well what time are we supposed to get to Morecambe then?'

She shrugged. 'The porter said if we get the connection we should arrive somewhere about, oh, eleven, maybe a bit later.'

I put my head in my hands. 'Oh bloody hell!' I said despondently.

The events of the last few days were rapidly catching up with us. The long Christmas Eve with Midnight Mass, a longer Christmas day, followed by another restless night, and now, what looked like being the longest day of all! Although we were so miserable we just had to laugh, and prayed that nothing else would go wrong.

Our prayers were answered. The journey to Preston was uneventful, and the change of trains equally smooth. At eleven fifteen we staggered, exhausted, out of the station and into a waiting taxi for the short journey to Aunt Louise's where, silhouetted against the sitting room light, she watched anxiously at the window. In suppressed anxiety she fussed over us as she came to the door.

'Oh,' she exclaimed, her thin sad face drawn with worry, 'whatever happened to you? You must be dog tired.'

Bleary-eyed and shattered, we staggered into the welcome warmth of the sitting room. With minimal introduction, I flopped on the couch as, with gentle affection, her arm round Antoinette's shoulders, Aunt Louise chattered her way into the kitchen to make a much needed cup of tea. As I sat, still in my outdoor clothes and staring at the roaring fire, it seemed barely a moment before they were back, Antoinette with the pot, and Aunt Louise with a bottle.

'This will warm you up,' she said, uncorking the bottle.

I shook my head. 'Thanks, but a cup of tea will do just right.'

She handed me the cup instead and, still gazing into the fire, I sipped luxuriously. I have no idea how long I sat, lulled by the warmth into a fitful doze, but Antoinette's high-pitched giggle suddenly aroused me. The bottle of wine I noticed dazedly was more than half-empty, and they were both in fits of laughter.

'Come on, wake up,' said Antoinette rising and standing over me. 'You nodded off.'

I dragged my eyes open and gazed dully at her smiling face. Her eyes, so recently tired, seemed very bright. God, I thought, with a glance at the half-empty bottle, she's tiddly! I looked across at Aunt Louise, emptying the remains of her glass. She didn't look much better.

'Come on luv,' I suggested, 'let's get to bed, I'm shattered.'

Antoinette laughed. 'Alright my love, in a minute, I'm just telling Aunt Louise about er, er, well you know, er, about today.'

I sighed and slumped back as she rejoined her Aunt. She was still talking as the clock struck half past twelve, with the bottle nearer empty than full. Like me, she wasn't used to alcohol, and it showed! Giggling her head off I half carried her up the stairs. Laurel and Hardy had very little on us as we staggered about the darkened room getting ready for bed. I finally made it as she went off into the bathroom still giggling, then nature took its inevitable toll and I went out like a light. Next morning I was still, according to strict Canon Law . . . Single!

12

Biddy

Aunt Louise, tall slim, with deep blue eyes set in a pensive face, and widowed for many years, proved to be a slightly eccentric treasure. Quiet and gentle, with a fanatical love of animals, her walk, or rather glide, could have a very unnerving effect when she materialised at your side without warning. But there lay beneath that solemn exterior an engaging sense of humour. Sharing the large house with her, and accompanying her almost everywhere she went, were Shep and Mandy, her two collies, not to mention The Captain, a cat of doubtful parentage and piratical aspect, who clearly disliked strangers and, from the attention paid to it, had definite plans for the ageing budgie. But the oddest of them all was Biddy, the most emancipated hen I ever met, who, bought some little time before to provide a gala dinner for the honeymooners on their final day, had now become fully established on the unit strength. Biddy and I were to become very close before the week was out.

Our first meeting, however, was traumatic as I walked down the stairs on the morning after our arrival, with Antoinette following close behind. Blending well with the carpet, she lay contentedly on the bottom stair, and all hell broke loose as, with my head turned talking to Antoinette, I trod on her. She rose with a heart-stopping squawk as I tumbled to the floor in a heap. Seconds later the small and already crowded hall was jammed as Antoinette collapsed on the stairs, laughing, while our fellow honeymooners, quickly followed by Aunt Louise, rushed to see what was happening, inadvertenly blocking Biddy's escape.

'What are tha doin theere?' an amused voice queried.

Still confused, I looked up into the laughing face of George, short, heavily-built and broad Yorkshire. Alongside, jammed against the doorpost, with Biddy frantically trying to get between her legs, Edith, his dark and diminutive wife gazed at me wide-eyed.

'Tha's fallen over the'en then, 'ast tha?' she asked.

George gave her a disparaging look. 'Nay lass,' he said with a grin as he helped me up, ''e allus comes darn like that, don't thee lad?'

Antoinette wiped her eyes as she helped pull me to my feet, whilst her aunt, with Biddy now safely in her arms in the background, cooed soothingly to the distraught bird.

'Ah,' said Antoinette, 'the poor bird. Didn't you see it?'

I felt irritated. Cor blimey, I thought, never mind about me! I reacted without thinking. 'Well,' I began, 'I didn't expect to find a flippin' . . .' I felt her aunt's sad eyes on me. 'No luv,' I ended lamely, as Aunt Louise cooed her way into the kitchen with Biddy.

'I did warn you, didn't I?' Antoinette reminded me as we sat at the table. 'She just loves animals, so you'd better keep your eyes open, my love.'

With brief introductions over amid the seductive aroma of bacon and eggs from the kitchen, George, calloused hand grasping the teapot, took over as master of ceremonies. His method of pouring tea was unique, his aim unerring as he gradually raised the pot several inches as he poured, so as, he explained straight-faced, 'to put a head on it'. And each time Edith made what proved to be her main contribution to the conversation for the rest of the week, 'Oh George . . . Don't!' Such complete opposites, they matched in a strange way, into a perfect, unrehearsed comedy-duo, with the 'missus' as the perfect foil for George's lugubrious humour.

I was still laughing when a long arm appeared round my shoulder, as Aunt Louise silently laid my plate before me. I glanced at her sad face and wondered guiltily if I had upset her over Biddy, now clucking her way round the room. I whispered my fears to Antoinette as the slim figure moved away.

She smiled. 'Oh no, I wouldn't think so, love. After all, you didn't do it on purpose did you?' I forgot all about it and tucked in, but, although her aunt was quite normal for the rest of the day, the same thing happened at breakfast the next morning. This time I knew it had nothing to do with Biddy. Antoinette was puzzled too, but George, now a firm friend, laughed when I mentioned it.

'Nay lad,' he said comfortingly, 'don't thee tak' on about it now. It's Percy, tha' knows, that's all.'

'Percy? Who's Percy then?' I asked.

George's smile spread from ear to ear as Edith dallied with her bacon. 'Th' pig!' he replied with a laugh.

I was surprised, I hadn't seen any pig in the garden, large though it was. 'Ah,' I said sympathetically, 'what's up with it then? Sick?'

He shook his head. 'Nay lad,' he answered solemnly, 'dead.'

'That's funny,' broke in Antoinette, puzzled, 'she never mentioned anything to me.'

George burst out laughing, while his wife looked glumly at her plate. 'Tha's eating' it, yeh daft ha'porth,' he said, pointing at my plate.

I looked down guiltily. Oh my God! I thought, as Antoinette began to giggle. 'D'yeh mean t'say . . .?'

'Aye,' replied George, 'that's 'im alreet, an' a right nice mouthful 'e is, too.'

'Oh George!' exclaimed Edith, pushing her plate away. 'What a thing to say.'

Antoinette collapsed in a fit of laughter. 'Oh that's Aunt Louise all over.' She exclaimed. 'I told you, she's dotty on animals.'

For a few moments, with Edith sitting in thoughtful silence, we howled with laughter as Biddy, forever on the prowl, rose from her box near the fire and clucked her way into the kitchen. George followed her progress with a wicked gleam in his eye, as he popped the last of Percy into his mouth, then flicked his head at the vanishing bird.

'Aye,' he observed meaningfully, 'an' I don't fancy 'er chances much cum Saturday neither, Li.'

His 'missus' frowned heavily. 'Oh George!' she exclaimed disgustedly.

My heart went out to poor Aunt Louise, as her terrible dilemma became more apparent.

With rationing still strictly enforced, and a living to make as a boarding house landlady wishing to do well by her guests, she had bought Percy to fatten him but, like Biddy, he had become a pet. Under Ministry regulations, and long before we had arrived, poor Percy had been removed for his official demise, with the bulk of him being kept by the Ministry and the rest returned to Aunt Louise for her own use. He was gone, but was definitely not forgotten. She must have felt terrible, cooking him each day. I shuddered to think of how she would feel when Biddy's turn came.

By Wednesday we all felt as though we had known each other for years. Even Edith, the same age as her miner husband, and mouse-like by nature, had opened up a little. Each morning, in pairs or as a foursome, we battled our way along the windswept promenade in biting weather, or explored the deserted town accompanied by the dogs, seeking the meagre entertainments offered by a seaside resort in the depths of winter and finding little but our own high spirits. On Wednesday evening, still sorry for Aunt Louise and her problems, I suggested we all went to the local

Music Hall to enliven the proceedings, a visit made memorable by both George's piercing laugh and Aunt Louise's high-pitched giggle. I lost count of the number of reprimands George received from the 'missus' as he roared at the antics of Nat Jackly, the 'India-Rubber Man', on stage.

Our journey home in a crowded taxi, through driving rain, only served to heighten the fun. It had been a hilarious evening and we were still laughing as we tumbled into bed. Next morning Aunt Louise received another surprise. Biddy, off-colour for the past few days, had laid an egg. I rolled my eyes as we were called into the kitchen to see it, and joined in the congratulations, half-way through which George dropped another clanger.

'Aye,' he said thoughtlessly as Biddy snuggled in her mistress's arms, 'it's a right pity she's agoin' tomorrow, in't it?'

Edith's rejoinder was predictable and Antoinette volunteered to put the kettle on to break the sudden silence.

Breakfast on Friday was more solemn than usual, as our landlady announced a hitch. The man next door who was to see Biddy off, couldn't manage it. He would be out fishing all day; therefore, unless Biddy decided on suicide, George or I would have to do it! George, despite his eagerness to eat her, drew a definite line at killing her.

'Nay lad,' he said, much to Edith's relief, 'aah could'na do it. Tha do it, tha's bin a soldier. It shouldn't be nowt t'thee!'

In vain I tried to explain that I hadn't been trained to kill chickens. Men yes! But a chicken, in cold blood, oh no! He remained adamant and, if Biddy was going to be guest of honour, the only thing he would agree to would be to give me a hand in arranging the execution. This agreed, we discussed several ways to accomplish it, and each time Biddy walked past us we felt a growing guilt. I suggested chopping her head off while he held her legs. But who would hold her head? Suppose I missed? I could have his hand off, he insisted. At last it was solved and, with neither of us up to wringing her neck, it was decided he would hold her legs and I her head while I chopped. Execution was set for four o'clock and the women would go out to town to be out of the way. I felt miserable all day.

At four, with the sky darkening outside, Biddy, with some sixth sense, headed for the garden. A frantic chase followed as we located, then tried, without success to catch her. For five exhausting minutes, the air filled with feathers and piercing squawks, we raced about from one hiding place to another until a sardonic voice called over the fence.

'What yeh tryin' t'do —?' it asked, 'frighten it t'death?' We stopped, exhausted, and gazed at the grinning face crowned with a sou-wester. I explained what we were doing. His grin broadened. 'Aye, I know. I should've done it this mornin' but couldn't. D'you want me t'come round and' wring it's neck?' We agreed gratefully. 'Oh, hang on a minute,' he added, vanishing momentarily below the fence then reappearing with half a dozen flukes on a string. 'Take these, will ye. I knew Louise had guests so I thought she'd like a few.'

I felt a surge of relief as I took the fish. 'Look,' I added after thanking him, 'don't bother about Biddy. Leave her where she is.'

'What about dinner tomorrow?' asked George.

I held the fish up and grinned. 'Let's make it fish an' chips, eh?'

The neighbour burst out laughing. 'God,' he said, 'you're as bad as Lousie!'

At four thirty we met the ladies at the gate with prearranged solemnity. Aunt Louise was far from happy. George gave Edith a slow wink as she gazed at him accusingly.

'Have you done it?' whispered Antoinette sadly.

'Come and see,' I invited without expression. Moments later the house was filled with laughter as the door opened and Biddy clucked her way into the kitchen. 'Fish and chips tomorrow,' I announced, holding up the flukes.

It had been a wonderful week, quiet, simple, and with a great deal of unexpected merriment. We parted with the reluctance of old friends and dear, gentle Aunt Louise, with Shep and Mandy alongside her and Biddy safely in her arms, watched in what I believe was genuine sadness, as we entered our joint taxi for the station. Even the Captain, aloof as ever, tail high in the air, had the good manners to come to the gate. Only Percy was missing, and even he, in a manner of speaking, was still with us. At the station, with mutual good wishes, we parted from this outwardly dour and most unlikely couple, never to see each other again.

With just one more trouble-free journey behind us, we were home to a greeting as warm as the parting, with our rooms, so thoughtfully prepared, quite beyond our expectations. Half an hour later, my new mother-in-law knocked discreetly at the door.

'What with one thing and another, Li, I nearly forgot,' she said as I opened it. 'I met your Teresa down town the other day. She told me to tell you there's a letter for you.'

My heart leapt, then sank again as she told me, in answer to my query, that she had no idea who it was from. It must be from the Coal Board, I thought. No one else would write to me, as far as I knew. I wanted to go immediately but she wanted to know about our holiday.

Antoinette agreed with her. 'Mum's right,' she said. 'It won't run away. Besides I'm starving and so are you. Let's go after tea.'

Reluctantly I agreed.

At seven we were in our second home. They were all

167

there, including Con, looking as grim as ever. Mam and Teresa couldn't get Antoinette into the parlour quick enough to hear all her news.

'Hey,' I called as they were leaving the room, 'what about the letter then?'

Mam turned. 'Oh it's on the mantelpiece, behind the clock.'

Con watched in puzzlement as I dashed across to retrieve it, while Dad sat in silent expectancy. Fingers fumbling in excitement, I ripped it open and felt a surge of relief as I scanned its brief contents.

'I've got it!' I yelled dashing through to the parlour to spread the news. All three were delighted and I left them talking animatedly. I gave Dad a broad grin as I handed him the letter. Con's frown deepened.

'What's all this about?' he demanded. 'What's all the excitement?' Dad passed the letter across to him. His temper rose as he read it, then he blew. 'An' warrabout yeh job down there?' he demanded angrily. 'I worked damned 'ard t'get that for yeh.'

I tried in vain to pacify him, as Dad sat forward in his chair irritably. I knew he had tried hard to get me fixed up. I knew he wanted me to settle into the old routine. I told him so and tried yet again to explain that I simply wanted something with more prospects, that's all. But I might as well have talked to the wall. He was beside himself with anger. Instinct warned me that a row was but a word away. I didn't want that.

'It's his life!' snapped Dad venomously. 'So you mind yer own flamin' business. Good luck to 'im, I say.'

Con glared at him furiously. 'Yeah, maybe, but why the 'ell didn't 'e tell me, hey? That's what I'd like t'know.'

My patience, never of the quality of Job's, was running out fast. Ignoring Dad's warning look I flew at him. 'I'll tell you for why, Con,' I snarled. 'Because they're too bloody sarky by half down there and you know it!'

'Hey,' broke in Dad, half rising from his chair, 'that's enough of that . . . Just watch yeh tongues, both of yeh or you'll answer to me!'

Oh bloody hell, I thought as I sat down. Here we go again! What should have been a happy reunion was going badly wrong.

I tried to calm things down again. 'I'm sorry Dad,' I said, 'but honest t'God, 'e gets up my flamin' nose sometimes. Every time I . . .' One look at Con was enough to tell me I'd put my foot in it again. He nearly went purple, and the women, disturbed by the growing altercation, couldn't have picked a worse time to come and see what all the noise was about. Con gave Antoinette a filthy look as she came through the door first.

'Big ideas, that's your trouble, mate,' he said sarcastically, 'big ideas . . . An' it's all 'er fault! College this, an' colle . . .'

That was it! In the act of sitting down, the accusation stung me as my seat touched the chair. I rocketed to my feet again in a searing temper. Everything seemed to happen at once as I made to cross the room to him; Dad shot to his feet, white-faced and angry, while the women stood dumbfounded.

'That's enough!' he snarled, looking from one to the other of us. 'Now knock it off both of yeh . . . Siddown' he ordered me. I sat, seething. 'An' as for you,' he snapped at my brother, 'you ought to be damned well ashamed of y'self!'

Con, now tense and drawn as he faced the sudden hostility around him, lowered his eyes as Dad turned to Antoinette to apologise. Face white with temper, she tried to smile as she laid her hand gently on his arm.

'That's alright Mr Sullivan,' she said quietly, 'I understand. Sit down. Please.' She turned to me with a warning look as the women looked on, then to Con, sitting angrily on the edge of his chair.

169

He was outnumbered and he knew it. Nor could he blow as he would do at work, or with his mates. Oh no, not at home with Dad watching and waiting, and Mam, her arm round a worried Teresa, just itching to go for him. I felt genuinely sorry for him as Antoinette, quiet but determined, castigated him.

He, not she, was the snob, and the very worst kind of snob, she told him. 'An inverted snob.'

He gasped at the accusation. Him . . . a snob!

'Don't be so bloo . . .' He stopped as he caught Dad's look.

'Oh yes,' she continued, 'a real snob. To you, people who don't dirty their hands at work are rubbish, useless, aren't they? If that's not being snobbish I don't know what is . . . Everybody works, Con, clean hands or not they work alright. The trouble is, you're about fifty years behind the times.' Con sat bolt upright at this and was about to retort when she quelled him with an imperious gesture. I felt proud of her. 'No,' she said politely, 'with respect, just let me finish!' Then she challenged him to give a reason why I shouldn't try to get on a bit. What the devil was wrong with that, she wanted to know.

His lips were still framing an answer when Mam beat him to the punch. 'Yes,' she demanded. 'Why the hell shouldn't he? It's his life isn't it?'

'Our life, Mam,' I interrupted quietly, giving Con a filthy look.

'Yeah,' he growled, 'that's warr'I mean, big ideas! Wants t'step outa 'is class.'

'Rubbish!' snapped Antoinette, finally losing her calm.

Suddenly Teresa, pale and anxious, took an unexpected hand. 'Oh Con!' she sighed. 'What's up with you, for God's sake?'

A worried Mam tried to calm her down. In her state of health, family trouble was the last thing that was needed. But Teresa for once had her dander up, and all hell wasn't going to stop her having her say. Con looked worried as she went for him. He loved her as much as we all did and tried to calm her as she laid into him and his politics.

'I'm sick and tired of it,' she announced, glaring at him. 'Every time you've stepped through the door since Li's come home, it's been trouble. If it's not one damned thing it's another, and all t'do with politics, or unions or . . . Oh damn it!'

I rose angrily, putting my arm round her protectively as she burst into tears. I could feel her shaking. Releasing her, I took a step forward as Con, visibly upset at the thoughtless havoc he had caused, stood up. Dad misinterpreted my movement. From my expression he must have thought I was going to thump Con, but it was the furthest thought from my mind. Dad was taking no chances in the charged atmosphere, however.

'Siddown!' he snapped, but Con had had enough.

He gave me a ferocious look. 'Ah, t'hell with yeh,' he barked. 'Do what yeh want. I'm goin'!' Without another word, he nearly took the door off its hinges on the way out.

For a few moments there was an uncertain silence as Dad ran his hand wearily across his forehead, flopping into his chair.

'God almighty,' he sighed, 'I dunno what the hell's got into that feller lately, honest I don't.' He turned to Antoinette. 'Don't take any notice of 'im luv, will yeh? He's a good lad really.'

'Runnin' with the wrong flamin' crowd, that's his trouble,' opined Mam.

Antoinette laughed and shrugged. 'Well, I'm sure I don't know what I've done to him, and that's the truth.'

Dad looked at her knowingly and tried to explain. It wasn't her, he said, it was her background. She laughed at the suggestion, but he persisted. She was right when she said that Con was suspicious of anyone

171

who didn't dirty their hands, and, since she was going to college, she was one of them. The trouble was that Liam wanted to do the same, and to Con that made him a traitor to his own class, and all hell wasn't going to change his views on that.

'That's the way it is, luv,' he ended. 'Daft it may be, but it won't change.'

'Silly buggers,' broke in Mam without thinking. 'Oh, sorry Antoinette!' she added.

Antoinette giggled. 'I couldn't have put it better myself,' she said with a grin.

Suddenly Mam remembered the letter. 'There!' she exclaimed. 'We don't even know where he's goin' yet. Come on Li, read it again.'

I obliged with great relish. It seemed I was heading for some kind of a village called Todmarsh in the Colchester area, and I would have to report on the eleventh of the month, which gave me just enough time to hand my notice in, with a few days to spare. After further discussion we decided it must be one of the many derelict Army camps, of which there were a great number about, most of them in or near scattered villages. But I didn't care if it was in Timbuctoo. It would be the chance I craved, away from the mind-boggling boredom and hassle of my present job, and that was all I asked.

*   *   *

With my notice safely in on the following morning, we had a stroll round the ever-lively market, then a long comfortable walk to our new home. My in-laws had been as delighted with the good news as we had been and the time passed quickly for us in a hectic week. I met Con again on the Monday. He was distant but wished me luck.

Now on my own, with Antoinette back in college on the Thursday, and with the agreement of my in-laws, I went back home for the remainder of the week. On Friday night, as though nothing had ever happened, Con walked in and talked his head off about everything under the sun except trade unionism. Now that the die was cast, we agreed amicably that I was, as Teresa had said earlier, a square peg in a round hole with my current views, and that the move was probably all for the best. On Sunday after Mass, and a final meal together as a family, Con and Dad walked to the station with me, our individual views still firmly held, but equally firmly suppressed. We parted as good friends, and I was happy.

13

P.T. Walla

After a smooth, uneventful journey, during which I had
the old sensation of returning from leave, I arrived at the
ancient garrison city of Colchester for the second time
in my life, having seen it briefly from a convoy lorry, as I
passed through it to the South Coast early in the war.
This time, as I tramped the narrow streets to the bus
station for the final leg, I was able to take a closer look at
the important Roman town upon which Boadicea had
rendered such havoc so long ago.

A short journey and I alighted at the familiar gates of a
run-down camp. There were no whitewashed stones
outside the old guardroom, no bustling Swaddies to
give it life and purpose, not even a flag to inform me that
I was in friendly territory, just peeling paintwork, a few
broken windows and, perhaps the most heinous crime
of all, bank after bank of weeds! God, I thought, what a
dump. Suitcase in hand, I cast an experienced eye over
it and did a rapid calculation. Yes, Sergeant Major
Spencer, my old boss, would have been in his element
sorting this lot out. Two weeks with a couple of fatigue
squads under him and the weeds would have been
frightened to grow! But then, he had been a pre-war
soldier, not 'dressed-up civvies', like us.

Instinctively I knew where the Orderly Room would
be, and headed straight for it, knocked and walked in.
It was just as tatty inside as it was out. On the far side of
the sparsely furnished room, an extremely well-
upholstered blonde of about thirty sat at a paper-littered

trestle table, gazing at me from a pair of limpid blue eyes set beneath eye lashes any 'Chunka Walla' would have been proud to use to keep the room cool.

'My name is Sullivan,' I announced crisply, putting my case down.

Her full red lips, glistening with lipstick, pursed as she gazed back dumbly. I repeated the statement. Still no response. Instead, still watching me, she placed her palms on the table and rose to her feet. I watched in admiration as her bursting bodice was fully revealed, when she straightened up. Strewth! I gasped silently.

'I go,' she said, pointing to a door on her right. She did and she looked just as seductive from the rear as she wiggled away. Moments later she returned, followed by the tall, elegant figure of what was obviously an ex-officer. By reflex I stood to attention. Laughing, he raised his hand.

'Stand easy Mr Sullivan,' he said. 'This is the Coal Board, not the Coldstreams.'

I flushed momentarily, then joined his laughter. 'Old habits die hard sir.'

He smiled and nodded. 'I know,' he replied, indicating I should follow him. 'Sit down,' he invited as we entered a smaller and equally untidy room. With a nod and a smile he dismissed the blonde as I sat, once again enjoying the provocative wiggle on the way out. As the door closed I turned to see a grin on his face as he leaned back in his chair. 'A fine woman,' he said with the merest hint of a leer. 'Teaching her to be my secretary. No English of course, but she'll learn ... Czechoslovakian you know, unpronounceable name. Just call her Ledy, she'll understand.' Blimey, I thought, I'll lay ten to one that's one Czech that'll bounce!

'Now Liam ... It is Liam, isn't it?' he added checking a form in front of him.

'Yes sir.'

He smiled and shook his leonine head. 'Well, it's all

175

very informal here of course Liam, as you might guess, so we can drop the sir. John will do.'

I hesitated before replying. I liked authority clearly defined, with respect to those above and below me, then everyone knew where they were. I never believed, certainly not in the services, that you could call a bloke sir one minute and mate the next, especially when trouble arose. It was bad for discipline.

'I think I would prefer Mr Williams, if you don't mind,' I answered, remembering the name I had to report to.

He smiled and nodded. 'As you wish. I quite understand.'

'And the duties, Mr Williams?'

He took a deep breath, then pursed his lips. 'Well, it's pretty disorganised at the moment, as you can guess, but your duties will be mainly to organise recreation. However, we are all just feeling our way. The main thing is to get this Basic English across as quickly as possible . . . You know, of course, the job is short term?'

I acknowledged this and asked him about equipment. His answer was discouraging, just a couple of footballs, an old badminton net and a few odds and ends.

He looked at me apologetically. 'I'm afraid you will just have to, er, well, you'll know exactly what I mean!'

I did. I would have to do the same as we had in the field battalions for recreation equipment. Make it up as you went along. I sighed inwardly. 'Are there any indoor facilities for bad weather work?'

Again the head shook sadly. 'Not much. Just see what you want . . . Except the huts used for classrooms of course.'

He rolled his eyes when I asked how many men there would be. The current two hundred would be doubled and more over the next week or so. Oh charming I thought. Five hundred odd and no equipment. That should be fun. Then I put my most vital question.

Discipline? With several nationalities involved and all from camps, they were not going to jump for joy at organised physical work, and that was a fact. We both knew there could be problems, maybe between nationalities, maybe grudge fights, anything, and I wanted to know just how far I could go if there was. Now was the time to sort it out.

'Well,' he said after some thought, 'I'll be quite honest, Liam. We will have to play it by ear for the moment. It's a very mixed bunch and we don't really know what we've got yet, so all I can say is that I will back you to the hilt on this question. If there is any nonsense, they can always be removed, and quickly! But I'm sure with your experience you'll be able to cope. However, you can rest assured, you will have my absolute support. Are you happy with that?'

I gave a relieved grin. 'Just wanted to know where I stood, Mr Williams, that's all.'

'And quite right too, but if . . .' The door suddenly opened and the blonde's head popped round, flashing a brilliant smile.

'Mee-ster . . . Ben'on, Mee-ster Vil-e-ums.'

'Mr Benson,' corrected the boss. 'Send him in.' She looked puzzled. 'In,' he repated. The head vanished as a bouncy, tousle-headed, tweed-cladded figure beamed his way in, stopping short as he saw me.

'Oh!' he exclaimed, 'I didn't . . .'

'Oh that's alright, Johnny. This is Liam, Liam Sullivan. Just joined us. P.T. Walla.'

'Oh my gawd!' exclaimed the newcomer in mock horror. 'Don't come near me for anything,' he said with a grin as he came forward, hand outstretched, 'I've got flat feet!'

'You've just come at the right moment,' broke in the boss. 'You can show him where to put his kit. By the way, what was it you wanted?'

Johnny shrugged. 'Oh nothing really. Just finished a class and thought I would pop in.'

'That's alright, then. Just show Liam around.'

I thanked him, especially for his backing.

My new friend nudged me in the ribs on the way out. 'Talking about discipline were you?' I nodded. He grinned cheerfully. 'You'll be alright. He's a good'un, ex-colonel you know. He won't stand any nonsense. If he says he'll back you, that's just what he'll do. Nice to know, just in case, eh?'

'Yeah,' I agreed. 'Looks like a real mixed bag,' I said, looking at some of the students walking between classes.

'You're not joking my friend,' he replied. 'East Europeans mainly, with other odds and sods thrown in. A rum bunch, laddie.'

'That secretary?' I queried. 'She's a Czech isn't she?'

His eyes rolled appreciatively. 'Ah Ledy! What a cracker she is, eh? Only been here a week and has been, what one might say, seconded. Yes, she's a Czech alright and,' he added with a lecherous wink, 'I have a strong suspicion that our good friend the Williams sahib, is going to cash it very shortly!'

I burst out laughing. 'Are there many women? I thought it was for miners.' He grimaced and explained that there were a few, for cooking, cleaning etc. 'And Ledy?'

He gave a slow wink. 'Let's say she's been promoted, eh?' He gave me another nudge as we reached the staff quarters, 'Come on, I'll introduce you to the rest of the teaching fraternity.'

And what a fraternity it was! Six in all, including me, with more to come later I gathered, and all except one, were larking about like a crowd of high-spirited schoolboys.

Two of them, about my age, and like me ex-service, were waiting to go to Teacher Training College. Two more, posh-speaking clones of Johnny, and a fifth, a dear old boy of about seventy, hunched deep in a chair by the roaring combustion stove, puffing away on an enormous Meerschaum pipe. For a moment I had the feeling of being 'home' again in this familiar atmosphere.

'Silence gentlemen, please,' announced Johnny ceremoniously. They quietened down and looked at me. 'May I introduce our 'muscle man', Liam, whose duty it will be, believe it or not, to entertain the blighters. Games, exercises, and God knows what-all abominations.'

'Chuck him out,' suggested one of the budding teachers.

'I warn you gentlemen,' continued Johnny amid a howl of protest, 'stay clear of him. His complaint may well be catching, and exercise, as you are well aware, is bad for you . . . You have been warned!'

God, I thought, as they crowded round to shake my hand, what a crew! Not since I had left the Mess so many long months ago, had I seen this kind of spirit. If only for this, the move was well worth while, short term or not. But my biggest pleasure was still to come as Johnny walked me over to the quiet figure in the chair and straight back into a world of Dickensian courtesy.

'Liam,' said Johnny solemnly as we halted at the chair, 'meet our guide and mentor, our esteemed Guru, Mr Milton. Mr Milton . . . Liam Sullivan, P.T. Walla.'

The guru did not move. Instead he scrutinised me silently with a pair of twinkling blue eyes, peeping mischievously from beneath bushy white brows. Then, slowly, the rosy unlined cheeks creased into a beaming smile as he finally hauled himself slowly out of the chair and stood, slightly bent, eyes still watching me as he held out his slim hand.

'My dear boy,' he said in a small piping voice, 'what great pleasure it is to meet you. I do hope you had a comfortable journey. Do sit down, please,' he invited, as Johnny obligingly pulled a chair alongside for me, 'and tell me all about yourself.'

179

It proved to be a very happy hour indeed. A retired academic, brought in especially for the organisation and running of the scheme, he was a real gent, one of the 'old school' and, with a shoe on one foot, and a slipper on the other, a little eccentric and forgetful perhaps. Not once in the slow conversation did he talk down to me. I was so comfortable I felt I had known him a hundred years. I was to remember Mr Milton long, long after the scheme was dead and buried, for he taught me a great deal before I finally left.

His personal lodging on the camp, just down the corridor from me, was a veritable junk shop of books, scattered in wild disarray in every nook and cranny. His dress sense was in similar vein. His clothes, of beautiful quality, hung about him in a variety of clashing colours, startling in their effects, with his pipe forming an integral part of whatever ensemble he happened to be wearing. Later, near the end of the scheme, we were to receive a VIP visitor of some renown, and Mr Milton, from the esteem in which he was held by all, was given the honour of greeting our guest. Even on this occasion he remained true to his sartorial eccentricity and forgetfulness, when, with great aplomb and exquisite courtesy, he greeted the guest in pin-stripes, bowler hat, and slippers! No one said a word. Even the VIP merely raised his eyebrows slightly. He lived in a world entirely his own, yet his work was brilliant. With five languages at his command he was the only one in camp who could actually converse with the students on a personal level. Dear Mr Milton. What a generous soul he was.

With a good and happy staff to live with, I wondered what lay in store for me with the students. From those I had seen, I got a strong impression that I was among the Maquis, they looked so rough. I was even less favourably impressed the following morning when, with the agreement of the boss, and the help of the rest of the staff, I had the full complement assembled in the large dining room to, as Montgomery would say, put them in the picture. Hell, what a crew they looked, I thought, as they sat in rows across the room, chattering in half a dozen languages and, in the age-old habit of homeless people everywhere, seemingly carrying all their possessions with them in a variety of battered bags and suitcases.

Standing on a home-made platform to get a clear view and also so that they could see me, I gazed at them solemnly and with a sinking heart for a few seconds; even if I'd wanted to, there was no escape now. With three bright students who could speak a few words of English plus three or four other languages fluently alongside me, I launched in and called for silence. Nothing happened. I tried again. The English teachers looked at me sympathetically. Still nothing happened.

Johnny wagged his head. 'You'll have to shout Li,' he advised.

I refused. Shouting in that situation I had found over the years was the last thing that was effective. I pointed to Barry Johnston, one of the two ex-service men, who, with a bad foot, was at present using a walking stick.

'Ask Barry to lend me his stick,' I requested.

Moments later, stick in hand, and a ferocious look on my face I crashed it on the table top in front of me. For a few seconds we just looked at each other, until the noise died completely. Then, in absolute silence, I started. I explained, via the interpreters, who I was, and what I was there for, and, as each item was translated and the students passed the information around, moans and groans arose. Within twenty minutes the message was across, and the first fifty reluctant humans, complete with suitcases and assorted bags, were assembled outside ready, but not eager, for work.

With no gym and no equipment there was little I could do but 'run' them. First, though, I had to get rid of the suitcases. With the freezing cold and many without top coats, although they had all been issued with good boots on their arrival, I got some murderous looks when I insisted that the baggage should be returned to their barrack blocks. I was not popular, and this was only the first of the four squads I would have to deal with. By the time they re-assembled to start the run, it was almost time to come back and begin the operation all over again with the next lot. However, despite the ensuing chaos to teaching schedules on the first day, all the runs took place. They were not a success, and, for a short time not at all popular but, exercise they had to be given, and, until facilities improved, exercise they would get!

For the first week, with the bad weather continuing, indoor work limited to small groups in the confines of the largest available hut, and with the lethargy of the camps from which they came still upon them, it became a straight battle of wills. They came forward in dozens, with a thousand and one excuses why they should not run, or do any exercise, but I had heard it all before. To give in would be fatal.

Nicky, a Yugoslav of about thirty, and one of the three who were with me on the platform the first day, gave up all his spare time to help me get across to them, and at the same time improve his own English; but there were always the bright boys, the spiv types and inevitable layabouts. In the Army their feet wouldn't have touched the ground on the way to the guardroom, but here it was different. I knew exactly what I would like to do but couldn't, so I needed time to infuse a spirit into them, to breed friendly competition between them to give them aim and purpose. But with the weather and other limitations it was difficult. Through Nicky I dropped the first gentle hint that if they were not willing to work, it was possible that they could be considered unsuitable for the work they had come to do. The message went home and things quietened down, my popularity going down with it. Several bright boys remained, however, and a show-down was bound to come. On the tenth day of my arduous tenure it did.

With almost a third of the total camp-strength lined up outside the camp in a freezing wind, and gradually increasing snowflakes falling about us, Nicky, at the far end of a disgruntled column, was talking excitedly to a small group who had detached themselves. I went to see what the hold up was, as the remainder stamped their feet.

'They 'ave not their . . .' he struggled for the word 'boots' as he pointed at their battered array of slippers and plimsoles.

I looked at the half-grins on their faces. It was a 'try-on'. They had either hidden or flogged their boots. If I was soft and excused them from the run, it would be taken as weakness and I might just as well pack my bags and go home, and I would rather have died than that. There was only one answer. I took my boots and socks off and, giving them to Nicky turned to them. I pointed to myself then my bare feet.

'No boots . . . I run . . . You run! Get back into line.'

Nicky interpreted. Scowling heavily, they ran, plus an extra mile for luck! They didn't try it again, but I must admit, it was bloody sore on the feet, despite the practice I had had as a lad.

Another ploy came within a week — dodging the column. With a long line of men I could only be in one place at a time, and, after a quick check on return from the runs at the end of the second week, I found less returning than had started out; not many, but enough. It had to be stopped and quickly. With the boss's help it was relatively simple.

Mr William looked up as I walked into his office. 'Hello Liam, how are things going?'

I shrugged disconsolately. 'Not so good,' I admitted, then moaned about the continuing bad weather and lack of indoor space which made the runs inevitable. 'They hate them,' I told him. 'Still,' I added more cheerfully, 'I've been able to cut them down to two a week now I've got the football going. Mind you, they haven't the foggiest idea of how to play, but it's good exercise.'

'Oh, don't worry yourself about it,' he advised with a smile. 'We knew it wasn't going to be easy, and there are quite a few passengers among them, and that's a fact. Quite honestly I shall be surprised if some of them ever go down the mines. Still, that's not my problem . . . What was it you wanted to see me about?'

I explained about the new game they had. Was he willing to help? He most certainly was, but how? I checked to make sure that he was able to withhold the few shillings a week they received as pocket money. He grinned. Oh yes he could do that. All I had to do was to produce the culprits and that would be that, no money, or a reduction, whichever was suitable. With this assurance the rest was simple.

He burst out laughing, when I asked to borrow his date stamp and pad. 'Well,' he said with laugh, 'I'll give you one thing Li, it's novel!'

It was. At mid-point of the run I stamped the back of every man's hand in the squad. On inspection of the re-assembled squad at the end of the run, four had rejoined as we came into camp. They were hauled up immediately and the boss did me proud. Word got round quickly and that was the end of it.

Despite the working problems, due mainly to weather and lack of facilities, both of which were improving as the days passed, life was exceedingly pleasant. With Antoinette, whose letters arrived almost daily, well occupied in college, no house of our own to worry about, and everything at home, according to Dad's letters, in good order, except for Teresa's uncertain health, I really was happier than I had been since leaving the Army. In the Mess, with a lively and happy crew to share the long dark evenings, and a growing number of friends among the students, things were settling down very nicely. Among the foreign domestic staff I found, quite by accident, one of life's real treasures: Wilhemina, a short rotund, near-sixty-year-old Estonian, who cooked the finest steamed pudding I ever tasted! How she came to be at the camp at all at that age, I never found out, for the remainder were comparatively young. But she had managed it, and I was glad of it, even though her mangled English did come one laborious word at a time.

At first she was very nervous when she came into the staff quarters to cook for us, but Mr Milton, with his old-world courtesy and fluent German, soon put her at her ease, for they all had a smattering of this tongue. Within days, with a long slow wink and a smile from me every time I saw her, we soon became friends. She found I liked tea, and made me a cup every time she clapped eyes on me and, whether I wanted it or not, I always drank it. The same with puddings. Always she gave me a little extra. Gradually, as the days passed and her nervousness with them, she would return my wink, shyly at first but with growing boldness. Her round chubby face would beam when I came into the kitchen, then her liquid brown eye would close conspiratorially, making us both laugh. But what tragedy lay behind that laugh!

Only after weeks of patient bridge-building did I get her halting story. She had lost everything when the Germans had invaded. Small crofters, their world had crashed to pieces one bright, sunlit day in just two hours, as the troops moved in and through their tiny village. Her husband was dragged from the nearby field and shot in front of her. Her sixteen year old son, pleading for his father's life, was cut down without mercy to lie across his father's body, and all the while Wilhemina was forced to watch. Then, punched and kicked with the remainder of the survivors, they were herded like cattle for endless miles to be dumped, like so much garbage at a collecting point, for the slave camps. Poor Wilhemina! What a dear lady she was, so eager to please, so eager to be friends. Of them all, I was glad *she* was in England.

But if I was glad for her, my feelings did not embrace all of the remainder. Some were pure spivs, others, well most ex-service men wouldn't trust them as far as they could throw them, and I was no exception. For that kind, always in a small minority, England was a soft touch — as it had always been. There were two in particular who, if they were potential miners, would have made me a potential Papal Nuncio! I'd have laid a hundred to one that the moment they had shaken the dust of the camp off their feet, they would be into the Black Market like a couple of Brambies on a dead Malay! They were two 'Beauts' and they hated my guts because I made them work. I also noticed after a very short time that they seemed to be sporting a fair amount of new gear, shoes, shirts and so on, and wondering why, I asked Nicky. He grinned broadly when I mentioned it and rubbed his finger and thumb together. I probed deeper and was amazed. They had a racket going in bread, and it had to be stamped on quickly. It was all very simple really. The people in the European camps had not seen white bread in any quantity, if at all, for years. There was plenty available in England and, with appetites wetted for it, demand had grown, despite the generous allowance within the camp for bread. These two were on to it like a flash with a bit of Black Market trade, and for some days had a right old time. I tipped the wink to the boss, who immediately assembled the camp and informed everyone of the correct price and availability of bread should they wish to purchase any in the village. The local baker co-operated and refused any exhorbitant orders until he had checked with us, and that was that. I had no idea how the students sorted them out, nor was I fussy, but both looked a little worse for wear by that weekend. However, being the kind of blokes they were, they'd soon find something else, I had no doubt.

With so much to do, so much to learn, the time just flew along. Already a month had gone by with things generally sorting themselves out and, despite our frequent letters, I began to miss Antoinette more and more. The chances of getting home to see her were nil for some time to come, and the chances of her coming to see me were even less. Even if she did, there would be nowhere for us to stay.

It was on the Friday of the bread-busting week, feeling a bit in the dumps and looking forward to a quiet evening by the stove in the Mess, that I refused an invitation from the other instructors to go to the local pub, on the excuse that I had some letters to write, and settled down to read. Within half an hour Mr Milton arrived and sat down beside me.

'All alone tonight, Liam?' he asked in surprise.

I looked up. It was always a pleasure to see Mr Milton. He could talk on a thousand things and never bore you. 'Oh yes. The lads have gone down to the pub, but I've got a good companion here,' I added, holding the book up. He leaned over and looked at the title.

'Ah, old Bertie Wooster, eh? Good old Bertie, always guaranteed to cheer one up. A very droll chap is our Mr Wodehouse. Oh, by the way,' he added, changing the subject, 'I take it you will be going home for the weekend of your wife's half-term?'

'No,' I answered, putting the book down. He looked at me closely.

'Oh!' he said, surprised. 'Am I at liberty to enquire why not?'

'That's easy,' I replied airily, 'I can't afford it, not for a weekend. By the time I got there it would be time to come back.'

He gazed at me thoughtfully. 'Quite,' he said. 'Incidentally,' he continued after a moment's hesitation, 'you don't mind my talking to you on a personal matter do you?'

I laughed. 'Not at all. Fire away.'

'Well,' he continued, still very serious, his pipe forgotten and his glasses perched on the end of his nose, 'you were telling me of your marriage at Christmas, and-er, I-er, naturally thought you might-er, take advantage of the half-term to see your lady wife.'

I shrugged. 'I'd love to, of course I would, but I've got to be practical, haven't I?'

'Quite,' he said again, thoughtfully rubbing his chin. 'Just so. Nevertheless,' he persisted, 'you are just married and-er, well!'

I burst out laughing then shrugged resignedly. 'That's life Mr Milton. Money doesn't grow on trees, does it?'

'No,' he agreed, pursing his lips for moment. 'But . . . Now you're sure you don't mind my speaking?'

I leaned across and touched him gently on the arm. 'Now you know I don't. I told you. Fire away, I don't mind, honest.'

'Well,' he continued after a moment's hesitation, 'I think it is important that you should see each other, for both your sakes.'

I was surprised. A bachelor himself, ninety per cent of his time he was completely lost in a world of his own and the turn of conversation puzzled me. He mistook my silence for disapproval and looked concerned.

'Please, do let me go on Liam, I rather think these things are important you know, and what I would like to do, with your permission of course, is to-er, so to speak, arrange a visit at my expense.' I stared at him in stunned surprise as he rubbed his nose absently. 'Yes, yes,' he muttered to himself, 'absolutely, capital.' The full import of what he proposed struck me and I made to protest. His forefinger went up admonishingly. 'No, no Liam. I will take no objections my boy. Let us say it is a small present, shall we? It has not been easy for you, we are well aware of that, therefore let us say this is my appreciation, shall we?' I felt astounded, delighted, and struggled for words as rowdy voices broke the silence outside. He put his finger to his lips. 'This is our little secret,' he said conspiratorially, as the door burst open and the staff tumbled into the room.

And so the surprise of my life was arranged. In two weeks the half-term break would come and I would see Antoinette! Next day Mr Milton confirmed that he had booked us in for three days at a small hotel on the camp side of Colchester. I truly believed in fairies again!

Creeping into my second month, the first frustrating traumas safely behind me, except for the continuing poor weather, things were beginning to settle down. But the spirit I so desperately sought, to weld my disparate collection of humanity into a cohesive and industrious whole, was not easy to engender. The language barriers between the students and, more importantly, between them and myself, had not proved as difficult as I had thought it might, for most of them could communicate with each other through either German, French, or one of the other European languages. With Nicky's invaluable help, suitable demonstrations and gestures, I too found a lessening difficulty as the days passed. Unfortunately, with their turbulent, and for some, terrifying backgrounds of hardship, deprivation, constant fear of their lives, and the final enervating sojourn in the camps from which they had so recently escaped, the adjustment to our English ways must have been the ultimate confusion for them. But come what may, I had to find and nurture this spirit somehow, and quickly.

I agonised for hours over it. If only the damned weather would pick up a bit, I could get them outside more often . . . But wait a minute! Perhaps the very difference between them could be turned to good use?

189

The different nationalities certainly stuck together like glue, although they all seemed to get on well enough. I felt suddenly excited. Yes, why the hell not I could set them against each other in organised competitions on national grounds. I knew scores of games large and small, suitable for indoors or out, apart from the football already in full swing. Volleyball, scramble tennis, quoit tennis, heading voll . . . Oh hell, no end of them, and then, when the season came round, cricket! by the cringe, that would fox them and no mistake. Then there were small side games if I could wangle enough derelict huts; dodge ball, ground handball, padder tennis, ring the stick, shinty, oh yes, that was a good one, they'd like that alright. But what about equipment? Ah, no problem. I'd do the same as we did in the Army when we were stuck: make the damned stuff as we went along. There was plenty of junk about. Suddenly my frustration fell away from me, my mind teemed with plans, providing the flaming weather picked up. That's all I asked for, dry weather.

Within days I had wangled the use of a couple of extra huts, prowled the grounds in the pouring rain to earmark suitable sites for rigging the volleyball courts I had planned, the shortened football pitch I hoped to get marked out, and another to dig a long-jump pit for those athletically inclined. All I needed was for the heavenly taps to be eased off and to arrange with the boss for smaller squads for official periods, except for the now weekly runs. The individual skills for the keener ones I could take in the evenings in the huts, until daylight lengthened for outdoor work. Come what may, I would somehow have that spirit. Once there, it would feed itself. I was so fired up I even forgot to write to Antoinette for two nights in a row, but she wouldn't mind. In less than a week I would see her, and I knew from her replies to my letters telling her of the arrangements, that she was as excited as I. But that was a week away. In the meantime I had to put my plans into a structured programme.

14

Madame Gymnastica

Time is an amazing phenomenon. One waits in a fever
of suppressed excitement, like a child awaiting Christmas, apparently such a long way away. It arrives, and
whoosh! It is gone. Our long weekend was no exception. For an hour I had haunted the station before the
anticipated time of her arrival, and tortured myself
with a hundred questions. Had she caught the train?
Would she catch the right connection? Would she . . .?

Suddenly she was there, and it was good to hold her
in my arms once again. Tired but happy she told me
how things were at home. Teresa, my main worry,
could be better but was as cheerful as ever. Mam and
Dad were fine but, as expected, Dad was already fed up
being retired after just two weeks, and Con, of all the
screaming twits, had finally gone on strike over who
should bore the holes in the long-running dispute,
while Bernadette was her usual capable self.

With my mind settled about home, the pathetically
short time just vanished in a blur of introductions,
descriptions of what we were doing, and a long
detailed discussion with our benefactor Mr Milton,
who, in the event, doted on Antoinette. For the rest, we
walked and talked the hours away as we wandered the
ancient streets, or sat in some quiet spot, planning,
planning. Suddenly the dream time stopped. She was
gone and I was thrust back into reality.

Renewed and refreshed, I flung myself into my
schemes and spent hours, with the help of volunteers,

making and rigging equipment, scrounging for odds and ends of anything that could be pressed into service to provide recreation, and it worked. Cock-eyed some of it may have been, but it provided an outlet for surplus energies.

Football they loved, although the precise rules remained sketchy to them to the end. The number of volleyball courts rapidly increased from two to four, and all were in constant demand with games fiercely contested. The small team games, earmarked for indoors in bad weather, provided hours of fun, especially the scramble tennis, played with the simple equipment of an old tennis net, scrounged from the village tennis club, and bundles of paper tied with string. There was only one rule in the game, which insisted that every bundle had to be grounded on the opponent's side to win. Very few games were won outright, but the energy consumed in trying was enormous.

My objects were simple, to keep as many men occupied and exercised as possible but, as with all groups of men, reactions to the scheme were mixed. The natural dead-legs and layabouts used every dodge in the book to avoid work, but I was not particularly bothered. The bulk enjoyed themselves voluntarily, and the dead-legs I could well and truly nail during official periods, on the Army principle that if they were breathing, they were fit for work.

Now was the time to put their national rivalries to good effect. On a voluntary basis, teams were formed for all the main games, and knock-out competitions organised with some hilarious results as teaching staff, unused to this kind of work, enthusiastically joined in to help out with refereeing or judging. Football skills became the rage with the younger ones, but their tackling, when excitement carried them away, left a lot to be desired. The greatest favourite was volleyball. They would practise for hours, if allowed. It was as a result of this that a potentially dangerous situation suddenly blew up.

With half an hour's free time after a training session, and with games in progress on all the volleyball courts, I was making my way to the Mess where I knew Wilhemina would have a cup of tea for me. Nicky, pale and excited, raced up and grabbed my shoulder.

'What the hell's up with you?' I gasped in astonishment.

'You come. Quick, quick! They fight!'

Oh Jesus! I thought as we turned and ran back. What happened when we turned the corner of the hut to where the volleyball court was, was not so much action as reaction. The only thing that was clear as we dashed into a tense, silent crowd, was a tall, fair-haired lad, backed up in terror against the net. A couple of feet or so away, crouching, legs well apart, and bent forward with one hand half raised, the other wielding a jack knife, was a powerfully built figure, a manic expression on his broad Slavic features. I knew this was no time for finesse. This needed action, and without stopping I took it. Crossing the court, I caught him straight in the groin with my foot. A startled expression clouded his face as the knife dropped and he clutched himself in agony. A split second later a dozen hands grabbed me. Pandemonium broke out as I was swept into the air and carried shoulder high amid babbling voices. It was an amazing reaction on their part. Even as they put me down, the whole kaleidscopic incident seemed unreal. The very act of a knife being used in a fight in England was itself rare, but that was not the real problem. With the culprit now being held in the office, awaiting the boss, the question was, how many more had knives? This was solved the following morning.

With everyone assembled, a tight-lipped and angry boss castigated them through the interpreters. This was England, he rammed home. No weapons of any description would be tolerated here and, more important to them, if anyone was found in possession of one, let alone using it, the police would be called in to deal with the matter. They knew what that meant. Normally debonair and a gentleman to his boots, I had never seen Mr Williams so angry. As for Mr Milton — he tutted sadly for a week following the incident. However, unsavoury as the episode had been, it had done a lot of good. At last they now knew exactly where they stood and, if I had inhibited the knifeman's marriage prospects, well, that was just too bad.

By the end of that month things were running smoothly. The scheme was going well and the weather no problem. The compulsory runs, so unpopular, but so necessary at first, and already reduced to one a week, became walks, although still in columns, as we toured the surrounding countryside. Only on the last half mile or so did I insist that they marched in good order, and for this I used the age-old standby of soldiers the world over — singing. This they enjoyed immensely, with the Ukranians revealing their qualities both of singing and the knowledge of some rollicking marching tunes. These walks, taken in the gradually warming sunshine, I look back on with infinite pleasure, for I knew that to sing with such spontaneity they must have been happy. At last I had found the spirit I had worked so long to instil.

At the end of the normal football season, with the country turning its mind to cricket, our season was still in full swing with our own international programme. Day after day, with official work over, we were on the field practising skills, or racing up and down the field with either me or a staff volunteer doing our damnedest to see that most of the rules were observed. Excited spectators, carried away with enthusiasm for their teams, caused chaos as they ran on to the field at every opportunity. I stopped this by arranging that three consecutive blasts on the whistle would stop the game stone dead until things quietened down, so they kept their enthusiasms to the sidelines.

We were discussing this enthusiasm in the Mess one evening when, for no apparent reason, the conversation turned to rugby, a game I had never played and about which I knew nothing.

'I'm surprised, Liam,' said Vin Ford, in his way-back voice, from the depths of his armchair, 'that you don't teach the blighters a proper game, a real man's game.'

'Oh, and what's that then?' I asked, looking across at the heavily built, elegantly clad personal friend of Mr Milton's who, like Johnny, was waiting to go to university.

'What else?' broke in Johnny Benson. 'Rugby, of course. Rugby, dear boy.'

I laughed. 'Rugby! You must be joking. It takes me all my time to keep them separated at football . . . What d'yeh want, casualties?'

'Nonsense,' broke in Vin disparagingly, 'utter rubbish! They'll love it. What d'you think Mr Milton?'

Reading quietly on the fringe of the circle round the empty stove, Mr Milton looked up absently. 'Oh absolutely dear boy, absolutely . . . What was that now?' We smiled as he gazed at us enquiringly.

'Rugby,' repeated Vincent. 'I was just telling Liam here that I think he should . . .'

Mr Milton nodded. 'I quite agree, Vincent. Very sensible, I assure you. Oh yes.'

'There you are!' cried Johnny triumphantly. 'He's all for it, too.'

'Look Li,' interrupted Vincent, 'I'll tell you what. I'm going home this weekend, so I'll bring a ball back, then you can give it a try. I'm sure it'll be a success.'

I blew through my lips then tried to dissuade him. 'I don't know Vin. They're a rough crowd and, anyway, I don't know the rules.'

Johnny brushed this aside airily. 'Oh that's nothing Li, Vin and I can sort that out. Anyway,' he added, 'so long as they get it over the line, what the hell?'

I didn't like the idea one little bit. They didn't know

them like I did. I turned to the boss for his opinion. He smiled broadly and replied that I was the P.T. Walla, so it was up to me. I reluctantly agreed.

With a ball that wouldn't bounce straight, and a couple of scratch teams of fifteen East Europeans bent on mayhem, it was the worst agreement I ever made, as I found out the following Monday. Vincent, with three interpreters trying to convey his words, outlined the simple objective of getting the ball over one or other of the goal lines. With even greater ambition, he demonstrated a scrum and what it was for, to the half-dozen nationalities involved. With the boss grinning like a Cheshire cat beside me, we watched him physically place everyone in position. The whistle blew. Seconds later there was a writhing mass of bodies as every player piled in. He blew the three consecutive blasts as I had advised him in the event of trouble. The game stopped and I walked across to give him a hand. Without knowing I was there he blew for a restart. The ball came in my direction and without thinking I caught the damned thing, then thought the world had come to an end as an avalanche of foreign bodies swamped me, pulling, pushing and swearing in a variety of languages, while the whistle blew and Vin shouted his head off.

'Come on chaps!' he roared above me. 'Play the bally game, now. Come along there!' Impossibly jammed beneath the mass I heard the three sharp blasts, and the pressure gradually eased as the bodies slid off, one by one. 'I say Li,' he said in astonishment as I came to light, 'how the devil did you get there? I thought . . .?'

'You and your flamin' rugby!' I snorted as I looked over at the boss doubled up with laughter on the side line.

Vin shrugged despondently. 'I quite see your point old boy,' he admitted. 'They're not quite ready yet, are they?'

However, it was not the last time we used the ball.

With suitable adjustments to pitch size, and with our own rules, we had some hilarious six-a-side internationals, though they never got used to the shape of the ball.

As April slipped into May the whole camp had taken on a different aspect to its previous spartan conditions and, with a long dry spell setting in, all sorts of small games came into their own for those who wished to occupy their spare time, with yet another activity that had been impossible before — gardening. In this the villagers were a great help. With a camp in their midst throughout the war, they were well used to soldiers, but these weren't soldiers. They were civilians, but most important they were foreigners and, of course, villagers being what they are, their reception was neither joyous nor immediate. However, with the staff using the local pub occasionally, to pass away the dark winter evenings, we made contacts which grew, tenuously at first, and were particularly pleased when two of the students also broke the ice.

Politely tolerated, but never fully accepted, the contacts we made were valuable, for through them I was able to scrounge all sorts of odds and ends that were put to good use for equipment, and it was a couple of old spades which unexpectedly came in that gave me the idea of gardening a piece of ground at the back of the camp. I put it to the students whether they would fancy a bit of ground to themselves to plant if they wished. Quite a few did and so, with more tools acquired by the boss, another very satisfying activity was added, giving the camp a more homely feeling as the gardens took shape. Even I, for the first time in my life, had one just outside the Mess. I remember how chuffed I was when I saw something I had planted actually grow! Just a couple of rows of potatoes, it's true, but I guarded them like a mother hen with her chicks.

It was a new type of life and I began to love it. Yet, as

May slipped quietly into June there was a sadness behind the pleasure, for I knew that by the end of August at the latest, it would all be over. I consoled myself with the present. Tomorrow would look after itself.

It was as a result of the growing village contacts that cricket came on to the agenda, and it was as I was working on one of the two bats and a set of wickets which the boss had acquired from somewhere for staff use, that the second and last major crisis dropped on me. It was a beautiful afternoon as I sat in the sunshine outside the Mess with an hour's free time, cutting and shaping a copy of one of the bats as a pattern for Nicky to pass to the students to copy, if they got the cricket bug. I was just finishing the shoulders and handle of the bat and admiring my work when Harry Lewis, ex-service like myself and waiting to go to teacher training in September, dashed through the gate and skidded to a stop in front of me. He looked pale and worried.

'Hey Li,' he gasped, 'you'd better come!'

I looked up enquiringly. 'What's up? Not another fight is it?'

He shook his head. 'No, a nutter! He's locked himself in the projection room.'

'A nutter? What d'yeh mean, a nutter?'

'What I say,' he replied with growing urgency. 'Bloke gone round the bend, mate, smashing everything in there, he is. Come on, hurry up Li.' Hell, that's just what I needed, a flamin' nutter! But, since I was the P.T. Walla, I didn't have much option. Blast it! Just when things were going nicely!

We dashed into the camp and joined the crowd of students and teachers around the Nissen hut used as a projection room. From the sound of crashing furniture from inside, whoever it was, was having one helluva time. I stood on tiptoes and peered through the small, half-opened window on the front of the hut. It was chaotic, as though a cyclone had hit it, and at the far end, tousle-haired, face strained with effort, was one of the previously quietest students in the camp, but who was now glaring frenziedly about him.

'Bloody 'ell!' I said as I got down, 'you're right mate. He is round the twist!'

'I told you that!' Harry snapped. 'But what are yeh gonna do about it?'

I looked at him, nonplussed. 'I'm not a flippin' trick cyclist! What the hell can I do? You want one'f those fellers in a white coat.'

Harry agreed but insisted. 'But you're the P.T. bloke, Li. You'll have to get him out. He's wrecking the joint.'

I had no option. 'Right, send Nicky for the boss, I'll see what can be done.'

With just a small window about head height either side of the door, it wasn't going to be easy. If I smashed the door, then a lot of valuable equipment couldn't be secured any more. I decided to try the window, although if he caught me half-way through, God knows what would happen! I decided on a bit of strategy just as Johnny arrived.

'Look Harry, you nip round the other end with a few blokes and distract him, will yeh?'

'But what shall I do?' he asked.

I gazed at him irritably. 'You can whistle Annie Laurie if you want!' I snapped. 'Just keep him busy.'

'Won't that make him mad?' he asked innocently.

I glowered back. 'He's already flamin' mad, isn't he?' Harry shot round the back.

'And what are you going to do?' asked Johnny interestedly.

I explained that I was going through the window to try to get the door open before he spotted me, then they could all grab him.

He smiled, 'And jolly good luck to you dear boy,' he said sympathetically.

With the boss now present, I explained what I

wanted. He reminded me the window was small and I might get caught half-way. I called Nicky over and told him to get a couple of big blokes to hold me horizontally and put me through the window backwards.

'Feet first?' queried the boss. I told him that if the boys at the other end couldn't hold his attention and he came after me half-way through, I would feel easier if he knocked hell out of my feet rather than my head. 'Makes sense,' he said worriedly, 'but be careful. I've sent for the doctor.'

With two holding the window as high as it would go, and the other two holding me horizontally, I was ready, but reluctant, to go. 'Don't forget,' I reminded Nicky, 'get me through quickly!' He nodded and the hairs on the back of my neck rose as the uproar behind me increased. 'Now!' I snapped. From the length of time it seemed to take, I must have grown to about twelve foot long. Thank God I could still hear him walloping the door at the other end. Suddenly my shirt front caught on the short piece of metal used for fastening the window, as my feet scrabbled for a hold. There was a tremendous crash behind me, I tried to turn and the movement ripped my shirt free, dropping me unexpectedly to the ground. I bounced up by reflex action and hurled myself at the door to turn the key as the madman crashed his way towards me over the debris. We collided as the door opened and the impetus pitched us both through it. It was all over in seconds, but it took four men to hold him down until the ambulance arrived a few minutes later. No one ever quite knew what had gone wrong with him but, according to his friends, he had had one helluva time during the war and, although I had always found him quiet and pleasant, he had, it turned out, been on the blink for sometime, until something, God alone knows what, had finally snapped. God help him!

With our poor friend hopefully in safe and caring hands, things settled down into their now steady rhythm. Evening cricket became the rage with the staff, whilst students watched and muttered about this strange English ritual. To us it was a gentle relaxation. To them, when they practised what they saw with the home-made bats that had sprouted among them from my original pattern, it became lethal. They used as balls anything small enough to be thrown and hit. Even Ledy, the boss's secretary, tried her hand with the staff team, but the general opinion was that she was built for more exotic pastimes.

Among the student spectators there was often a curious and amused villager or two, and one of these Johnny jokingly challenged to a match against the village. To our surprise it was accepted and, for me, was to have far-reaching consequences. Two weeks later, after assiduous practice, our team, including all staff except Mr Milton, plus one or two of the keener students to make up the numbers, assembled on the local ground. It was disaster! We batted first and made just ten runs between us, with Johnny the highest at a glorious five. The game was watched with unholy glee by the howling villagers on one side and completely mystified Europeans on the others. However, if the result was a foregone conclusion, the dividends in goodwill were immense. For me it was a night I would remember for a long, long time, for I made a friend of a man laughing delightedly beside me. In the course of conversation, after I had been clean bowled for a duck he told me that his son, of the same age as myself, had emigrated to Australia.

During our return to camp in high good humour Mr Milton, in a quiet moment, asked me whether Antoinette would be coming again for a visit during her long summer holidays from college. It was not until a few hours later, thinking about the match and the fun we had had, that the two items of conversation connected to form an idea, an idea that grew in exciting prospects the more I thought about it. After all, with his son gone, he must have a spare room. If I could work it, I might see Antoinette not just for a weekend but for weeks! I was a long time getting to sleep that night.

With the village so small I had a fair idea where I might find my friend the following evening and, with just three pubs in the place my search did not take long. Sure enough, there he was sipping a quiet pint in the Horsehoe, not a stone's throw away from the camp gates. His eyes lit up as I walked towards the counter.

I stopped in feigned surprise. 'Well,' I said, 'fancy meeting you here!'

He laughed and pointed to a seat opposite him, inviting me to have a drink. I refused, saying I'd just popped in for some cigarettes, but offered him one instead. He insisted I had a chat when I returned with it. Up North I would have broached the subject uppermost in my mind within minutes, but South it was not quite so easy, especially with new acquaintances in small villages. The average villager, I had found, does not like to be rushed, and above all he does not like strangers on his floor. I had to tread warily. Though I disliked drink, I eventually accepted his offer of a pint, reduced on my request to a half, then with a few sips of the bitter liquid inside me, I put my question in conversational form.

'Where's your son gone, then?' I asked when we finally got on to the desired subject.

'Melbourne. Met some people while he was servin'.'

I suggested that he must miss him badly. Well yes and no. He'd been away a long time in the war, so it wasn't too bad. His mother missed him very much, though. I sympathised and pointed out that most mothers missed their children very much, adding that at least he had the rest of the family for comfort. I got the answer I needed. He was their only son, and no, he wasn't married . . . Was I married, he queried.

'Oh yes. Married on Boxing Day last.'

He looked at me in surprise. 'And you're separated from your wife . . . Already?'

I grimaced and shrugged my shoulders despondently. He was definitely on the right lines. 'No wish of mine, I can tell you.' He raised his eyebrows questioningly. 'The fact is,' I continued, 'she's at college at the moment, and will be for another year.'

'Well,' he said, finishing his second pint off with a flourish, 'fancy that . . . Not much of a marriage for you, though, is it?'

I agreed and picked up his glass. He protested. I wouldn't hear of it. 'No that's alright. I'll get them in . . . Same again?' He nodded. I turned at the bar with the drinks and my heart sank as someone plonked himself in my seat and started talking to him. I needn't have worried. The stranger left as I returned.

Mr Green, my new friend, flicked his head at the departing figure. 'Works with me on the farm,' he explained. His next words cheered me up no end. 'Why don't you bring her down to see the place?' he queried. 'Do you both good,' he suggested chattily.

'And where would she stay!' I asked, anxiously watching his face as he thoughtfully sipped his beer. 'We can't stay in the camp, that's a fact.'

It seemed an age before he put his beer down and answered. 'Look,' he said, with an uncertain glance at me, 'I'll 'ave a word with the missus if you like?' Hairy as he was, I could have leaned over and kissed him.

'What?' I asked innocently. 'You mean stay at your place?'

Another long pause as he weighed his words. 'Well, yes . . . I'll have to have a word with the wife first, of course. Look, I'll tell you what. You come round to our's tomorrow night, then we'll see, eh? Y'know where we live?' He laughed, 'Course y'don't! Anyway it's 'Hillside', thatched place, down near the church. Y'can't miss it. About seven, alright?' I was delighted!

His wife, in her latish fifties like himself, proved to

203

be a short, buxom, and spotlessly clean woman who treated me with the distant, inbred caution of country folk. Within half an hour, however, helped by a glass of potent, home-made wine and a cup of tea, she had relaxed, and within an hour the deal was done. All I had to do was to let her know when Antoinette would come, and for how long. I floated back to camp!

A frantic week of letters between us solved both problems. I would have her all to myself, in board and lodgings, for four whole weeks! At that moment I wouldn't have called the King my uncle. Mr Milton, too, having what you might call a proprietary interest, was as pleased as Punch, for he also, ever since our weekend, had received a note from her enclosed with her letters to me. Then, almost at the end of June, and with growing excitement over her arrival the following month, he casually discussed another subject which was going to have an even greater impact on our lives.

Actually I was not even taking part in the heated discussion going on in the Mess on a miserable, drizzly evening which had put paid to our cricket, but sitting comfortably alongside Mr Milton, engulfed in pipe smoke. Because Antoinette was at college and they were arguing about education, I listened interestedly as battle lines were clearly and predictably drawn. Johnny and Vincent, both privately educated and awaiting university, were for private schools. Harry Lewis, ex-service and working class, ever a blithe spirit and also awaiting teacher training, thought the whole argument codswallop, as he said, but Barney Matthews, in exactly the same circumstances as Harry, was laying the law down, the 'other end' of our Con . . . Rampant.

Mr Milton, alongside me, puffed in silent fury, driven occasionally to retort with a reasoned comment to some of the more outlandish of Barney's statements, as the boss grinned benignly on the far side of the circle . . . 'Balderdash' . . . 'Rubbish my dear boy', or 'Hear,

hear' on the odd occasions when Vince or Johnny managed to get a word in.

Fresh from my recent battles with Con and his mates, it all made me feel quite at home and even less inclined to join in. A couple of times, frustrated by the opposition arrayed before him, and knowing my background, Barney turned to me for help. With no axe to grind, I merely smiled and shook my head. I would get more than enough of that when this job finished and I returned home, the real stuff too, not academics! Only once did Mr Milton, stung by one of Barney's remarks about private education, feel impelled to clarify a point.

'I have a friend,' he declared quietly, 'who runs such an establishment, dear boy, and has done for many years and, may I say, with jolly good results, too.'

'They should abolish the lot!' stated Barney vehemently. 'With respect,' broke in Mr Milton again, 'that is utter rubbish, absolut . . .'

'Hear-hear,' chorused Johnny and Vince in unison. 'Jolly well said sir,' added Vince with an approving nod.

'And furthermore, Mr Matthews,' added Mr Milton with genteel irritation, 'I would venture, with all respect of course, to say that your experience is totally inadequate for such a definitive judgement. In my opinion, there is a need for both forms of education. One does not condemn, merely because something which one disagrees with is there . . . That is complete balderdash!'

Barney was rapidly getting hot under the collar. I winked at Johnny opposite to me and made a sign of drinking, as Barney leaned forward to speak again.

He got the message and stopped Barney stone dead. 'O.K. Barney my son,' he said jocularly, 'if you want to waste the whole bally evening arguing the toss, we don't . . . Let's go for a pint.' Minutes later the room emptied.

I turned to a slightly agitated Mr Milton as the door closed. 'Some argument, eh?' I said with a smile, as he re-lit his pipe.

'Hmn!' he grunted. 'I don't know what some of these young men are coming to, really I don't.'

'Oh, take no notice of Barney. He'll learn, don't worry. He's young yet.'

'Hmn, possibly, possibly.' He looked at me keenly as he pressed new tobacco into his pipe. 'I noticed you offered no opinions, Liam?'

I grinned. 'No thank you very much. I hear enough politics when I'm home, believe me.'

'And Antoinette? What are her views on these matters?'

'Same as mine. All we want is some peace and quiet. That's why I like it here. Who wants trouble unless it's forced on them?'

He mused for a moment. 'Yes, I must say, you seem well settled. Do you enjoy teaching, Liam?'

'Love it!' I replied emphatically, 'I just wish I had Barney's chance to go to college, that's all.'

The subject veered slightly as we talked for a few moments about teaching in the camp, and the spirit that had developed since the first difficulties I had experienced on my particular job, and he admitted that he and the boss had been well aware of them. They were particularly pleased with the relations with the villagers. That, I found out, had been a worry for them because the students had been an unknown quantity. I was flattered by his kind words in relation to my work with them. He thought the cricket match had helped a lot in opening up friendships, and for a while we enjoyed in retrospect the fun we had had that evening. As he said, winning wasn't important, but meeting the people was.

Suddenly he changed the subject again. 'Would you like to teach as a career?' he asked.

I laughed. 'Chance would be a fine thing!' I replied cryptically. 'Even half a chance would do.'

He cocked his head to one side, giving me a quizzical look. 'Oh you never know, my boy, you never know!' He turned to Antoinette's coming visit and how he was looking forward to it.

'That was through the cricket match,' I said, explaining how it had all come about.

He smiled delightedly. 'There you are! What did I say? It did help relations, didn't it?'

I assured him that as far as I was concerned it had, and that she would be down in the middle of July. 'Oh yes,' I added, as a thought struck me, 'have you any idea when the scheme actually finishes?' 'Thirty-first of August,' he replied without hesitation. 'Why?'

'Oh, just wondering,' I said disappointedly, hoping against hope that it might have been extended a bit. 'It's a pity. Still,' I added resignedly, 'I can always go back to the shipyard, I suppose!' He gazed at me long and thoughtfully, then shrugged.

Another visit to my friends the Greens settled the details of Antoinette's visit. She would come down for the last two weeks of July and the first two of August. Great! I wasn't sure who was the more delighted, Mr Milton or myself. For me, during the remaining time, until her arrival, the job took on a whole new aspect. The period was one of great enjoyment, the only sadness being that I knew in my heart, that whatever job I finished up in, it would not, could not give me the same satisfaction as teaching. This was what I wanted to do!

Keeping busy all day, and most evenings spent arranging both normal lessons for five or six hundred men, plus a variety of off-duty games and skills practices, the time of Antoinette's arrival came a lot quicker than I could have imagined. The day before her arrival, strangely nervous and excited, I moved out of the camp amid good-natured leg pulling, and into our new lodgings. By the following afternoon, with George our landlord still at work, we had settled into the tiny but very comfortable room to begin our first spell of married life. The two women, one buxom and motherly, the other young, slim and normally reserved, had given me some cause for concern as to whether they would get on. My fears were groundless. Even George, on his return from work, could not have been more friendly. It was only the next morning, as I paraded a large column for the weekly walk, that possible trouble dawned. It was Nicky who drew my attention to it, as the squad stood waiting to move off. He nudged my arm as I settled the ranks furthest away from the village. I turned as he pointed to the other end. Every head was turned towards an approaching figure. It was Antoinette!

The order to be quiet froze on my lips, as jealous anger consumed me like flame. Dressed in a light summer dress she looked an absolute picture, and I knew, with growing anger, just what they were thinking. I roared for attention. Nicky looked at me, startled and puzzled, as I waved Antoinette over to me. I had been in the Army too long not to know the thoughts in their minds, and was determined to stamp on any nonsense now. They watched with curiosity as she joined me, flushing scarlet. I felt sorry for her as I took her hand, but it had to be.

'This,' I said to Nicky, 'is my wife.' His large brown eyes opened in surprise as I turned to the students gazing at her lecherously then, followed by Nicky, I walked her to different points of the long column to tell them who she was. Just to make sure, Nicky repeated it in whatever language he thought necessary, with instructions to pass it on to students not present. 'And tell them this,' I added, glowering, 'if anybody, anybody, even looks sideways at her, I'll slit his flamin' throat! Do you understand?' I asked, drawing my finger across my throat.

Nicky grinned broadly and repeated the instruction as I walked with him down the column, then returned to Antoinette. A short, chubby, and always cheerful little Estonian left the ranks as we rejoined her, then, with a broad smile stood in front of her and bowed.

'Good morning Madame Gymnastica,' he said with dead-pan seriousness. The column dissolved into laughter as the others bowed too. And so named, she remained all the time she was with me. She was safe, and I was peaceful in my mind.

So the weeks passed, busy, happy and for us idyllic. I even had a few flowers in my impromptu garden. Nor was I the only one happy; Mr Milton was equally delighted, and treated her like a father, always thoughtful, never intruding, and patently concerned for our future.

It was on the final weekend before she returned home that the staff had arranged to go to a cricket match. Antoinette, never having seen a village cricket match before, was looking forward to it. As we gathered in the Mess prior to going, Mr Milton popped his head round the door. Could he have a word with me? I suggested Antoinette go on ahead, but he wanted to see her as well, if she didn't mind. With the boys gone, the three of us settled down and he reminded me of the conversation we had had after his argument with Barney. Antoinette laughed as I explained what it was all about.

'Oh you should hear them at college,' she said to Mr Milton. 'I just keep out of it.'

He smiled. 'So does your husband,' he replied. 'However,' he continued in a business-like tone, 'you will also remember, Liam, that I mentioned my friend who has a boarding school.'

I nodded as he put a match to his pipe. Amid a growing cloud of smoke he wanted to know, now that Antoinette was with me, did I really mean what I said about wanting to teach? Would I, should the chance come to me, take it up? He seemed anxious for my answer. I repeated what I had said previously, that half a chance would be enough. He wanted Antoinette's view on it.

'It would be too wonderful to think about,' she told him.

He seemed delighted, then dropped a bombshell. 'Well,' he said, eyes twinkling as he polished his pipe on his cheek, 'it may not be quite as impossible as you think, my dear.'

In growing excitement we gazed at the cherubic face, as he carefully inspected his pipe. 'What d'you mean?' I exclaimed.

He became cautious. 'Well, at the moment there is a possibility . . .' he waved his pipe warningly, 'a possibility, no more mind you, that the School Sergeant . . .' I had never heard the term before. He explained that in private schools this was a title by which the P.E. instructor was often known. 'Anyway,' he continued, 'the present incumbent is, we believe, likely to leave very shortly for domestic reasons and . . .'

'How d'you know?' I queried in astonishment.

He smiled. 'Well I don't know his reasons, of course, the whole thing just came up during a telephone conversation with John last night . . . You remember? I mentioned he ran the school. However, that is not important. What is important is if he leaves, and John will know by this evening, are you prepared to step in?'

Antoinette and I looked at each other, thunderstruck delight spreading over our faces.

'Oh love!' she gasped.

'Well, would you?' he insisted.

'Would I?' I exclaimed. 'Just you say the word!'

He beamed as he eased himself out of the chair. 'That's all I wanted to know. Now you wait here,' he added, 'I'm just going to the phone.'

In the brief time he was away we made a million plans. I felt so excited I could have danced about. Within ten minutes he was back, beaming like a schoolboy. We knew it had, unbelievably, come off.

'Well,' he said, determined to suppress his delight, 'the Sergeant is leaving at the end of term, as a matter of . . .' We didn't hear the remainder of his words, for we were on our feet hugging each other excitedly. 'Well,' he broke in, watching us benignly, 'at least I know you're both happy!'

Happy! What a paltry word for what we felt. We were so overjoyed, I had forgotten all about getting time off for an interview. I put the question to him.

He laughed. 'Oh there's no need for that, my boy. John and I were at college together. My recommendation is enough. Anyway,' he added after a little thought, 'if it will make you feel easier, we can settle the introductions now. If you will excuse us, my dear?' Antoinette nodded and I followed him out of the room.

Minutes later over the phone in the boss's office, I was talking to my new boss. I mentioned an interview. He brushed it aside and said he looked forward to seeing me in the first week of September. Everything would be confirmed in writing within the week. Thanking him, I handed the phone back to Mr Milton and, without waiting for him, dashed back to a rapturous Antoinette.

'Come on,' I said, as he walked in, in high good humour, 'never mind the cricket, let's go to the pub and seal it with a drink. And,' I added, 'the drinks are on us!' Once again Mam's philosophy had proved right. It wasn't what you knew in this world that counted, but who you knew!

It was a happy evening as Mr Milton, sipping daintily at his drink, filled in some details. The school, in a large old house, was called St Benedict's Preparatory School for Boys, and stood in its own grounds not far from the sea at Hastings. To us, coming from a noisy, heavily industrialised area, it sounded idyllic, but, despite my happiness, one thought niggled relentlessly at the back of my mind. If, as I would have to, I went straight to the school after the camp closed, it would mean that I couldn't get home until at least Christmas and, for all Antoinette's reassurance that everything was alright there, I *was* worried about Teresa. I mentioned this to Mr Milton.

'Oh don't worry now,' he assured me. 'Just leave it with me, I'm sure I can arrange something suitable. I quite understand . . . Look, I'll have a quiet word with Mr Williams, then, when you finish classes tomorrow morning, pop into the office on your way to the Mess. Will that be alright?'

With Mr Milton escorted back to camp, puffing contentedly on his pipe, we went for a long, talkative walk, and were still discussing our amazing turn of luck as we crawled into bed. Within minutes Antoinette was fast asleep, but my mind, filled with a thousand Utopian possibilities, spurned sleep completely. Nothing, but nothing had ever come to me so easily in my life. There just had to be a snag somewhere! Surely fate wasn't going to give up that easy?

15

Home Leave

With the job safe and my mind only half on the activities I was conducting, it was an anxious Monday morning as I awaited the coming interview with the boss at lunchtime. It was short and devastating when it came. How they managed to jiggle it, I never found out but I was to be released, not for a few days to allow me a quick visit home, but on the coming Friday! We could travel home together and be together until Antoinette returned to college. Not in my wildest dreams had I expected so much, and could scarcely find words to express my thanks.

All the worries of the past few weeks of what might or might not have happened when the camp closed down, all the silent envy I had felt for the remainder of the staff whose futures were so clear cut, was swept away. Oh how I had envied the good fortune of Johnny and Vince as they joked light-heartedly about university, and Harry and Barney their embryo teaching careers; the boss himself, seconded from other work for this temporarary scheme, who would return to his well-ordered and well-heeled lifestyle, having enjoyed this new experience, and dear Mr Milton, who had made all this possible, who would return to the genteel solace of his books in pleasant retirement, to while away his time in academic pursuits of his own choosing. Oh yes, I had envied them all, but now, against all the odds, I was to join them . . . It couldn't be true! But it was, and I had to tell Antoinette immediately.

They were drinking tea at the laden table as I appeared, like a grinning genie, through the back door of the cottage. Antoinette, cup half-way to her lips, eyes wide open, gazed at me in astonishment.

'I'm coming home with you!' I announced gleefully.

'No!' she exclaimed in delight. 'How . . .?'

'Been released two weeks early,' I interrupted.

'But . . .?' I smothered her enquiry with a kiss, then winked at a startled Mrs Green. 'I'll explain it all later,' I added, straightening up and heading for the door. 'I've got to get back.' They were still staring at me, dumbfounded, as I reached the door and stuck my thumb up. 'Great isn't it? Cheerio then, see you later.' Their startled expressions remained, as I dashed out.

It was the beginning of a very, very happy week. With the future seeming to be settled beyond all expectations in the direction I wished to go, I could not, and would not dare to ask for more and yet, in a reversal of emotions, I found to my surprise that I did not want the week to end. I would miss the camp and especially the camaraderie of the Mess. I would miss the job, hard and frustrating though it had been at times, but I would miss, above all, the peace and quiet of Todmarsh itself, not to mention our good and homely landlords in their Dickensian cottage, with its bucket toilet, oil lamps, and the steeply-sloping thatched roof that made one cautious of leaping out of bed in the mornings.

There was one more surprise awaiting us before our final departure when, with cases packed on the Friday evening, and all our goodbyes made to the camp earlier, we paid a final visit to Mr Milton's quarters for a quiet chat. He suggested that we would be more comfortable in the Mess. To our surprise the smallish room was full when we arrived, not only with staff but also three or four students who had been so helpful with early interpreting. In a corner, busy laying sandwiches and a few drinks on a trestle table, was a beaming Wilhemina. She spotted us at once, and came across to greet me with a bear hug.

'Aah, Meester Suleevan,' she said with a frown, 'you go ah? You no come back, no?' I gave her a hug in return.

Johnny Benson, blithe spirit that he was, joined us with a wink at Antoinette. 'Jolly good job you're here my girl,' he said gravely, nodding towards Whilhemina. 'Those two would have been off, y'know . . . Oh yes. First full moon and whoosh, they'd have gone. Had my suspicions for some time now. Hey,' he added, with a nudge, 'Nicky wants to say cheerio.'

I untangled myself from Wilhemina and looked at the tall, sallow, and ever-solemn Nicky, who had proved such a good friend. He was holding a folded piece of paper.

'Hi yeh Nick?' I said in my usual daily greeting. He looked embarrassed, and held the paper out, as the boss and Mr Milton looked on. I unfolded it and burst out laughing as I passed it on to Mr Williams. It was a drawing by some talented joker among them, showing a column of men in chains, with me walking alongside with a whip and Nicky in close attendance. I looked at Nicky as the staff dissolved with laughter as it was passed around, and his normally grave face broke into a slow and very broad grin.

'God,' I said, 'surely it wasn't as bad as that?'

He shook his head. 'They not like very much . . . Cold, werry 'ard, but, you go too, so alright I think.' Still I thought, I hadn't fancied the early runs either, but it had to be done.

It was a great night. The portable gramophone that had whiled away the winter evenings screeched away again, as we joked and reminisced on this short and most unlikely interlude in our lives; but with midnight approaching and a very early start in the morning, we had to leave. I was disappointed during the final handshakes that Mr Milton was missing. We left our regards for him but it was unnecessary. He was waiting outside.

'Just thought I'd have a private word before you vanished, old chap,' he said, as we joined him under the street lamp. We tried again to thank him for all he had done, but he wouldn't hear of it.

'But we are grateful, Mr Milton,' insisted Antoinette. 'You don't know how grateful.'

'The pleasure is mine, my dear,' he answered gently. 'Your career is assured. Let us hope that this will give Liam a similar opportunity. And now there are one or two things I would like to say. I may be a little blunt, Liam. I do hope you won't mind?'

I assured him that I was well used to that. He smiled and went on to describe my new life and to warn me that a private school was like a private world. That I would find it completely different to the background I had described to him. I must give myself time to settle before making any judgments on it. I found it a comfort when he handed me his address, just three miles from the school, with instructions to contact him immediately if I had any problems.

'And now Liam,' he continued with a grave expression, 'I must remind you of one very important thing.' I listened with equal gravity as he told me that I would be dealing with children, not men. That they could be absolute devils at times, so I must watch my temper! Although the head would normally administer punishments, there would be occasions when I may have to. If I did, I must not punish in a temper. I must be calm about it, otherwise the purpose of the punishment would be lost on the child receiving it. He must know why he was being punished. Did I understand that? I assured him I did and would follow his advice.

'That is not to say,' he added with a twinkle in his eye, 'that you must stand any nonsense from the blighters, oh no! The trick is, the three F's.' I laughed.

He looked over his spectacles and added. 'Yes, the golden rule in teaching, Liam, is to be Firm, Fair, and Friendly, and you will be a good teacher as opposed to an instructor. Do you understand that?'

Again, I assured him that I did, as he apologised for the lecture. Then, after a long and affectionate hug from Antoinette, we watched the tiny figure, head bent forward, fading into the blackness beyond the circle of light. We owed him so much. I just hoped that I could fulfil his faith in me. Most certainly I would try.

*   *   *

The journey home, though on a crowded train, was made in virtual isolation, and we planned in exquisite detail our future of untroubled bliss. I would take the long-awaited opportunity to study; with Mr Milton I'd have a pillar of wisdom to whom I could turn for guidance, ready and willing to help me. Then, when Antoinette finished college, she would come down to join me, perhaps even in the school itself but, if that was not possible, she could get a job nearby. Eventually we would get a place of our own — nothing grand, naturally, a couple of rooms maybe, then, who knows? Maybe a house even! There were no end of possibilities.

Recalling that journey with painful clarity, I blush at the memory of our child-like naïvety, the eager simplicity with which, with our wordly possessions amounting to fifteen pounds hard cash, a small amount put by in the Post Office, a few wedding presents and virtually what we stood up in, we planned our alluring future with rock-like certainty. By the time we reached Lime Street station, we had it all settled and assured. Our parents would be delighted with our good fortune. All our fears for the future, so black just a week ago, had vanished like snow before the benificent rays of the sun.

Our euphoria remained, and was even enhanced when we arrived at our temporary home, for Antoinette's parents reflected our own hopes. Nor was it dispelled, when, after a wash and a meal, we went home to spread the good news. They were all there in force to greet us, with Teresa looking not nearly as well as I would have liked, but chirpy enough. The biggest surprise was to see Con, still on strike and dressed out of overalls. It could not have been better if I had stage managed it myself!

Aunt Min was predictable as she stood back after her greeting. 'Ah,' she said fondly, 'don't they look well, God luv'em.'

Mam expressed delight with my new job as I gave her a hug, then made to follow Teresa into the back kitchen.

I turned, bumping into Con as he rose to come over. 'Whoops-a-daisy,' I said jocularly, taking his out-stretched hand. 'How are you?'

He grimaced. 'Oh, I'm well in myself like, but er . . .' I knew what the 'but er' meant and didn't speculate. Instead I winked at Dad sitting in his chair in case he got run over in the crush.

'See yeh in a minute!' I said to Con. He sat down again as I worked my way through to Dad. He too, now retired, was out of overalls for the first time for many years at this time of the day.

'How are yeh?' I asked above the chatter.

He smiled as I clasped his hand. 'Oh not bad, thank God, Li. Just seems a bit funny not workin' any more, that's all!'

I pushed him on the shoulder and clucked. 'About time you put your feet up, isn't it? Enjoy it while you can, I say.'

Within minutes, the first chaos of the greeting over, the crowd thinned a little as Bernadette announced her departure.

Con rose as she spoke. ''ang on a minute, I'll come

with yeh.' He turned to me, 'I'll be round termorrer night, Li, OK? Gorra meetin' on t'night.'

I crossed over to him. 'Sorry you're going. You look well, anyroad. Remember me to Edie, will you?' I was glad he was going before I had to talk about my new job. Since I was going over to his 'enemy', so to speak, it could have been tricky especially since he was on strike, which no one had mentioned. I caught Dad's expression as he left, and he didn't look very pleased at all. I'll bet there'd been some right up and downers about it. Thank God I was out of it all.

With everyone who was 'going ashore' having gone, and the tea cups filled again, the conversation turned to us, and especially my new job. Only one was not absolutely delighted about it.

Aunt Sarah, as usual, had grave misgivings. 'Funny places, them there toff's schools, y'know. They tell me . . .'

Aunt Min clucked disgustedly. 'What the 'ell are yeh tryin' t'do woman? Purr'im off?'

I laughed. Now I knew I was home. I left Antoinette to argue the point, and nipped into the back kitchen to catch Teresa on her own. She stood quietly washing up.

'Well,' I said quietly, 'come on now, how are you . . . Really?' I looked closely at the unusually brilliant eyes set in a drawn face, as she raised her head with a smile. Slowly and deliberately she struck a match from the box in her hand and lit the gas before replying, then, a ghost of a smile lighting her face she poked me in the ribs.

'You worry too much!' she said softly. Without smiling I repeated my question. She put her small hand on my arm affectionately. 'I'm alright Li . . . Honest I am.'

I grimaced. 'Well,' I replied bluntly, 'you don't look it! Now what does the quack say?'

She told me. It was heart trouble, something to do

with the valves. There was nothing they could do, just give her pills and advice to take it easy. If I didn't believe her, she added, then go and ask Mam. I warned her I would, and advised her not to do anything daft like lifting.

It was her turn to laugh. 'Oh don't worry, Mam won't let me. Y'know what she's like? Honest Li, I just get a bit short of wind now and then, that's all . . . Go on, get back in there while I make the tea, and stop worrying! . . . Oh, Li,' she added, putting her finger to her lips as I turned to go, 'now don't go worrying me mam, will you?'

I turned, then stopped again and waited for her to finish filling the pot. 'What's all this about our Con on strike, then? What did me dad say?'

She rolled her eyes. 'Don't talk t'me about it, Li. We're sick and tired of the whole damned thing . . . Ask me dad if you like, but don't get into any arguments about it . . . Please!'

I grinned at her. 'Don't worry, I won't! Come on,' I added, 'I'll take the tray in for you.'

She pursed her lips and refused. 'I'm not a flippin' invalid, y'know!'

'Who said you were?' I demanded jokingly.

She laughed and tossed her head. 'Right. Come on, then,' she said, picking the tray up. I followed her into the noisy kitchen.

'Come on,' said Dad as I handed him his cup, 'let's go in the parlour. 'We'll never get a word in edgeways 'ere with this lot.' We left them to it.

*   *   *

This short and totally unexpected home leave was for me a strange period of studied ambivalence. Having left a slightly unrealistic world, I found myself part of, yet detached from, the domestic currents surging about me: a relaxed yet restless period during which

221

many tensions revealed themselves in a dozen different ways, but which remained largely unspoken. My new job itself was a flashpoint, and would be spoken of at two different levels. At Antoinette's it was a source of unreserved delight, and its possibilities discussed for hours with her parents. At home, depending on the company, there were mixed feelings in which all except Con, and predictably Aunt Sarah, were as delighted as my in-laws.

Over all, the ever-present and malignant spectre of the strike, in which Con was taking part, hung like a restless spirit, bringing silent strife between him and Dad, whose chat with me had revealed total opposition. Not least in the tensions was my own relationship with Con, and the class treachery, which he felt I was showing by taking my new job. In short, it was a potential minefield for the hurried word, or an opposing opinion. With such a powder keg, one does not deliberately strike matches, so whenever Con was present, I walked carefully and my words were conciliatory. I had no wish to take with me to my new world the memory of a conflict left behind. Two worries would, however, remain with me: Teresa, so happy now that Antoinette was home, and with whom she spent hours, and Mam and Dad. Teresa I could do nothing about, but Mam and Dad I could.

Now that Dad was retired their income, never high, had dropped considerably, and I decided to have a word with Mam about it at the first opportunity, despite her fanatical independence. With arrangements already in hand for Dad and me to decorate the front room the following day, and with everyone else out, I caught Mam quietly ironing in the back kitchen and, after a general conversational lead-in, put my question to her.

'How does Dad like being retired, then?' I asked her, knowing damned well he didn't.

She shrugged and continued ironing. 'Oh, y'know

your father . . . Restless as usual. When you've finished the front room tomorrow, he'll 'ave nowt t'do. He gets on his own nerves.'

'Ah well, it's only natural, isn't it?' I replied consolingly. 'Still, he likes reading.'

She clucked. 'Can't read forever, can 'e? But there, he'll 'ave t'get used to it, won't 'e?'

I put the delicate question I had been angling to put. I knew the answer too. 'How d'you do for managin', then?' I asked cautiously.

She carried on ironing without looking up. 'Oh we'll manage,' said airily. 'Other's 'ave to, an' we're no different.'

'But-er, it's a bit of a drop from wages to old age pension, isn't it?'

She looked up at me quizzically. 'What you askin' all this for?' she demanded.

'Oh just wonderin', that's all. It is a drop though, isn't it? Bound to make a difference?'

She agreed that it would, but ordered me not to worry about it.

I ignored her advice. 'But Mam, first my wages went when I got married, now me Dad's finished. I thought, well y'know . . .'

She smiled and put the iron down. 'Now luk, Li, ta very much for thinkin' about it, but your first job is your wife, and don't you forget it, so . . .' I made to protest but she cut me short. 'But nothing!' she broke in bluntly. 'I'm well used to managin', you know that, so stop yeh worryin'. You get your own 'ome t'gether. We'll be alright.'

Her answer was no surprise, but the problem would not leave me. I discussed it with Antoinette that night. The answer was simple. Send her a postal order each week and, if she sent it back, as she probably would well, fair enough, just keep bunging it back until she cashed it. In the event, after the first couple were returned to me, then sent straight back to her, she got

223

the message and it worked well. At least I was happy on that score. Only Teresa remained a worry.

After my abortive attempt with Mam the previous day, the house, with everyone out except Dad and me, was quiet and, with neither of us the greatest decorators in the world, we got down to papering the room. About three o'clock, as I stood on a chair waiting for Dad to pass me the length of paper he was just pasting up, Con walked in.

'Oh great,' I said, 'come to give a hand, then?'

He grinned and shook his head as Dad finished off the pasting. 'No, just passin'. Thought I'd drop in, like. Gorra meetin' on, y'know.'

I looked across at Dad, hoping he would answer, because I resolutely refused to mention the strike, but he didn't. He just grimaced. 'When are yeh goin' back, then?' asked Con, knowing damned well I was going the following weekend. With the paper fully pasted and soggy, Dad folded it over to give to me just as Con spoke again. 'Wanna them private schools then, is it?' he asked with heavy sarcasm. I nodded and held out my hands to Dad for the paper. 'About time they abolished that lot!' he continued, leaning casually against the door. 'Warrabout the poor ki . . .'

Dad rounded on him angrily. 'You keep your opinions to y'self!' he snapped, unconsciously raising his arms to admonish him. The paper slipped and finished up on the floor in a heap. He blew! 'Holy Sailor!' he ejaculated, 'now luk what you've flamin' well made me do.' Con looked on sympathetically as Dad tried to retrieve the paper without tearing it. It ripped! With a thunderous expression, Dad looked from his pasty hands to Con, then cut loose. 'Bugger it!' he snapped, rapidly losing his temper. 'Now luk at it . . . Ruined, and we've only just got enough to finish . . . Damn the flamin' strike!'

My alarm bells jangled instantly. Those few words could be fatal, as Con glared at him angrily.

'What d'yeh mean, damn the strike? What's that got . . .?'

Furiously Dad glared back. 'If yeh weren't on bloody strike, you'd be at work, wouldn't yeh? Then it wouldn't 'ave 'appened, would it? Anyroad, it's about time they settled the damn thing,' he added, thoroughly fed up and releasing his pent-up feelings about it. His next words made it fifty times worse. 'Daft buggers!' he snapped, wiping his hands on his overalls. 'It's all about nothin', anyway!'

I looked anxiously from one to the other and realised the tensions there must have been while I was away.

Desperately I tried to calm things down. 'Look Con,' I pleaded, 'just leave it, will yeh? Me Mam'll be back soon, so just let's get the job done, eh?' It was no use, they were both strung up. I watched helplessly, as hidden passions burst through.

'If I wanted t'go back, Dad,' he snapped, 'then I'd go! It's the principle.'

With the women out, Dad suddenly let rip in a flaming temper. 'Principle!' he snarled. 'Don't talk so bloody daft. If yeh did, you'd be a scab! Your life wouldn't be worth livin' down there and you know it. And don't try to kid me otherwise. That's why yeh can't go back, not bloody principles, my lad! You can stick that where Paddy stuck 'is ninepence!'

I honestly felt sorry for Con as Dad let himself go. Neither of us had seen him like this for years, and nothing was going to stop him. I groaned inwardly as he reminded my brother that up to now he had thrown away six good weeks' wages, with no end of it in sight, and all because two trades couldn't agree over a job.

He taunted him with a question. 'An' what's it all about, eh? Go on, tell me.'

Tight-lipped and angry, Con told him that he already knew that it was about the holes, and who would drill them.

225

Dad snorted disgustedly. "Oles!' he snapped sardonically . . . 'arse'oles more like, an' you flamin' well know it. Is this what you want for him?' he demanded, jerking his thumb at me, perched on the chair. 'Well, is it?'

'You've gorrit all wrong, Dad,' answered Con defensively.

Dad laughed scornfully, then renewed the attack in colourful shipyard language. Con was left in no doubt regarding what it was really about, as we both got an unexpected lecture on shipyard politics. He pulled no punches, nor glossed over any hard truth, as the pent-up words bubbled out. And all the while my fiery brother, held only by a deep and genuine affection for Dad, despite all their arguments, stood furious but silent under the tirade. Only Dad could have lashed him like that.

At last, passion spent, Dad's tone softened a little, but with a warning. 'Your mother's sick of it,' he said, 'an' it's not doin' Teresa a helluva lot'f good either, so don't mention the strike in this house again. As far as I'm concerned, enough's enough, so knock it off or stay away. Take your pick. An' by the way,' he added, 'I don't wanna hear anymore sarky remarks abut Li's new job, either. If yeh feel like bein' sarky, just go an' talk t'yeh flamin' self for a minute or two, right? Now,' he added as I suppressed a smile, 'as far as I'm concerned, that's an end to it! You stick to your views and I'll stick to mine, and so will he. But here,' he added, pointing to the floor, 'I want peace, an' I'll bloody well 'ave it. OK.'

I took advantage of the altered tone. 'Hey Con,' I said jocularly, 'forget the meeting t'day. Go and make a cuppa. We could use one.'

For the first time since he had arrived he smiled, then looked at Dad. 'Sorry Dad,' he said as he took his coat off, 'I didn't think!'

Dad shrugged as he examined the soggy paper on the floor. 'F'gerrit,' he said.

I sighed with relief. It was over, with no damage done and Dad a lot easier in his mind. With a fresh cup of tea inside us and Con's help, it was quite like the old days, as the three of us worked happily together to get the room done. Even the piece of paper that had caused the flare-up was put to good use, in a place where it wouldn't be noticed. By the time the women returned we were close to finishing.

Antoinette must have thought she had suddenly acquired a new brother-in-law, Con was so chatty! He even questioned her with interest about college. With tea over, Con gone, and Antoinette more than happy to stay and chat with Mam and Teresa, Dad asked me to walk down to the club, ostensibly to see Uncle Matt but, as it turned out, he wanted a chat. I knew he was anxious and agreed, but I hadn't realised just how anxious he was. His main concern was that Con and I shouldn't fall out. In all the arguments Con and I had had since my Demob, this had always been a great worry to him. Most of the things he wanted to talk about, we had already discussed many times on our occasional walks, but his concern was very real and I listened patiently with the odd interjection. I told him that Con sometimes got up my nose a bit with his politics. Personally I just wasn't interested in them. All I wanted was a bit of peace to get on with things. But his real worry, as indeed was mine, was Teresa. She couldn't stand trouble these days. I asked about Mam. He laughed. She was more than able for Con: any trouble, and he got his marching orders on the spot! Not that Con ever took any offence at it.

Nor did I escape entirely as he pointed out that I was just as pig-headed. He even accused me of egging Con on at times. I protested vehemently.

He laughed. 'Oh don't come the innocent with me. I know yeh. I've seen yeh do it.'

'Well,' I admitted, 'sometimes maybe, just for a bit'f divilment.'

'He's a good lad,' he emphasised, as we strolled the last few yards home. 'Give you the shirt off 'is back if you needed it. It's just the bloody crowd he's in with, that's all.' I agreed on the generosity Con had always displayed, and vowed that whatever happened, I wouldn't fall out with him.

Dad looked relieved. 'We won't be 'ere forever, y'know Li!' he stated as we walked up the pathway.

I joshed him light-heartedly. 'Oh come on Dad! You're only a lad yet . . . An' Mam — well, she's like a two year old.'

'Aye maybe, but trouble like this afternoon won't help. Still, it had to be said, more's the pity. Now perhaps things'll settle down a bit, so don't worry while you're away will yeh? And,' he added as he turned the key, 'make sure you write to 'im, OK?' The promise made, we walked into the house at peace.

On Tuesday of the final week Dinny came round to see if we were still at home. He was fed up to the back teeth, although he had managed to get himself a part-time job to keep him going while the strike was on. He was delighted with my turn of luck. As he said, perhaps it was better that I should get the hell out of it, with my views. Then with a few wry comments on his efforts to stop the dispute, he was gone.

All too soon it was Friday night. Tomorrow I would seek new pastures and, to be honest, I was getting a bit nervous. It had been a happy second week, with Con a different person, even volunteering to escort Antoinette over to Liverpool to catch her bus on the Sunday evening after I had gone. I was grateful. Perhaps he would get to know her a bit better, too. I hoped so.

With farewells said to my in-laws, we went home to a full reception and, as usual, the house was crowded to see me off. Perversely, with them all around me, I didn't want to go. But the die was cast so, amid the usual jokes, dire warnings from Aunt Sarah and jovial hugs from Aunt Min, I turned for a final farewell to Mam.

'Luk after y'self now,' she said as I embraced her, 'and don't forget to write.' Bernadette, too, gave exactly the same advice. Teresa, misty-eyed as always when I went away stood torn between two emotions, delight that I was going to teach, and sadness that I would be so far away. I, too, wished I could have been nearer as I gazed at the small, thin figure with its crown of auburn curls.

I glanced at the clock and could put it off no longer. 'Don't get drunk now!' I warned her solemnly, as I always had when leaving home. She put her arms round me and laughed. I caught Antoinette's anxious look at the clock as Teresa gave me a long, long hug. I would miss her. I would miss them all.

'Come on you two,' broke in Dad jocularly, ''urry up or you'll have the train gone.' Teresa freed her arms reluctantly.

'Now don't do anything daft,' I told her. 'No liftin', nothin' like that.'

'Don't worry, she won't,' promised Mam.

'She'd better not!' warned Bernadette, with a fierce look.

'Right,' ordered Dad, holding the case out to me, 'you'd better get your skates on. Go on.' We followed him down the hall. Holding his hand out at the open door he smiled. 'I'm glad you an' Con are hittin' it off better now, and so is your mother.'

'Speak of the divil,' I said as Con came up the pathway.

'Sorry, got 'eld up. All the best now,' he added holding his hand out. 'Hope y'do well!'

'Thanks. Look after y'self, give our best to Edie . . . Right then, all bein' well I'll see you all at Christmas,' I said. Dad nodded silently and watched us until we turned the corner.

The journey over the water away from home was

229

never a happy one. With a hundred and one instructions to each other, interspersed with periods of thoughtful silence, we reached my platform. I hated this moment, but it had to be and, with an assurance from Antoinette that she would keep her eye on Teresa during her weekend visits, I reluctantly boarded the train as the guard blew his whistle. Hanging through the open window, I watched the trim and much-loved figure grow smaller as the train picked up speed, and vanishing as we rounded a bend. Alone in the compartment, I wondered what the future would bring.

16

St Benedict's

Although Mr Milton had described the place to me, I was still amazed as I came to a halt in a broad, tree-lined avenue on the outskirts of Hastings and stood, suitcase in hand, staring through the wrought-iron gates at what appeared to be a solidly built Tudor type mansion, squatting with ageless comfort at the end of a shortish drive, and guarded on either side by gnarled old trees. Hell! I thought, suddenly nervous, fancy me workin' in a place like this!

The contrast with the harsh industrial background I had just left was startling. I felt like pinching myself to make sure it was true. To make absolutely sure, I stepped back to examine once again the gold-painted notice board screwed to the railings: ST BENEDICT'S PREPARATORY SCHOOL FOR BOYS With all doubts removed, but still decidedly edgy, I marched through the gates and headed for the main door, a dozen conflicting thoughts chasing themselves through my head. Suppose they were a toffy-nosed lot, as Con predicted? Suppose someone tried to take the micky? I just hoped not. Diplomacy was an art I was only just trying to learn. For the first time in my life I felt uneasy about my background, my limitations, my speech. I felt like an expert clog dancer suddenly transferred to the corps de ballet, and just as liable to tread on someone's toes.

Riven by doubt, I stopped half-way along the drive, my mind tumbling about. If only I could talk without opening my mouth! A reversal of emotions made me feel ashamed. Why the hell should I be uneasy about my background? I wasn't ashamed of it. Why should I be? It was all the luck of the draw, and anyway Mam and Dad had done a good job, against all the odds. I was proud of them, very proud. No, to hell with 'em, I thought, they can take me as they find me, even if I do talk funny. Other doubts arose and were immediately dismissed. I'd do as I always did, cross the flamin' bridges as I got to them.

I took my own advice and pushed the doorbell. A maid opened the door.

'My name is Sullivan,' I announced.

She smiled and opened the door wider. 'Would you follow me sir, please? Mr Patterson is expecting you.'

'Sir' followed across the wide, tiled hall, up a broad staircase, nostrils assailed by a long established odour of wood, polish and food, all in a subdued atmosphere of quiet order. We came to a halt outside a door on the first floor. She knocked discreetly and entered in response to a sonorous command from within.

Mind still partially blank, I followed her into the headmaster's study-cum-office-cum-sitting room, to be greeted with a beaming smile as Mr Patterson rose with outstretched hand. Shortish, with a pair of pince-nez balanced on the end of his prominent nose, his thinning hair brushed to one side to make the most of it, he was affability itself, enquiring whether I had had a comfortable journey, as he sat down again.

'Clare,' he continued to the waiting maid, 'would you be so kind as to bring some refreshments?'

She glided noiselessly away, to return very quickly with a laden tray. I scrutinised my new boss. In his late sixties, more portly, and slightly less donnish than Mr Milton, he had the round, unlined face of a well-fed academic, and a most charming manner.

For fifteen gentle minutes, as we sipped and chatted, he expertly weighed me up with a series of softly spoken questions that left me totally relaxed. Without warning the door silently opened and a severely dressed lady of generous proportions manifested alongside me. I rose instinctively, but she waved her bejewelled hand imperiously.

'Do sit down Mr Sullivan, please.'

I obeyed, feeling suddenly tense as I did so. I didn't much like the regal manner, nor the steely blue eyes set in a stern but handsome face. I knew instinctively just who the boss was, when I was introduced to his dear wife. For a fleeting moment I felt sorry for him. She was massive, with a very close resemblance to Aunt Aggie of my youth, and, if I was any judge, just as formidable.

'I take it you had a comfortable journey, Mr Sullivan?' she asked.

'Yes, thank you.'

Her embryo smile faded as she looked at me. Her husband coughed gently. 'Hmn, er. It is the, er custom within the school Mr Sullivan,' he said with a hint of apology, 'for the staff to address my wife as Ma'am. I trust you understand?'

I flushed in embarrassment, but managed to sit on my natural reactions. 'Oh, I'm very sorry,' I replied calmly, 'I didn't kn . . .'

'Quite alright Mr Sullivan,' she replied, the smile returning, 'quite alright. Clare will show you to your room directly the headmaster is finished.' With another automatic smile she left, like a galleon easing majestically into a turning tide. It was impressive and I wondered idly just how many guns she was rigged with. Another gentle cough brought me back to the present. He was smiling. I felt easy again.

'You will soon get used to our little ways, Mr Sullivan,' he said reassuringly. 'A little strange to you perhaps but, er, well we do have a rather regulated life in these establishments, you know. But there, after a day or so, you will very quickly settle down, I'm sure.'

'Oh yes sir, I'm sure I will.'

'Of course you will. I have a feeling we are going to get along very well together, and I must say, Mr Milton was quite enthusiastic about your work.' I coughed, slightly embarrassed. 'Now,' he continued in a business-like tone, 'your duties.'

I listened carefully as he reeled them off. All games, for formal and recreational purposes, general discipline, supervising Prep (whatever that was) whenever rostered for it, dormitory duties when rostered, supervising walks (again a mystery), plus other, seemingly numerous lesser duties from time to time, of which I would be informed as and when they arose. In addition, when the weather improved, I would also teach swimming in the school's outdoor pool. All in all I got the impression that I was in for one hell of a busy time, in return for which I would receive the magnificient sum of four pounds, ten shillings a week, with board and lodgings found.

He was sure that I would maintain the high standards of both the school and the previous Sergeant, and I was equally sure that I would have a damned good try, after which, in response to a bell button on his desk, Clare reappeared.

'Oh yes, one other thing,' he added as I rose to go. 'Supper will be served at five thirty.'

I thanked him but remained puzzled as I left the room. Supper — at five thirty? That's a funny time to have supper, I thought, as I followed Clare up the stairs. She turned left at the top and stopped almost immediately, opened a door and smiled shyly.

'This is your room, sir.' Suppressing an instinct to pull her leg about the 'sir', I assumed an air of gravitas, thanked her and walked in.

Not exactly the Waldorf, my new domain was long and narrow, situated at the rear of the building but, austere though it was, it was more than adequate, with its single bed, small chest of drawers, wardrobe, and tiny handbasin with a single cold water tap, jammed inconveniently between the wardrobe and a small, fixed writing table, all along one wall. I had seen and slept in a whole lot worse. From my window I gazed out at the quiet spacious playing fields beyond the swimming pool. Apart from odd buildings here and there, it was virtually open country down to the sea. It was beautiful, peaceful and a whole world away from what I had left behind. Deep down I felt I was going to love it. It was an unexpected chance, and I determined to make the most of it. I decided to introduce myself to the few boys on the playing field, but the door suddenly opened and a cheerful face popped round.

'Ah,' it said with a grin, 'you're here then?' The face developed into a short fat body, as the newcomer, still talking, came in. 'The old boy told me you'd arrived. Thought I would pop round, sort of thing, make you welcome so to speak . . . Jurgens,' he added, his hand outstretched.

'History,' he clarified, as I shook it. 'Mine's Liam,' he looked puzzled, then brightened.

'Ah yes, I'm with you. See what you mean. Silly of me. Unusual though isn't it? Can't say I've met a Liam before. I'm Alfred. Blighters call me King Alfred. Take no notice of them, that's my advice. Absolute menaces all of them. You'll find out.'

I had the feeling of talking to a Bren gun, firing in short bursts, but I did manage to get a couple of words in.

'So, you teach History then?' I queried, gazing at the round, cheerful forty-odd year old.

'Oh absolutely, old chap.' He suddenly grimaced. 'Complete waste of time of course . . . Philistines the lot of them! You'll never believe it, old boy, but I set a test last term for the Dominic's.' I looked at him, puzzled. 'Oh, didn't the Head tell you? . . . Typical, absolutely typical. All saints' names here of course, St Dominic's, St Hugh's, St Francis, St Anthony. Where was I? Oh yes. This question I set. Simple, old chap, rock-bottom simple. Patron saint of France. Who was it? Do you know what one blighter told me?' I shook my head, not quite sure myself who it was. 'Frankenstein!' he said in disgust. 'Would you believe it? Frankenstein! Felt like resigning on the spot. Oh by the way, have you bumped into Boadicea yet?'

'Who?'

'Mrs Patterson, largish lady, gimlet eyes etcetera. Forbidding is the mildest word I can think of. You must have seen her, surely!

'Is that what you call her?'

He grinned in high glee. 'Oh rather. Absolute stickler. Boys terrified of her. Confidentially,' he added with a broad grin, 'so am I. The old boy's alright though, one of the best, but watch her old chap, watch her.'

'There's a fair amount to watch,' I said.

He went off into fits. 'Oh I say, jolly good. Yes, you'll fit in alright my boy. Come on, I'll take you down to the Common Room, introduce you. Not many about today, though. Sort of free time today. You'll find out. Come along,' he added, 'Winifred might have a pot of tea ready. Usually has about this time,' he ended, checking his watch.

Minutes later, still a bit punch drunk from the rapid, one-sided conversation, I followed him down the stairs, past the Headmaster's office and into a large room at the end of the corridor. He burst in cheerfully. In the far corner, bent over a small gas ring, a tall, slim, sad-eyed lady glanced towards us, resignation on her solemn face. Her eyebrows raised slightly as she saw me.

'Ah,' said my companion cheerfully, 'tea ready? Well done.' Taking me by the arm he introduced me. 'Winifred, Mr Sullivan. Mr Sullivan, our Common Room treasure. Winifred — Music and other things.' She smiled gently, unconsciously smoothing her short straight hair as we shook hands.

236

'You're very welcome Mr Sullivan,' she said in a low voice. 'It is nice to see a new face.'

'Ah Horace,' exclaimed Jurgens behind me, 'there you are. I wondered where you'd vanished to. I knew you couldn't be on the field.'

A long, cadaverous figure, pale face adorned with thick, steel-rimmed spectacles, surmounted by a short thick crop of iron grey hair, rose like an emaciated wraith from the depths of one of the three deep winged armchairs, and looked solemnly at my companion.

'Alfred,' he said in an admonishing tone, 'why are you always so damnably cheerful? Don't you realise that this wil . . .'

'Ignore his remarks,' advised Alfred, unabashed. 'Always like this at the beginning of term. Charming fellow, really. Let me introduce you to our Mathematical genius, Horace. This is Liam Sullivan, new Sergeant, disciplinarian par excellence, I hope!'

His huge hand engulfed mine in a firm grip. 'Delighted,' he intoned.

'And this,' continued Alfred, with a dramatic sweep of his arm round the room, as Horace resumed his seat, 'is our oasis. The one corner of this ancient pile which is free from the blighters. Here we, and no doubt you, in the near future, avoid total madness. Here . . .'

'Oh do be quiet Alfred,' pleaded Winifred with a laugh, as she brought the tea tray. 'Really, you'll scare the living daylights out of the poor chap. Please Mr Sullivan . . .'

'Liam,' I corrected.

She smiled, 'Very well then, Liam . . . Just ignore him Liam. He's always like this at the beginning of a new term, and,' she added mischievously, 'for most of the term as well!'

'Winifred!' he exclaimed in mock horror, as he took the proffered cup. 'That is tatamount to slander. How could I not prepare him when, to the simple question, "What do you know about Henry the Eighth?" I get

237

from Williams Minor the answer that he is a cruel man! Why, Williams Minor, do you think he was a cruel man? I asked. Do you know what the cretin said, Winifred?' She shook her head with a smile as I listened, amused. 'Why? Because he pressed his suit on Ann Boleyn! I ask you, would you believe it?'

Even Horace, slumped behind a newspaper, burst out laughing. He lowered his paper and gazed solemnly at Alfred. 'You are well aware, I presume Alfred, that the class is the mirror of the teacher!'

'Touché!' replied Alfred, sitting down with a grin as Winifred, searching her handbag, withdrew a piece of paper and passed it across.

'If you think Henry the Eighth is bad, Alfred, then I would consider this sacreligious, wouldn't you?' Alfred put his cup down, examined the paper and convulsed with laughter as he passed it to me. 'That,' Winifred informed me, 'was the result of a small exercise requesting them to draw their impressions of the Flight into Egypt!'

I examined the childish drawing, depicting a small biplane with two passengers and a small head between them, from which a long arm dangled, holding a suitcase, with the letters J.C. on it.

'Now will you agree with me?' demanded Alfred. 'Maniacs — that's what they are. Maniacs!' I suggested, handing it back to Winifred, that the artist had shown imagination.

Alfred snorted disgustedly. 'You'll learn my boy . . . You'll learn,' he warned.

With good company, a cup of tea and a book-lined room, all thoughts of visiting the field had momentarily vanished, but eventually my conscience pricked me and I felt that at least I should put in an appearance. I said as much to Alfred.

Horace, now in the cosy circle with us, looked at me horrified. 'Good God!' he exclaimed. 'Do I sense unwonted keenness?'

Alfred grimaced. 'I rather fancy you do, Horace.' He turned to me with a grin. 'My suggestion Liam, should these feelings arise unexpectedly, is to recharge your cup, remain seated, and wait until they have passed. What do you think, Winifred?'

'Oh absolutely, Alfred,' she replied without a flicker of humour, 'very sound advice.'

'Such feelings,' suggested Horace, with equal gravity, 'could, if mooted abroad, and spread among the remainder of the staff, do incalculable damage.'

I looked from one to the other of the serious faces, then laughed.

'Believe me,' said Alfred, serious this time, 'you will get more than enough of duty before term is out, and these moments, my dear chap, are beyond price.' There were general nods of approval as he went on, 'Once term starts on Monday you will not have time to breathe, except for your official and precious half-day holiday each week, and even that is not always sacrosanct!' Again they nodded agreement.

Hoorace leaned forward. 'You'll see,' he said warningly.

I did. The current recreation on the field was free-time for the early arrivals, for, with more staff and boys still to arrive over the next twenty-four hours, the routine had not yet started. When it did, it proved frenetic.

The afternoon passed in illuminating conversation, during which I said little and learned a lot. The full teaching staff of twelve would all have arrived by early evening, when there would be a general meeting with the Head and his wife to discuss the new term, after all the pupils had been settled in for the night. Matron of course was in a category of her own, as were the domestic staff, but as far as I could gather, all would be revealed that evening. The intervening time for me at least was free and, when the teapot finally gave up as more staff arrived, Alfred suggested that he should take me on a tour of the school.

For me, in such an alien world, it was quite an experience. The school proved to be much bigger than it looked, with nooks and crannies all over the place, from long dormitories high up in the building, to poky little rooms in the oddest places and over all a feeling of age, solidity, and order. Alfred chattered incessantly, and I discovered I had entered an isolated, more or less self-contained world, with rules and regulations as tight as any service unit, in some ways even tighter. Most, like me, lived in. Others, conveniently local, lived out and some of these, I learned later, provided another sort of school during the long holidays. For those who lived in, I gathered, the job never finished. One was on call, should the need arise, both day and night. Even a normal day started early and finished late. As Alfred said, it would be no sinecure, but strangely, different though it was for me, I felt I was going to like it very much. I loved the place itself, and those I had met so far had been more than friendly. The fact that I spoke differently and was nowhere near them academically, appeared not to make the slightest difference. By the time we returned to the Common Room, now more crowded, I felt completely relaxed. My only worry now was could I handle the pupils successfully without losing my rag? I was to have my first full encounter the following morning at breakfast.

Waking up on my first Sunday to a discreet knock on the door, I was surprised to see a strange but pretty young face pop round the door in response to my call to come in. She smiled as I instinctively pulled the blanket higher, and handed me a cup of tea from the tray she was carrying. Surprised but grateful I took it, then, remembering I was going to Communion, put it down.

'What's your name?' I asked

'Jenny, sir.'

I pointed to a small brass watering can on the tray. 'What's that?' I asked.

She smiled. 'Hot water, sir,' she explained. I expressed surprise. 'I bring this every morning, sir,' she continued shyly. 'Only the cold water tap, you see,' she pointed to the wash basin with its single tap.

I felt a bit of a twit. I had never been waited on in my life before and didn't quite know what to say. Normally up North, there would have been a quick exchange of repartee, but here I felt dumb.

'Thanks,' I said with an involuntary wink. She giggled as she left. Flippin' 'eck! I thought, fancy that! Bringin' hot water up.

I vowed to be up and dressed in good time the following morning. God alone knows why, but oddly enough I found myself embarrassed. Nor was it the only time I was going to experience the feeling that morning.

Half an hour later, I met the boys for the first time as they sat, en masse, in the private chapel. I knew that I was, as a new master, an object of curiosity as I took my place with the rest of the staff. Everyone was there. Short of death itself, nobody misses Mass in a Catholic school. My first real sight of them, in serried ranks of grey uniform, was as I returned from the altar after Communion, and I could almost feel the speculation, as scores of beady eyes followed me up the aisle.

Breakfast in the long, oak-panelled dining room was, as all meals proved to be, a fairly formal affair, with Bodicea, the Head and the housemasters sitting at the top table, placed squarely to give a clear view over the whole to those sitting at it, with the remainder of the staff spread among the boys tables. I was on the table nearest the Head, with eight boys. It was at this meal that I got my first among many surprises for, instead of the English boys I had naturally expected, they seemed to be from all nations and of several different colours. Not that that bothered me, coming from a seaport. Even the English boys were not all from England, many coming from overseas, where their parents served in the colonial services or the Armed forces. All that they seemed to have in common was that they were Catholics.

On my table that morning were just two English, no less than five French, and one dark skinned little bloke from God knows where but, like me apparently, a new boy, and a very silent one at that. Not the French, though. They jabbered like ten year old monkeys amid the general murmur of voices. Suddenly, two of them, within arms' reach of me and with half an eye on me, started pinching each other. I felt Bodicea's eye on the table. Glancing towards her I found my instinct correct, then looked to my right at Alfred, two tables down. Catching my eye he grinned, pointed to the boys, then ran his finger across his throat. I took the hint and threw the boys a filthy look. They stopped and all was relative peace until the maid brought the cereal in a large bowl and placed it before me. With a glance round I got the procedure and likewise started to dish out with a serving spoon. No sooner had I filled one plate than the two terrors started again and grabbed as I put the plate down. I felt it was a challenge and reacted spontaneously, rapping both their knuckles with the spoon. The effect was immediate and they sat rubbing their knuckles and scowling heavily until breakfast was over. I congratulated myself as, the meal over, the boys filed out for a short break before changing for their Sunday morning walk. Alfred had just caught up with me when I felt Bodicea materialise at my side.

'Mr Sullivan,' she said quietly, 'may I have a word?' She had a glint in her eye. I waited. Within minutes the room had emptied of all but the Head, Bodicea and myself. 'I noticed a slight altercation at table this morning, Mr Sullivan.'

God I thought, she doesn't miss much! 'Yes Ma'am. Two of the boys . . .'

'Yes,' she broke in quietly, 'I had noticed Mr Sullivan. However,' she continued, 'I would point out that,

242

much as I admire your sense of discipline, I would be grateful if you would refrain from using the cutlery as offensive weapons . . . You do understand, don't you?'

I flushed in sudden silent fury, but bit my lip. 'Yes Ma'am, I understand.'

Alfred, waiting outside and guessing what had happened, laughed as I told him what she'd said. 'Typical,' he said with a grin. 'Not surprised at all. Headmaster's job to lay it on old boy. You can glare, rollick, or give stacks of lines, but don't lay a finger on them. Mind you, those French blighters would try the patience of a saint sometimes. Just keep their noses to the grindstone old boy, they'll soon get fed up. Trying you out, that's all. Only natural really. New master, you know. Always happens. Probably nickname you "Basher" or something. Mad you know. All of them. I did warn you?'

'Yes,' I agreed, 'you did. Are they always like that?'

He nodded sagely. 'Oh rather. Will be until they get to know you. Don't give them a chance, dear boy. Stamp on the perishers. Punish them which way you like, but don't touch them. We all have our methods. You should see Horace when he gets mad. Awesome my dear chap, awesome!'

'What does he do?'

He shrugged. 'Nothing really. He just stands over them and glares! You've seen Horace, six foot three in his socks. Has an electrifying effect on the boys. How would you like to be three foot nothing with Horace standing glaring at you?'

I tried to imagine. 'I wouldn't,' I replied with a laugh. 'Scare the life out of me.'

He gave a grin. 'Does them, too.' He glanced at his watch. 'Good Lord, look at the time!'

We both dashed up to our rooms to get our outdoor kit on. It was walk time, a ritual I had never heard of before. This communal walking, I was to find, formed a very essential exercise and release from the close

243

formal atmosphere of the school and now, with Mass and breakfast over, I was to experience it for the first time.

I was quickly to find out that Sunday, far from being a day of rest was, for me at least, the exact opposite for, without the formal daily academic pursuits, the boys naturally had more free time. Unfortunately, boys with free time can very quickly get into mischief, be they posh or otherwise and, as Sergeant, it was part of my job to see that there were no idle hands, apart from those voluntarily pursuing their studies, or were sick. For those fit and active I would have to provide useful and purposeful alternatives, but that would all come later. Today, I was looking forward to the walk.

With off-duty staff safely tucked away in the Common Room or elsewhere, the remainder of us chivvied the boys into lines. For this, my first trip, I would share a 'crocodile' with one of the regular staff, a tall, fair haired, gangling young man about my own age, whom I had briefly met, but not been introduced to at the staff meeting.

'Ah, Mr Sullivan I presume,' he said with a laugh, as he came towards me, hand outstretched. 'Burgess . . . Harry to you. Sorry we didn't get a chance to talk last night but . . .'

'Liam,' I broke in, taking his hand as the boys fidgetted about us. 'Just a second,' he interrupted as they became more restless. 'Come along now,' he said sharply, 'come along. What the devil's going on? Absolute rabble this morning. What's the matter with you? Now into line and jolly quick about it.' I watched in amusement as he shooed them into a loose but orderly line. 'And no noise!' he added warningly. 'Remember, people will be watching you. I want no nonsense, understand?'

With a chorus of respectful 'Yes Sir's', we were off. He grinned as we fell into step. 'Always give them a pep talk, just to remind them, otherwise they would be all over the place in no time.' I still wasn't sure what the exercise was all about. Did they have to learn anything during it? Did they go to look at anything special? He laughed when I asked him. 'Oh no, nothing particular. We just walk.'

'Anywhere special?'

'No, not really. We all have our favourite walks, of course, but I usually give them a choice, otherwise it's boring for them. It's up to you really. Today they've asked for their favourite, along the promenade. They love it.'

And so did I. It was a lovely September morning and with my new friend in a chatty mood, a very instructive one, too. I learned a great deal about my new life. With an occasional stroll along the line, we exchanged personal histories. He, lucky devil, was awaiting the same teaching course as the boys at Todmarsh, and for the last two terms had been filling in to get some first hand experience. Apart from assisting with English, he also helped with the games and, to my delight, was a rugby fanatic. He was interested to hear about the Coal Board scheme and even more about Antoinette at college. Never having been North himself, he seemed fascinated with Merseyside. However, it was his views on St Benedict's which shook me most. Too close, too tight a society for his tastes and, in his opinion, the hours were murderous. Always on call, working every holiday, including Sundays. Oh no he didn't like that. True, we got much longer holidays than state schools at term-ends, but for all that he didn't fancy private schools as a career.

Most surprising of all, I found that, instead of envying the boys the privilege of a private education, with small classes and detailed attention, he actually felt sorry for them.

'You know, Liam,' he said as we strolled along the sea front, 'some of the poor blighters never see their parents from one year's end to the other.' I expressed

245

disbelief. 'Oh but yes,' he replied emphatically, 'half of them live and work abroad, you know. Colonial service, that kind of thing, so even on Parents Day they don't see them. How can they? If I was a kid I wouldn't fancy that, would you?'

I had a mental picture of the first time Mam went into hospital, when I was a lad. At the time I thought the end of the world had come. 'No I would not!' I replied with equal emphasis.

'Look, I'll give you an example.' He went on to describe the Parents Day of the previous term, the flashy cars, their beautiful clothes and so on. To me they sounded loaded with the necessary. He agreed, then told me what happened after he had gone to bed, absolutely shattered, close to midnight. He said he heard a kind of sobbing noise, but thought it was one of the boys making a noise in his sleep as sometimes happens. Again he heard it and, being on Dorm duty that night, thought he had better check. Nothing wrong in the dormitories, he was on his way back. He heard it again, coming from downstairs. He went down.

'And you know what Liam?' I shook my head. 'Well I'll tell you, honestly I could have wept. There was this little chap, squatting on the bottom stair, sobbing his heart out. He wanted his Mum and Dad. All the other parents had been, he sobbed, why couldn't his? But how could they Li? They were in China!'

'Ah, the poor little soul. What happened?' I asked sympathetically.

'Oh I couldn't do anything with him. He was too upset, and it was late, so I dug Matron out. Now there's a real Mum! If anyone could comfort him, she could. But I'll always remember it. It seemed such a shame, but that's one of the penalties of being rich. I suppose they gain a lot, but they also lose a lot, especially the children.'

'But what about the school holidays?' I asked. 'Surely they must see them then?'

246

He laughed. 'You must be joking,' he answered wryly, casting his eye along the line for any mis-behaviour.

'Why?' I asked.

'Summer schools,' he replied enigmatically.

'Summer schools?' I repeated. 'What are they?'

He winked. 'Ah now, that's a good question. Well, as you probably know, half the staff live in the area, so in the summer a lot of them take in the boys who either cannot get home, or whose parents cannot be with them. Simple eh?'

I looked at him in astonishment. 'The poor sods!' I replied without thinking.

He shushed me quickly then blew through his lips. 'Language old boy! Watch your language! The Head goes mad over that.'

I clapped my hand to my mouth. 'Sorry, I didn't think,' I said apologetically. Hell, I thought. I'd have to watch it. This wasn't the shipyard!

'You've always got to think in this kind of school, Liam, especially with Bodicea. She's got ears like an African elephant . . . Oh, just a second,' he added as another crocodile, female this time, approached on the other side of the road. 'Just drop back gradually and remind the perishers "hats off",' he ordered.

Mystified, I began the process, but they didn't need reminding, really. Every red cap with its white piping, including our own two trilbies, were raised in solemn courtesy as the girls walked by, with the two mistresses in charge giving a slight bow in our direction as they passed. Obviously there were several private schools in the area, because the ritual was repeated no less than four times during the walk.

I was tickled pink. 'Do they always do that?' I asked in amusement.

'Oh yes, sticklers for manners round here, absolute sticklers!'

'Are there many private schools, then?'

'This area? Oh yes, no end of them. Not cheap either!' he added knowingly.

'Well, it must cost a fair bit, I suppose,' I said, 'what with food, lodgings, books, things like that to provide.'

He burst out laughing. 'The first two yes, but for the rest the parents pay. It's not like the state schools, with everything free. Oh no, not private. Even if they cough, they pay, literally. After all, there's Matron, isn't there? And there's always someone who needs attention, so yes, they pay alright, nor is it easy, either. These kids are under supervision all day, every day. Every move is watched and organised. No tearing off home for them when school comes out at four o'clock. Oh no, they still have work to do. I wouldn't like it one little bit.'

'I think you're right, Harry,' I agreed after absorbing all this. 'It's certainly nice, but it's got some snags, and that's a fact. I'll tell you one thing,' I added, 'if I ever have any kids, I'll want to see them every night!'

He laughed. 'Chance would be a fine thing, wouldn't it?' he said.

Still, it had been a beautiful walk and for me, a very valuable lesson on my new job.

*　　*　　*

Within two weeks, a routine had developed and I got to know the boys very well, but off-duty, the evenings were different. Unlike home, there was nothing to do, and except for the three or four whom I had met on my immediate arrival, and now Harry, I found the Common Room a strange place. Most of the staff were wrapped in their own private worlds, with any conversation usually sporadic and mainly on subjects containing little in common with me. What repartee there was, usually from Horace and Alfred was, to my background, laborious. The fast outright wit I was born into just did not exist. Until I knew everyone better, I felt it was safer to listen, to be silent rather than gauche, for as sure as God made little apples, if I let my natural instincts run, I would put my foot straight in it. Yet it was not unfriendly . . . Just different. However, all was not lost. We had a portable gramophone, a wireless set and, most important to me, shelves of books, and I determined to make full use of them.

At the end of the month I got a delightful surprise, as Mr Milton walked into the Common Room. It felt like receiving a visitor from outer space! Unfortunately, with a full programme, I could not talk to him for long, but arranged to visit him on my half-day off, and what a happy half-day that was. He had a lovely house right on the sea front, with a middle-aged housekeeper who kept both him and the house in strict order. He was full of questions, about Antoinette, about home. Was I coping alright? Could he possibly help in any way? And, most important, did I like the job? I was sorry when the time came for me to leave. It had been a nice change from the monk-like existence in the school. Unfortunately we would not be able to repeat the pleasure, because within a couple of days he would be away on further advisory work and wouldn't be home before Christmas. He gave me his new address. If I was stuck in any way I must let him know. I took my leave reluctantly and returned to my cloistered world.

September passed in a whirl of activity. Every day was overflowing with work and I enjoyed every minute of it. The House spirit, as far as games were concerned, was fierce. Then, out of the blue I went down with tonsilitis and, because of it, found another surprising facet of the school and Common Room. I had felt a bit rough for a day or two, then, with a full day ahead of me on the programme on the first Sunday in October, I came back to my pew from Communion and conked out. Throat swollen and head swimming I felt myself hauled from the pew and half dragged up the stairs where I was put to bed. Within minutes, it seemed, Mrs

Jessop our buxom, homely matron was at my bedside ordering me to open my mouth, followed by a spatula to examine my throat. I felt guilty and embarrassed as she clucked concernedly, then nearly choked as she painted the back of my throat with a brush. In a flash I was a lad again with Mam doing exactly the same thing. I didn't like it then, and I didn't like it any better now.

'It'll do you good,' she said, just like Mam.

With my head swimming I didn't argue. Within half an hour the doctor, on permanent call to the school, examined me, approved her action, pronounced I was not at death's door and left.

The episode, unexpected and nasty for me though it was, was also a revelation. I found that, closed society it might be, but they really did care. Even Bodicea, I found, was very much maligned. Martinet she might be, more observant than a bald eagle she certainly was but, beneath it, if her concern for me was anything to go by, she was a real lady. My protestations that I would be fit for classes the following day were swept imperiously aside.

'Until you are well, Mr Sullivan, you will stay exactly where you are! Is that understood?'

I nodded as well as I could in the horizontal position. 'Yes Ma'am,' I croaked.

'Good, if there is anything you require, just inform Jenny. Incidently,' she added, bending slightly forward like an overloaded jib on a tall crane, 'Matron informs me that lemon juice would be efficacious at this point?' Matron nodded in agreement. 'Good,' she continued, 'I will have some sent along immediately.'

The room suddenly seemed to increase in size as she and Matron left. Within ten minutes Jenny arrived, a look of concern on her normally cheerful face.

'Ah sir . . . Poor you,' she said sympathetically as she poured out some hot lemon juice and placed it on the chair. 'The Missus said you have to drink this. All of it!'

I struggled upright. With the command from on high I had no option.

I was unused to illness, and it was, thank God, a short-lived crisis. Within three days, still a bit weak at the knees but with a clear head, I was up and about, with my whole conception of the school completely changed. Everyone had been so kind. After all, I was new and a comparative stranger, but it had made no difference. Apart from my two special friends Horace and Alfred, several others of the 'live-in' staff had also taken the trouble to pop in and cheer me up. It meant a great deal and for the first time since I arrived, I felt that I really belonged. Before the illness I had just been there, another disconnected island among several islands in a semi-hostile sea. So, fit again, it was with an entirely new perspective that I stood in front of the boys in the Main hall on the following Thursday.

It also made a difference to the Common Room atmosphere. Things opened up a little, not much, but a little, and with cautious steps I began to join in the odd conversation and so relaxed and integrated more confidently. With the boys, things were slotting into place quite nicely. They liked the work I laid on, and, with the usual odd exceptions, threw themselves wholeheartedly into a variety of games they had never played before, in addition to the normal P.E. schedule.

With so much going on, and competition between the Houses increasing, the time sped away. All the worries I had had on my journey down had long since vanished. I was having the time of my life. Before I knew it, there was just a week or two to go before the long Christmas holiday and the boys, most of whom I now knew by name, were well used to me chivvying them for Matron's morning parade for those in need, then Mass, breakfast, a busy morning as the classes rolled through, lunch, afternoon work, a cautious eye on free-time activities between lessons and supper. Then Prep supervision when my turn came round, hot drinks and biscuits before bedtime, dormitory duty whenever rostered for it, followed by either the library, Common Room, or bed for the few free hours that were available. It was a tight, strictly organised life, but, with a natural liking for order and discipline, I took to it like a duck to water. Now I knew what I wanted to do. I had found a role, and was determined to follow it up with proper training and a teaching career. At long, long last I was happy, and the final days fled before term end.

The morning of departure for the holidays, just seven days before Christmas, was one of those rare December days of brilliant sunshine with an invigorating nip in the air. A perfect day to keep the restless, excited boys occupied with a few games in the Quad as they waited amidst a mountain of luggage for their parents to pick them up. The whole spacious ground was a fever of excitement, especially for the younger ones as they waited with growing impatience. Some joined in the games, others, too excited, danced about, chattering like monkeys, as staff constantly prowled to quieten the more boisterous. All the while cars arrived and departed to squeals of delight or shouts of 'Happy Christmas!' — 'See you next term!' Bodicea and the Head were surrounded by pupils, greeting or saying goodbye to parents and no doubt thinking of the peace to come. By ten thirty, the Quad was emptying rapidly, with just a few remaining boys to be picked up. Soon I, too, would have to go. Already I was cutting it a bit fine for the eleven-fifteen train for which Alfred had kindly offered to drive me to the station. I saw him signal, then walk towards me.

'Alright boys,' I announced to the few still playing quoits over an imaginary net, 'I've got to go now, otherwise I'll miss my train.'

'Ah sir. Just one more point . . . Please!'

I shook my head. Alfred was already stabbing his finger at his watch. 'Sorry lads,' I said regretfully.

'Have a nice Christmas. You'd better go over to the Head and check your kit, alright? Safe journeys.'

I put my thumb up as Alfred signalled again, and went across to pick up my meagre luggage and say cheerio to the Head and Boadicea. We shook hands and wished each other a happy Christmas. I promised them that I would have the proposals for a Parents Open Day and display for the next term all worked out by the time I got back, then, with a final wave I got into Alfred's battered Morris Eight and chugged through the gates. We parted with good wishes at the station and, content and happy, and sure in the knowledge that at last I had the job I wished for, I flung myself gratefully into my compartment and gave myself up to thoughts of home.

I was so pleased with life I could have hugged myself. Four weeks holiday to come. Antoinette all to myself for the whole of her holiday, and all the things I had to tell them at home. Teresa especially would be delighted that I had settled, because of all the family, she had encouraged me most to strike out for something I really wanted. I had done that and she would love it. I could hardly wait to see them all, and, on top of everything else, it was Christmas . . . God in heaven! What more could I want?

17

My Dear Teresa

Comfortable, delighted to be going home, and with a thousand and one things to tell them when I arrived, I gazed contentedly out of the window at the lush, sunlit countryside flashing by. Quite suddenly the brilliant light began to fade as the sun clouded over, and the landscape became more and more obscured as we ran into thickening mist until, within an hour, we were labouring through a blanket of thick, clinging fog, blotting the world outside completely. Snug in my corner seat and lulled by the rhythmic beat of the wheels over the rail joints, I couldn't have cared less what was happening outside, as I closed my eyes and gave myself up to the pleasures to come.

The further we went, the darker it became and gradually, imperceptibly, the train slowed to a crawl that seemed to go on forever until, a good hour late, we crept stealthily into a strangely subdued Lime Street station. I was bitterly disappointed. With the fog thick enough to cut into slices, I knew that the ferries would be stopped, and if there was one thing I loved above all else when travelling home, it was to complete the final leg across the river by ferry, for once aboard I could lean over the rail and gaze at the bustling traffic on the turgid brown waters and know I was home. It never failed to bring back memories of childhood days, and the illicit fun we had had on the boats.

Disappointed, I groped my way through the snarling traffic and struggling crowds to the nearby underground station. On the other side of the river it was just as bad a 'pea souper', if not worse. Barely able to see my hand held up in front of me, with buses not running, I was not looking forward to the long walk ahead in this clinging, choking, all-enveloping and sinister blanket. For two solid hours, on a journey that should have taken a quarter of the time, I bumped and crashed into fellow travellers as my clothes became ever more sodden. I repeatedly took wrong turns and cursed until I found the right ones. I knocked at wrong doors until finally, tired, irritable and thoroughly exhausted, I knocked on the right door, knowing that within the hour at the most I would have to retrace my steps to ease their minds at home.

'Ah, you poor love,' said Antoinette as she opened the door and stood bathed in the hall light, 'you're soaked!'

I was but I didn't care as we fell into each other's arms. All the trials of the journey fell away as we hugged, kissed, and hugged again, then, banging my trilby against a sodden trouser leg, we walked into the warmth of the kitchen to be greeted by my relieved in-laws.

'That's one helluva fog out there!' I opined, as Antoinette took my case.

'Yes, and God help the sailors on a night like this,' intoned my mother-in-law, automatically expressing the traditional reaction of all Merseysiders in bad weather.

'Well . . . How was it?' asked Antoinette, as her mother vanished to get the tea.

'Great! absolutely great. Honest, I've got so much to tell you love . . .'

'Get yourself warm and have a cuppa before you do anything,' suggested her father, pulling a chair close to the fire for me.

I shook my head. 'No thanks, I don't want to get too comfortable, I've got to go home yet.'

Mrs Kavanagh stopped pouring the tea. 'You can't go out again Li! Not in this weather. Leave it till the morning. They'll understand.'

Again I shook my head.

'No, I'd better go. They'll be on tenter-hooks. You don't know me dad! He'll worry his soul case out if I don't go.'

'But I was just going to cook you something,' she complained.

I shrugged apologetically. 'Well thanks all the same but honest, I can't not go. They'll only worry.'

She gave in. 'Alright then, I understand. I'll make you a quick sandwich instead.' I nodded my thanks and minutes later was enjoying the snack, when Antoinette took her coat off the door.

'Where you going, luv?' I asked in surprise.

Her eyebrows raised. 'With you of course!'

I gave a horrified look. 'Oh no you're not. It's filthy out there. You'll catch your death of cold.'

She laughed at me. 'Oh yes I am!' she replied defiantly. Her mother and father grinned as I clucked disapprovingly, but I could see she meant it and shrugged in defeat.

'Oh, alright then, but get well wrapped up now.' She smiled as her father leaned forward and tapped my knee.

'Take my coat Li. That one's soaked,' he flicked his thumb at the back of the door where mine was hanging. 'Oh yes,' he added, 'if it'll fit you, there's a trilby there too.

'Whose goin' t'see it if it doesn't?' I asked with a grateful laugh. 'It's dry, that's the main thing.'

Five minutes later, feeling better for the impromptu meal, we were off, arms tightly linked, mufflers hiding our faces, and hats jammed tightly on our heads, as we struggled through the impenetrable fog for a tiring and silent hour. Dad opened the door to us.

'Oh, thanks be t'God you're safe!' he said as we shook hands. 'We were worried stiff.'

'We thought it was our Teresa,' broke in Bernadette as we walked into the kitchen and completed the greetings.

'Why, where is she?' I asked, surprised she wasn't there to greet us.

'She's round at Maggie Saunders',' replied Mam with a hint of worry. 'Went t'see the new baby.'

I knew Maggie well. She was an old friend of my sister's, living in the next street. 'How long has she been gone?' I asked, taking yet another cup of tea from Bernadette.

'Couple of hours,' she replied. 'It wasn't nearly as thick as this then . . . I thought she would have been back by now, especially with you comin' 'ome.'

I tried to ease their worries. 'She'll be alright Mam, don't worry y'self,' I said lightly. 'Y'know what those two are like when they get gassin', don't you?'

'Hmn, maybe,' murmured Mam.

I could see they were both very worried. 'Look,' I said, 'as soon as I get this down,' nodding at the cup, 'I'll nip round and fetch her, OK?'

Mam sighed with relief. With just a mouthful of tea to finish, the door knocker hammered heavily. We looked at each other in surprise. It was a very heavy knock for Teresa.

'Sounds like the bailiffs!' said Bernadette jokingly, as I dashed for the door. It wasn't Teresa, it was Maggie. She looked drawn.

'Where's Teresa?'

'You'd better come, Li. I don't think she's at all well.'

'What's up?'

'Well she started coughin' about an hour ago an' 'asn't stopped since.'

'Jesus wept!' I ejaculated. 'Hang on, I'll tell them.' I dashed back, told them what she'd said and before anyone could speak added, 'I'm goin' round to fetch her . . . Now don't worry!'

They would, but I had no time to discuss it. Seconds later, leaving the door ajar, we were gone. The fog was like a solid wall. Maggie was in a terrible state as we hurried through the door into the kitchen. Teresa, half bent over, sat close to the fire, her hair hanging over her face as she gasped for breath after another bout of coughing. A second later, as Maggie dashed upstairs to comfort her crying baby, I was kneeling, arm round by sister's shoulders, stunned with shock as she raised her head painfully and looked at me with haunted eyes, tears streaming down her pallid face as she gazed at me helplessly.

'What's up, luv?' I asked in stupid reaction. She shook her head, made to speak and started coughing again as Maggie, with the baby quiet once more, stood anxiously by.

'Fetch her coat Maggie,' I said urgently.

'But warrabout the fog?' she gasped.

I was in a dilemma. I couldn't leave her there. She had to be taken home and put to bed. I comforted myself by thinking it would only take a few minutes.

'I'll carry 'er!' I snapped, tense with worry. 'Let's have one'f your scarves.' She dashed to a drawer and returned almost before I had finished. I turned back to my sister. 'I'm gonna carry yeh, luv, now don't worry!' I explained as we put her coat round her, wrapping her own scarf round her head and Maggie's round her mouth to keep the fog at bay. 'Look, Maggie. Could you nip down and tell our Bernadette to fetch the doctor?'

'But warrabout the . . .' I knew what she was thinking.

'Tell her t'go to Harry's. He won't mind her usin' 'is phone.' Without speaking, she was gone. Thank God the baby upstairs was still asleep, I thought, as I picked up the feather weight of my sister to cradle her in my arms. Then, head down to protect her, and snuggling her close against the weather, I crept my way forward, cursing silently as the fog caught her throat and made her cough again.

Anxious faces greeted us as, forewarned by Maggie, they made way for me, then crowded tensely as I laid her tenderly on the sofa. She looked dreadful. Maggie had been quick but Bernadette was even quicker. I looked at her questioningly as Mam bent over the painwracked figure.

Bernadette nodded. 'Doctor's on his way,' she said. 'Fog might hold 'im up, though,' she added, adjusting the coverings over Teresa while Dad, with Antoinette's arm round his shoulders, stood gazing in agonised disbelief at his favourite child. I hoped the doctor would get through. Within minutes our prayers were answered. Teresa had been his patient for years and there was no ceremony. One look at her, a quick examination and he announced his verdict. She was very ill. The ambulance would be ordered immediately.

'Keep her warm, but don't give her anything. Where's the nearest phone?'

'Harry at the corner shop. He'll let you use his.'

'Good,' he said, vanishing as quickly as he had come.

There are moments when time itself seems to stand still, when mankind, for all its arrogance, is revealed in its true pathetic frailty. This was such a moment, when all you could do was to stand, mind screaming in silent futility as a loved one is stricken and beyond the help you so desperately yearn to render. At such a moment the picture before your eyes becomes etched in the memory for the remainder of your life, and the seconds drip, drip away with agonising remorselessness, leaving only prayer as a last resort. All the time, eyes closed, Teresa turned restlessly as the spasms swept her. At last, at long, long last, I heard the subdued sound of a motor, and the tension broke as I dashed up the hall and opened the door.

'Sorry mate,' the ambulance man said as I stood aside to let them through, 'but it's murder out there!'

I nodded and followed. Within minutes, with tender efficiency, and wrapped warm against the raw night, they had her inside the ambulance, with Bernadette beside her.

I gave Mam and Dad a hug in turn. 'Try not to worry,' I pleaded, 'she'll be alright once she's in hospital.' I hoped I was right. Oh God, how I hoped I was right, as I watched them slump in their chairs like zombies. I went to join the ambulance, with Antoinette holding my hand. 'Try and comfort them, luv, will yeh? It's been a helluva shock for them. Go on now,' I added as the fog swirled through the open door. 'Get back inside.'

In the subdued light of the ambulance, the scene was unreal as Teresa, restless and moaning slightly, was soothed by Bernadette. The ambulance man, witnessing such things everyday of his life, sat on his little seat, concerned but as helpless as ourselves, while I, numb with shock at the terrifying turn of events, silently watched a scene in which I did not physically belong. Surely it was a nightmare from which I would soon awake?

I felt a surge of relief as the engine fired and the ambulance started forward on a journey that beggars description. It was at once terrifying and maddening. I felt like screaming at the halting progress and all the while, like the baleful wailing of a banshee, came the continuous deadened, but deep-throated roar of the foghorns, as ships, blinded and cautious, edged over the invisible surface of the nearby river. A journey which, even in the heaviest of traffic, should have taken no more than five or ten minutes, stretched, in the all-pervading fog, to almost an hour of nerve-racking tension.

Suddenly it ended and the tension broke in a frenzy of activity, as we drew up at the hospital reception. Without waiting for the driver, the ambulance man and I manhandled the stretcher to a waiting trolley. A nurse waited in the corridor as the driver joined us. Taking one look at Teresa she flew for the doctor and, leaving Bernadette at the entrance, we ran the trolley along the corridor, past startled nurses and into a reception room. The ambulance man looked at me sorrowfully as we came to rest.

'Sorry mate,' said the driver, 'I just couldn't go any faster.'

I touched his shoulder understandingly. 'I know. You did your best, mate, and I'm grateful. Thanks.' I looked at Teresa as they left. Eyes closed, deathly pale, with lips moving spasmodically, she looked awful as I leaned over and gently smoothed her tousled hair. 'Shssh! my love. The doctor will be here in a minute.'

Her lips moved again, I bent closer to catch her mumbled words. 'Don't let them take me away, Li, will you?'

I ran my fingers lightly across her damp forehead. 'Don't worry my love . . . I won't.' Her face relaxed and my heart plummeted. This was not the relaxation of sleep, she was slipping away. I had seen too many good friends slip away in these past few years not to know the truth of what was happening. Every nerve in me felt like screaming in helpless frustration as I took the limp hand in mine and stroked it gently. *Where the hell was that doctor?* It seemed hours since the nurse had gone to fetch him, but I knew in my heart it was only a minute or two. My heart pounded again as her face relaxed even more and her eyes opened slightly. My hand tightened on hers instinctively. With an awful certainty I knew it would not be long.

'Teresa!' I whispered with quiet urgency. Her eyes fluttered momentarily, then were still and a tell-tale, blood-speckled froth appeared between her pallid lips. It was over!

'Teresa!' I repeated desperately, knowing it was useless. Oh God no! Not Teresa! Urgent footsteps sounded behind me. The doctor, young, and obviously tired, felt for a pulse, close-checked her breathing, then slowly placed his hand on my shoulder.

'She's gone,' he said simply.

I nodded. 'I know,' I replied in a voice so distant, so

261

detached, I could not recognise it as my own. I could not even cry as I sat gazing at the small, still form in disbelief, then, by sheer reflex, I placed my forefinger and thumb over her eyes and closed then. The action seemed to release my frozen brain, and a thousand thoughts began to tumble in incoherent chaos. How could I tell Mam and Dad? Mam, I knew, would be strong and show little outward emotion, though she would feel it to a depth no one would ever know, for she had had to be strong. But Dad — Teresa was his special favourite. It would kill him. Suddenly I remembered Bernadette waiting in the corridor outside. How was I to tell her? I didn't know, I was too confused so, like a frightened animal that will always revert to familiar actions to console itself, I too, in this traumatic moment, allowed nature to take over and, gently, quietly, with my head in a whirl, methodically smoothed her rumpled hair, stroked her forehead and laid her arms one upon the other, before drawing the cover over her. She looked as peaceful as though she were sleeping, so, with a final kiss and the sign of the cross on her forehead, I left her.

With but a step to enter the corridor, and a terrifying message to deliver to an unsuspecting Bernadette, I hesitated, turned, and gazed at the silent bier, blessed myself in reflex ritual, then, dry-eyed, heart pounding, I stepped into the corridor. Bernadette, waiting at the far end, saw me and started forward. Helplessly I stood, arms held out from my side with palms facing her and shrugged in a gesture more eloquent than words. She stopped in her tracks, hands flying to her mouth in horror, then collapsed on to a nearby seat, head buried in her hands, sobbing like a child. Still I could not, dare not cry. There would be much to do and it would need a clear head; I would have all my life to cry. For Mam's sake I dare not.

I sat beside Bernadette and put my arm round her shoulders.

'Come on, luv,' I said softly, 'we'll have to get home. There's nothing more we can do here.'

'What about me Mam and Dad? How are we goin' t'tell them?'

I shook my head. 'We'll talk about it on the way home, luv. Come on, we'd better go. Let's hope the fog's lifted.'

It hadn't. We had to walk every foot of the way, which was really a blessing in disguise. By the time we reached home we knew exactly what we must do, and I would break the news.

With a sinking heart I opened the door. Antoinette must have heard it and came to meet me as I walked up the hall. It seemed a mile long. I heard my brother-in-law's voice in the kitchen. Obviously worried about Bernadette, he had come looking for her. I silently thanked God. He would be a big help. Antoinette's hand suddenly tensed in mine as I whispered the news to her as we walked into the kitchen.

I felt strangely detached as we walked in, yet startlingly alert. Every move they made, every fleeting expression etched itself into my memory, as all eyes turned to me.

'How is she?' asked Mam, sitting in her usual place near the wireless.

I shook my head slowly from side to side dragging the words from my very depths. 'She's dead,' I said simply, and was appalled at the effect.

'Oh my God!' gasped Mam with a peculiar flatness in her voice as she rose, walked to the kitchen door, turned, went back to her chair and sat down, frozen into dry-eyed stillness.

'Jesus, Mary, and Joseph!' cried Dad in disbelief, half rising then slumping back in a flood of tears.

Jimmy's arm went round his shoulders in fruitless comfort. 'Alright, Pat,' he said soothingly, 'lerr'it all go . . . It'll do yeh good. Come on old son,' he continued as Dad's shoulders heaved, 'you'll be alright.'

I felt helpless as Bernadette went to Mam. Mam shook her head as my sister bent over her. 'I'll be alright luv, don't worry now, just leave me alone for a few minutes.'

There was nothing I could do except watch. If only Mam would cry, I would feel easier. I gave Antoinette's hand a squeeze. 'Come on luv,' I said, 'let's make a cuppa tea . . . We could all do with one.'

It would, I knew, be a long, long night. Already late, there were a million things to think about and Jimmy and Bernadette would have to get home to their family. Antoinette would have to go, too. Already, with the dense fog, her parents would be worried stiff, but she had a ready answer. Their neighbours had a phone. She would find a phone box and set their minds at rest. I refused to let her go. It was so thick outside, she might have an accident, or get lost. I could not leave, not tonight, no matter what happened.

Jimmy came to my rescue. 'Give us the number, will yeh, luv. I'll nip down to 'arry's, 'e won't mind!' He went and I felt a lot happier. Within five minutes he was back.

'Everything alright?' I asked him. He nodded. 'What did Harry say?'

He smiled. 'Oh y'now 'arry, easy come, easy go. Anytime yeh want t'use it, 'e said, just knock.'

'Good,' I replied, relieved. That would be a big help. But the family had to be told.

'That's alright, Li,' said Jimmy, 'I'll see to that. I'll drop Bernadette, then nip round to Con's. He'll tell Aunt Min an' she can pass it on, right?'

I nodded gratefully. With immediate problems solved, the first terrifying trauma passed as they left.

I put my arm round Mam, as Antoinette comforted Dad. Still dry-eyed and silent, Mam relaxed a little.

'Are you alright, Mam?'

She shook her head wearily. 'I'll be alright Li . . . Don't worry y'self, lad.'

'Why don't you have a good cry?' I pleaded, as Antoinette anxiously watched Dad slumped in his chair, now dry-eyed but looking a hundred years old.

Again Mam shook her head at my question. 'Tears won't bring her back Li. If only they would. But there, that's God's will, I'm just glad you're home. There's a lot t'do.'

'Why don't you go up to bed, then?'

She moved her head sadly. 'No, no, I couldn't sleep t'night Li. I just couldn't!'

I turned to Dad for help. 'Come on Dad. Go up t'bed. Please!' I added persuasively, looking from one to the other. 'There's nothing you can do now, is there?'

'At least you'll get some rest, Mr Sullivan,' broke in Antoinette. A few more minutes' persuasion and they reluctantly agreed. My heart went out to them. What a cruel thing to happen to them after all they had gone through. It just wasn't fair.

With them safely upstairs and hopefully resting, I tried to persuade Antoinette to go to bed, but she refused to leave me alone.

'Alright then luv, stay down, but at least get a couple of hours rest on the sofa there. It's goin' t'be a busy day tomorrow. Come on, luv. Please.'

'What about you?' she asked worriedly.

I gave her a hug. 'Don't worry, I'm alright, honest. One night up won't harm me, I know. Anyway, I'll make another pot of tea. There's a lot of sorting out t'do before mornin' y'know: the undertaker, arranging to bring her home, insurance, all sorts of things. Now don't worry. I'll get a cat nap. Now you settle down there and I'll cover you up.'

Ten minutes later she was fast asleep with exhaustion, and the house fell into an uneasy silence.

It seemed an age since I had set out with so much joy from the excited boys in the sunlit quadrangle, yet it was but twelve hours. Was it possible to travel from heaven to horrifying hell in so short a time? Was it possible that all the things I had so looked forward to telling my dear sister would have to remain forever unsaid? What a cruel, capricious thing fate was. How unjust to strike at one so innocent, so happy despite her burden. To strike again at Mam and Dad in such a way after all they had gone through. A restless movement on the sofa brought my mind back to grim reality as Antoinette moved in her troubled sleep. I rose, kissed her gently on the forehead and thought again of Teresa. It seemed impossible that I had performed the same ritual on an equally unlined face such a short time ago. In the depths of my misery I silently ran through a prayer that had been a favourite all my life, and which had brought comfort in times of great stress during the recent war:

O Sacred heart of Jesus I place my trust in thee.
Whatever may befall me Lord, though dark the hours may be,
In all my joys, in all my woes, when naught but grief I see,
O Sacred heart of Jesus, I place my trust in thee.

In the peace and quiet of the silent house I sat down once again. The enormity of the tragedy hit me like a delayed thunderbolt, and the tears rolled down my cheeks unchecked.

18

Nemesis

Cramped and confused from a restless night of disjointed dreams in Dad's armchair, I awoke, not quite knowing where I was, until, exhausted and mentally recoiling from the full horror of what had happened the previous night, I struggled for long moments to bring my emotions under control, to bring order into the chaos of my mind. It would be a busy, soul-destroying day I knew, but, like a mountain that had to be climbed, simply because there was no way round it, I too, and without emotion, would have to encompass the task ahead. If I did not, then the burden would fall upon those least able to bear it.

With Con newly back at work after the strike, with his own home to see to and wages to earn, it would not be fair on him, even though it would traditionally be his responsibility. Nor would it be fair to Bernadette, with her first natural duty to her own family, although she would be a great help as always. No, this was my job, and I thanked God for the four weeks break I had at my disposal and prayed that the emotions tearing me apart would not be visible, emotions that were strange to me, despite the killing I had seen. This was personal. This was my own flesh and blood, my Teresa, friend and favourite from early childhood. Oh no, this would not go away — ever! But today there was work to be done and my feelings were of no consequence. Only Mam and Dad mattered, and they had burden enough.

A rustle on the sofa broke my thoughts, and I turned to see Antoinette rubbing her eyes.

I crossed the room and bent anxiously over her. 'Are you alright my love?' I asked as she awakened fully. She nodded and I kissed her.

'How are your Mum and Dad?'

I shook my head, I hadn't heard anything and hoped that they had managed to sleep. 'Look, you stay there for a few minutes, love, I'll put the kettle on.'

She moved her head wearily, her eyes misting over as reality came into her consciousness. She, too, would miss Teresa badly.

I smoothed her forehead and gently admonished her, 'Now don't upset yourself.' I continued quietly, 'It won't do any good if we break down now, will it? I'll just go and make the tea.'

She objected. 'No, I'll make it, I'll feel better.'

I agreed. 'Alright then, I'll just creep upstairs and see how they are.' Mam was wide awake and sitting up. But Dad lay huddled and silent. 'How are you?' I mouthed silently.

She shrugged dejectedly, her waist-long, iron grey hair cascading over her white-clad shoulders. 'It's your father I'm worried about,' she whispered. 'He's taken it bad!'

'Antoinette's makin' some tea,' I whispered back in an effort not to disturb Dad. 'I'll bring you one up in a minute.' She nodded as I crept out of the room. It was just half past five when Antoinette brought the tea in. I could hear Mam upstairs. She must be getting up. She never was one for lying in.

'Don't pour Mam's out. She'll be down in a minute,' I suggested. Sure enough, her footsteps sounded on the stairs as I took my first grateful sip.

Neat as a new pin as always, but deathly pale, she took the cup from Antoinette and sat in her usual place. I was shocked into silence. She looked haggard, eyes lacklustre and knuckles showing white as she grasped the cup.

'How are yeh, Mam?' I asked anxiously.

She gave me a wan smile as she looked into my worried eyes. 'Oh I'm alright Li. Now stop worryin', lad. It's God's will and that's that.' Antoinette suggested another cup of tea. She accepted it.

'Anything to eat Mam?' I asked hopefully.

'No thanks Li, I just couldn't gerr'it down, honest!'

I questioned her about Dad — was he asleep? She told me no. He was just lying there, staring blankly.

Her eyes misted up as she spoke. 'Honest t'God Li,' she said sorrowfully, 'I don't think he'll ever get over it. Y'know 'ow 'e loved Teresa. Always did, from a baby.'

'I'll take him a cuppa tea up. Have a chat with him, eh?'

She agreed. 'But,' she warned as I filled the cup, 'be careful what you say now. I've never seen him like this in my life.'

A few minutes later I knew what she meant. His craggy face had aged visibly as he sat up, staring straight ahead of him. 'I've brought you a cuppa tea Dad. How yeh feelin?'

'Teresa,' he said, as I laid the cup down, 'why Teresa? She never 'armed anyone in 'er life!' His voice was flat and subdued, as though speaking to himself. Remembering Mam's warning, I made no comment. He looked dazed.

'Come on Dad,' I said encouragingly, 'get that down yeh. It'll do you good.'

'Alright Li,' he answered without looking at me. 'In a minute son.'

I stood, desperately trying to find the right words when the doorbell rang. I dashed downstairs. It was Con on his way to work.

'I came round last night, but the place was in darkness, so I didn't want to disturb anythin' in case they were asleep. Jimmy told Edie you were 'ere,' he said in answer to my unspoken query.

'You were out then, early on?'

He grimaced. 'Yeah, flamin' Union meetin', went on for hours! 'Ow's me mam and dad?' he added as we walked up the hall. Without waiting for an answer he went straight over to Mam and put his arms round her. For the first time she broke down and they wept together. I was glad to see her cry. It would relieve the tension for her, but I was sorry for Con, as his shoulders heaved uncontrollably. ''Ow's me dad?' he asked, turning a tear-stained face to me, as Antoinette went across to soothe Mam.

'Rough,' I replied, 'I don't like the look of him at all. You know how fond he was of her?'

'I'll nip up and see 'im,' he said, wiping his eyes.

'Look,' I said warningly, 'don't let him see you upset now, will you? And if he's asleep, leave him, OK?' Without a word he left, returning almost immediately, face drawn with anxiety. 'What's up?' I demanded sharply, fearing God knows what.

''e's sorta dozin', like. Come an' 'ave a look.' We both flew upstairs. Dad was still half slumped in the bed, eyes closed, breathing gently. My pounding heart eased a little.

'Dad,' I whispered. He stirred uneasily as we eased him into a more comfortable position. 'He'll be alright,' I said quietly. 'Come on, let him rest.' Con refused to move. I tugged his arm as the tears began to flow again. 'Now look Con,' I whispered urgently, 'don't you upset y'self. You've got to go t'work. You can't take time off now, can you? And anyway, there's nothing you can do, so come on.'

I felt sorry, but we had to be practical. He was already on his uppers through the strike. Losing more money wouldn't help Teresa, but, like me, he was torn with conflicting emotions. Common sense won, but he wasn't happy.

'Now luk Li,' he said urgently as we reached the hall, 'for Christ's sake, if anythin' goes wrong with either of them, get down t'that bloody Yard as quick as yeh can, alright?'

I tried to calm him. 'OK, but for God's sake stop worryin' y'self. I've got four weeks holiday so I'll see to everything. It's no good you takin' time off, is it? There's nothing you can do that I can't, so you'd only be throwin' good money down the drain. Come on now,' I urged as he hesitated, 'use your noddle. Y'would, wouldn't yeh?'

'But I wanna help, Li! There's a lot t'do an' it's not fair on you.'

'Now luk Con,' I said firmly, 'you know as well as I do, that this place'll be like Crewe Station by nine o'clock. You won't be able to move, never mind help, so come on. Me mam's not daft, y'know. She knows you've gorra go t'work. You'll have to take time off for the funeral as it is, anyroad.'

'Alright then,' he agreed reluctantly, 'Edie'll be round as soon as it gets light. I'll go'n say tarrar t'me mam.'

Within minutes of him leaving, Mrs Hannigan, our next door neighbour, the first of a multitude of friends, neighbours and relatives, arrived. From that moment and for a week afterwards the house was never still, and while Mam chatted I took the opportunity of getting Antoinette on her own to try to sort out how we would arrange things. But first I wanted her to get some rest. Poor love, she looked and was shattered and I knew she had a lot of college work to do. At first she objected to my suggestion that she should go home and get some sleep.

'Oh Li, I couldn't!'

I pointed out that it wouldn't help if she went down as well. We were still discussing it when the bell rang again. It was Aunts Min and Sarah, with Aunt Min gasping like an old steam engine in the semi-darkness.

'Mother'f God!' she gasped. 'What a thing to 'appen! How are they?' Without waiting for an answer they

271

brushed past me into the kitchen. Moments later all three were weeping together by the fire. I went through to the back kitchen where Mrs Hannigan was busy making tea.

'Tell me mam I've taken Antoinette home, will you luv? I'll be back in about an hour.'

'Ah sure I'll do that f'yeh alright. Don't worry y'self now, I'll luk after things 'ere. Go on lad, off with yiz.'

With convenient buses, and Antoinette safe at home, I was back well within the hour. The kitchen was still full of subdued chatter and I was glad to see that Dad was downstairs, sitting in his chair and talking quietly to Uncle Matt beside him. It was a good time to get to work.

With the parlour made ready for her homecoming, and the carefully hoarded insurance policies taken from their resting place, I examined and made them ready to present to the insurance people. Then I was all set to go. It proved to be a weird, unreal and interminable trek round the cold and still foggy town to all the offices involved in the arrangements. Oddly, I felt resentful as I ploughed resolutely through the noisy, bitterly cold streets. Didn't these chattering people know I had lost my sister? Didn't they understand my family was desolate? What the hell were they so happy about? God knows why, but I felt hurt and disappointed in the cool, efficient offices, in the cold unfeeling way they unconcernedly sorted their papers, mouthing their emotionless sympathy as they methodically crashed their official stamps on the documents, then intoned 'Next Please!'. I'd seen more emotion in the Lairage and it made me mad. This was Teresa, our Teresa! Didn't they know that? It would be days before that odd resentment wore off and I realised that the world, busy with its own affairs, was totally indifferent.

With Saturday half-day closing, it had been a nerve-shattering rush to beat the clock, but, just coming up to one o'clock, I had completed it and returned to a packed house, exhausted. I met Con, still filthy from his work, half-way up the path, anxious to know how they were. I told him I'd only just got back, but we needn't have worried. Mam and Dad were surrounded by people. Even Sister Agnes from the nearby Convent was there, sleeves rolled up, seeing to people's needs, while Father O'Brien, over in a corner, talked quietly but earnestly to Dad, who, thankfully, looked a lot better than when I went out.

'Where's Antoinette?' asked Con in surprise.

'Sent her home to get some rest and some college work done. She'll be back this afternoon.'

'Very sensible. Have yeh been to the hospital yet?' He was upset when I mentioned that they had suggested an autopsy, presumably because she was so young, but he settled down when I told him I had refused. She had been under the doctor so there was no need, and I was damned if she was going to be cut up for no good reason. Had I told Mam and Dad about it? he asked. No I hadn't. They had more than enough on their plates without telling them that. Maybe I'd tell them later, I suggested, see how things went. He still felt guilty about not giving me more of a hand, but was reassured when I went through with him everything I had done, but he still felt guilty. I had an idea to settle him.

'I'll tell you what would be a help, Con. You could keep an eye on Dad over the weekend, because I won't have time to take him out for a jar. If he got down to the Club with his mates he might feel a bit better.'

Con cheered up. 'Don't worry about it,' he replied with relief, 'me an' Uncle Matt'll luk after 'im. You and your missus keep your eye on me mam. Don't worry, he'll be OK'

With a final confirmation to him that Teresa, Lord rest her, would be home on Monday, taken to Church on Wednesday night, with the funeral on Thursday after Requiem Mass, he made his way through the crowded room into the back kitchen where Edie, his quiet, mouse-like wife, was helping with the washing up, to tell her to hang on there because he would be straight back as soon as he was washed and changed.

At three o'clock Antoinette, looking a lot more relaxed, arrived with her mother and father to join the constantly moving visitors, who had come and gone in a continuous stream since first light. Everything that could be done had been done, so we decided to go for a walk. Mam said it would do us good. It did. I was glad to hear during it that Antoinette had managed to get a little sleep.

On Sunday we went to Mass, neither listening nor hearing, but thinking a lot. The resentment of yesterday returned, together with some cynicism, as I watched the priest perform his ritualistic homage to God. I felt suddenly bitter. Who the hell was this much-vaunted and supposedly just God, who could snatch away so innocent a life? Where was this justice meted out to the good? Teresa had been good! None better. She never complained, was always cheerful, and would help anybody at the drop of a hat, so where was the justice? Why should she have her husband and home blown to pieces, lose her only child, and now have her very life taken, if good is supposed to triumph over evil? This, I thought savagely as I knelt and watched, is nothing but claptrap!

Antoinette must have felt my tension. 'Are you alright?' she whispered anxiously. Suddenly my patience snapped.

'No I'm flamin' well not!' I hissed in reply. 'Let's get to hell out of 'ere. It doesn't mean a bloody thing!'

We left the church in angry silence. I didn't even bless myself in the Holy Water font on the way out. I felt angry, bitter, and rebellious, and it took all her patient coaxing to snap me out of it. By the time we reached home I was calm again but still bitter.

*　　*　　*

Monday dawned in a cold, misty drizzle that suited my mood to perfection. At ten, Teresa came home for the last time. With the world outside working a normal day, the house, except for Dad and me, was packed with women. It was an eerie feeling to see one, normally so jolly, so lively, lying so still, her waxen face smoothed in a timeless peace. With the candles lit, and first respects paid in tearful silence, I knew that this was a special moment for Mam and Dad, and quietly insisted that they should spend these final precious moments with her alone. What fearful, unexplained emotions they must have felt. To have brought a child into the world, to love, nurture and defend her through all the horrors of poverty, then, with all hardships overcome, to lose her in the prime of her years! With a final glance at her serene face I left them in the flower-scented room, heads bowed, kneeling before the silent form, praying quietly to their pitiless God.

All day they came, some were complete strangers to me, in a continuous, ever-changing stream to pay their last respects; and in the evening, all immediate family except Bernadette's two youngest, came to count their beads in the Rosary. With Con on my left, and Seamus my nephew on my right, Aunt Min, who couldn't kneel, sitting at the head of the coffin, and those who could not fit into the tiny room kneeling in the small hall, I led them in the Rosary, the long repetitive homage to the Virgin Mary. There is no more solemn time in a Catholic house than this, but human frailty does not recognise solemnity, and I could see out of the corner of my eye, that Con was uncomfortable and hoped fervently that he was not going to get cramp as he normally did if he stayed in one position too long. But he did! Mam and Dad kept looking at him anxiously as I prayed on with the first part of each Hail Mary, with the assembled mourners completing the prayer en masse.

With two decades of the Rosary gone and another three to go, each with ten Hail Mary's, one Our Father, and a Glory be, my heart went out to him as he squirmed and wriggled in pain. With decreasing concentration I ploughed on relentlessly. Seamus, ever a giggler, followed the prayers and responses by habit, though his mind was obviously elsewhere. Suddenly, half-way through a response, it happened.

'Ooh, OW . . . Oh God. Cor, flippin' 'ech!' exclaimed Con in a strangled whisper as the cramp took hold. Unfortunately the solemnity of death is lost on youth, and Seamus started to giggle. It was not his fault. I was the same at his age, but I gave him a ferocious look on principle. He quietened but it was too late. Con, tormented with pain, suddenly rocketed to his feet and ploughed unceremoniously through the kneeling mourners to relieve his leg. Despite myself I had to laugh, and was consoled by the fact that if Teresa could have laughed, she would have gone off into fits.

The unexpected chaos grew as the doorbell rang. With the hall jammed with kneeling people the door could be scarcely opened, but when it did, it was a saviour. Father O'Brien came in and seconds later the mourners, once more solemn, took up where they left off with the priest as leader whilst I joined Con tramping up and down the back yard trying to get his leg right. It all proved a point of hilarity later. For two nights we waked her in the old tradition. It was a strange mixture of sadness and quiet merriment as anecdotes from her life were recounted. A time of story telling of days long gone, of hopes achieved or dashed, tragedies overcome, a kaleidescope of flickering scenes on a verbal screen surrounding her, as she rested among her family and friends for the last time. O my love, what a tragic, tragic waste!

All too soon the evening of her departure came and I felt an irrational fear as they prepared Teresa for the long and lonely sojourn before the High Altar in a darkened church, in preparation for her Requiem on the morrow. She had always been afraid of the dark, but it had to be. All my bitterness and rebellion returned as we moved out into the clinging fog on the short, unreal journey. On the final day, bitterness still gnawed as the priest intoned the *De Profundis*. Not all the pomp, the prayers, the sprinkling of Holy Water could purge it from me, and again as the Mass proceeded, Antoinette asked me if I was alright.

'Don't worry,' I whispered, 'just a bit upset, that's all. I'll be better after the funeral . . .' I wasn't, though. Even the final solemnity of the burial prayers left me stone cold, as I stood holding Mam's hand, Con at my other side with his arm round Dad's shoulders. At last it was done, and with the final sprinkling of earth, the priest and his accolytes, with his Holy Water and book of ritualistic soporifics, took their departure. The mourners, too, would depart after the traditional small meal on our return. They also would pick up the threads of life, and the house would be silent. Then, and only then, would the memories come flooding back. For the first time the family circle had been broken and the consequences as yet unknown. Despite my bitterness and the futility I felt of prayer, indoctrination was too strong, and I placed my trust yet again in the God I had so recently cursed.

For two weeks the turbulence gradually eased, then settled. Mam, with the loving care of Antoinette, Bernadette, and the virtually constant company of Aunts Min and Sarah, fought back well, but Dad had received a blow which seemed to drain the very life from him. Then, with just two weeks gone, this strange God struck again. It happened with such terrifying normality that it was petrifying. With Antoinette due to go back to college the following day, and with Aunt

277

Min keeping Mam and Dad company, we had just returned from a peaceful walk. With welcome cups of tea in our hands we sat on the sofa, whilst Dad relaxed in his chair, eyes closed, empty cup on the floor beside him. Mam and Aunt Min, sitting quietly chatting at the table began to fill their cups when Mam, seeing Dad's cup empty, called across.

'Pat, d'yeh want any more tea?'

There was no answer.

'Oh, he's dropped off again,' said Aunt Min with a smile.

I looked at the top of his head over the chair in front of me and grinned at Antoinette. 'He's sure driving them home, isn't he?' I said. 'It'll do him good.' Then I looked again. He didn't seem very comfortable, so I rose to ease him in his chair. I stopped as I came face to face with him and fear clawed at me. I leaned over him. 'Dad,' I whispered, in case I startled him. He didn't move. I shook him gently. His arm dropped lifelessly from the arm of the chair and I went cold from shock.

'What's up?' asked Mam, as I turned to face them.

I shrugged and turned back in near panic to feel his pulse. There wasn't one! Then everything happened at once. Aunt Min heaved herself up faster than I had ever seen her move, but Mam was quicker. She leaned over, gently touching his cheek.

'Oh my God no! Not again!' she gasped.

I caught her as she went down and Aunt Min, white faced and shaking, collapsed into her chair. 'Go next door,' I snapped to Antoinette, sitting wide-eyed on the sofa. 'Fetch Mrs Hannigan. Quick!' She hesitated in bewilderment. 'Hurry up!' I snapped again, as I laid Mam on the sofa. With everyone in a complete daze, all hell seemed to break loose. Mrs Hannigan appeared like a Jack-in-the-box, took one look and dashed back for her husband. I started down the hall.

'Where are you going?' gasped Antoinette.

'Doctor!' I shouted back. 'Be back in a few minutes.

Go round and tell our Con — Quick!'

Poor Antoinette, I felt sorry for her, but there was no time for sentiment. She was still gazing at me as I dashed through the door. I was lucky and just caught the doctor at the end of his surgery. He dropped everything and bundled me into his car. We arrived in minutes, but it was all too late.

'I'm sorry, Mrs Sullivan,' he said to Mam, now sitting, badly shaken, on the sofa, 'I'm afraid he's gone.'

Con flew through the door, white faced and breathless. 'Oh my God!' he said as he wrapped Mam in his arms. 'Not Dad too? Come on, Mam, you and Aunt Min come round to ours.'

She looked at Dad and made to object. I added my voice to Con's.

'Con's right, Mam. Come on now, you can't do anythin' here for the minute. You go with him.'

'I'll stay 'ere Mary,' broke in Aunt Min as Antoinette helped Mam on with her coat. 'Oh luv,' she added to a shaken Antoinette, 'you go with her, will yeh? I'll be round later, alright?'

Antoinette looked at me. I nodded agreement. With Con's arm protectively round her on one side, and Antoinette on the other, they set off for the short walk to Con's.

'Now don't worry,' Aunt Min called after them, 'Mrs Hannigan and me'll see to things 'ere.'

With Mam safe for the moment, I headed for Bernadette's. She knew something was wrong the moment she set eyes on me, and her hand went to her mouth. 'What's up? Is it me mam?'

I shook my head. 'No it's me dad. He's gone!' I replied bluntly.

She gazed disbelievingly. 'Y'mean . . .?'

I confirmed it. 'Died in his sleep . . . Just like that!' I snapped finger and thumb together.

'Bloody 'ell!' said Jimmy. 'When?'

279

'Five or ten minutes ago. Mam's round at Con's with Antoinette. Aunt Min an' Mrs Hannigan's in ours. Will you come an' give us a hand, Jimmy? We'll have to gerr'im upstairs, somehow. Con should be there when we get back.'

Jimmy nodded and turned to Seamus.

'Y'mean me grandad's dead?' asked Seamus, before his father could speak.

'Aye,' snapped Jimmy. 'Now you watch the kids . . . Understand? Yeh mam's goin' round to Uncle Con's, an' I'm goin' t'yeh Grandad's, so I want no flamin' nonsense, right? Make sure the kids get t'bed and stay there. If they want their mam tell 'em to shurrup an' get back t'sleep, OK?'

Seamus looked at his short, pugnacious father. He knew him too well to disobey, and nodded silently.

It was a frenetic night. Between us we got Dad upstairs and on the bed. The women would lay him out, and there was nothing more we could do. With Con having a cigarette to quieten his nerves, I joined a still shocked Antoinette, who had returned with him, in the back kitchen making yet more tea. We looked at each other solemnly. I had two weeks holiday still to run, but I knew in my heart that there was no way I could go back now. Mam, already battered and aged beyond measure by Teresa's death, would now be on her own. I knew from long experience that she would not think of living either with Con or Bernadette, however much they wanted her to. All her life she had lived on her own floor where, as she said, she could close the door on her troubles. Only once had she broken that strict rule, when we moved from the narrow street where I was born, into a bigger house with Bernadette and Jimmy. Improvement though it had been for all of us, it had not been the greatest success in the world, with two fiery temperaments on the same floor!

My future path was clear cut. 'I'm not going back luv,' I said to Antoinette without preamble.

'What do you mean?'

'The school . . . I'm not going back.'

Her face dropped in disappointment. 'Oh Li! You said you loved it! What a — It's your mother, isn't it? You're worried about her?'

'Yes, luv. She won't leave here, and I won't leave her on her own, and that's that. She's had enough, more than enough. She's going downhill fast. You know that. I just couldn't rest if I went.'

'Yes,' she answered with a sigh, 'she's certainly changed, although she never complains.'

'She won't! She's used to trouble, but this! It's enough to kill 'er. I'm sorry my love, but that's the way it is. If I went back and anything happened, I'd never forgive myself.'

She filled the pot thoughtfully, then gave me a hug as it brewed. 'Don't worry, I understand. It's just a pity, that's all. You loved it so much. The main thing is, what will your mother say? You know how delighted she was with your job.'

I grimaced. 'I'll tell her later. That way she . . .'

'What's all this then?' asked Con, as he came in to see how the tea was going.

I told him, and his reaction, considering his previous opposition, was surprising. After checking with Antoinette he rounded on me.

'Don't be so flamin' daft!' he snapped bluntly. 'That's what yeh wanted, wasn't it? Why jack it in? Me mam can come an' live with us, if she wants, or with Bernadette for that matter.'

I disagreed, pointing out with equal bluntness that he knew damned well she wouldn't be happy on someone else's floor. She was too independent. He looked more hurt than angry, and, knowing what was in his mind I reassured him.

'Oh, don't worry Con,' I said gently, 'I know she would be well looked after, but it's not as simple as that.' I pointed out that she had her own little routines.

Then there were Aunts Min and Sarah, popping in and out when they fancied. All sorts of things.

'But she can do all that round ours, can't she?'

I agreed and disagreed. 'O' course she could, I know that Con, but how would she feel, eh? No, no, Con, she'd pine away inside!' He made to object again. I stopped him. 'And you know why, too! Because she'd be beholden to whoever took her, and Mam wouldn't be beholden to God, man, nor the devil, and you know it!' He finally admitted I was right. 'Anyway,' I continued, 'that's it, I'm stayin'. You can tell Bernadette, but apart from that, not a word from either of you, OK? I'll tell Mam myself when I'm ready.'

He looked at Antoinette appealingly but got no support there.

'Sorry Con, but I agree with Li. Our place is here. Your mother will be much happier in her own place. In fact, I think everyone will.'

'Yeh,' he replied resignedly, 'you're probably right. She's too old to change now.'

Relieved that a decision had been made, I suggested that Antoinette ring her college for permission to stay for the funeral. It would be a big help. At nine o'clock the next morning I rang a shocked Head and explained all that had happened. He was very understanding. Would I be able to manage with a couple more weeks off to settle things? No, I wanted to leave altogether.

'Oh dear, I'm so sorry to hear that Mr Sullivan. You're sure?'

I said I was and apologised again.

He sounded very disappointed. 'Oh well, if there's no other way. It's a great pity but, good luck Mr Sullivan. I do hope things settle down for you.' He said he would send my employment cards to me immediately.

With final apologies I put the phone down, to face an uncertain future once again. But first there was work to be done, and quickly.

In a partial dream, I retraced my steps of two weeks before, then dashed round to Bernadette's where Mam had gone for a break from Con's, whilst all was made ready. She looked shattered, but little Patricia was cheering her up. I told her about everything except packing my job in — it would only have upset her. I made her promise that she would stay where she was until everything was done, and try to get some rest. My aunts, like two supporting shadows these days, assured me that they would see that she did, and again, with that feeling of detached unreality, I went home.

The house was full as Antoinette and I prepared the parlour, and I was glad that she had obtained permission to stay. In spite of her quiet background as an only child, she was a pillar of strength. By six o'clock the following day Dad was laid out in the parlour, and I went for Mam. All went well. The stories told during the wake were of an older generation, fraught with the battles they had fought to survive, and for them, perhaps because of their long experience, there were tales that brought laughter as well as grief. Tales of a world long before my time, of Ireland, of Dad's days at sea in the distant past, while Uncle Mick, that blithe and unquenchable spirit, regaled us with riotous episodes of when they were sailors together.

Then an hour before he was taken into church, Mam went in to see him. I made to accompany her, but Aunt Min pulled my sleeve.

'No Li, leave her be,' she whispered. 'Just leave them together for a few minutes lad!'

I loooked at her misty, rheumy eyes and nodded. 'I understand, Aunt Min. I'll just take her to the door.'

For long minutes I stood anxiously in the darkened hallway, and from the other side of the door I could hear Mam's quiet, subdued sobs. At last a muffled thud as she knocked a chair warned me that she was leaving. Moments later the small figure was wrapped safely in my arms. I was glad I was not going back.

19

God's Will

In a week of virtual mental suspension we worked like automatons. All that had passed such a short time before was repeated in a state of dream-like disbelief, and I was almost terrified in the first few days to take my eyes off Mam. But with a strength and purpose, born and sustained through years of bitter hardship, she moved through the nightmare with a quiet efficiency that was awesome to watch and an example to us all. Then, with Antoinette's return to college at hand, and with Bernadette — so like Mam in many ways — in capable charge, I felt it safe to leave her as the moment of departure arrived.

For the thousandth time, it seemed, I asked her the same question. 'Are you alright, Mam?'

And for the thousandth time she looked at me with sympathy in her eyes and replied, 'Don't worry about me, Li. I'm alright. Honest I am.'

Aunts Min and Sarah, never far from her since the trouble struck, walked down the pathway just as we were about to leave. I embraced them both.

'How is she?' asked Aunt Min.

I shrugged. 'Well, y'know me mam. She always says she's alright, but . . .'

She squeezed my arm. 'Now stop yeh worryin', lad. It won't help. Just go an' see yeh wife off and don't be daft. We'll look after 'er.'

I felt reassured, but nothing could stop me worrying as we walked down the street. How could I stop

worrying? Even the thought of losing her was unbeara-
ble. It was bad enough with Dad.

Two or three times during the short journey
Antoinette quietly admonished me. 'Your Aunt Min's
right, y'know Li. Worrying won't help. Now promise
me you won't; otherwise I'll worry over you, and so
will your mother!'

I could have kicked myself. 'I'm sorry luv, I don't
mean to, but, well y'know, after me Dad. Anyway,' I
added, giving her arm a squeeze, 'I promise. Honest!'

She gave my arm a squeeze in return and knew, as
well as I did, that only time would ease my fears.

Half an hour later, with Antoinette reluctantly on
her way, I was back home with Aunt Min asking me the
question I was asked on Demob day, ten thousand
years ago.

'What yeh gonna do, then?'

This time, unlike then, I knew! As soon as I had had
a cup of tea I was, for the first time in my life, going to
the Labour Exchange. It was to prove a nasty experience. Mam had been shocked when I told her in a quiet
moment after the funeral that I was staying home.

'Oh Li!' she had exclaimed sorrowfully. 'That's
wrong! You've got to think about your own life, and
more important Antoinette's.'

But deep down I think she was pleased I would be
home, and anyway, as I pointed out, it was done, so
there was no use talking about it. Now I was about to
find out just what I had done!

With no experience of the Labour Exchange, and
completely ignorant of the ramifications of bureau-
cracy, I marched confidently in and joined the be-
draggled queue. The place was full. For many it must
have been as humiliating as it was for me. For others,
natural 'dead legs', who wouldn't work in convulsions
if they could avoid it, it was home from home. There
were several vaguely familiar faces as I looked around.
Fifteen minutes later I placed my Employment Card on

the counter before a tall, cadaverous looking young man who had cynic written all over his face.

'Name?' he asked, picking my documents up.

'Sullivan . . . Liam.'

'Registered before?'

'No.'

'Last job?'

I told him.

He gave me a cynical smile. 'Y'what?' he asked.

I repeated it as he sorted my papers, then he asked if I'd been sacked.

I reacted furiously. 'No I damned well wasn't!' I snapped, irritated by his attitude. I explained why I had left.

He showed immediate sympathy. 'Oh! I'm sorry, but I'm afraid there's nothing I can do for yeh. Rules.' he added enigmatically.

'Rules? What rules?' I demanded in growing dismay.

He explained them. If I had been sacked I would get dole, but since I left of my own accord, I would have to sign on there for six weeks before I received a penny. I was shattered.

'What's up, mate?' asked a voice. I turned to a dark-haired bloke behind me.

'Tells me I can't draw dole,' I answered automatically.

His cheery face grimaced as he flicked his head at the clerk and clucked loudly. 'Wouldn't give yeh last year's Echo 'ere mate!' he stated authoritatively.

The clerk reacted fiercely and glowered at him. Obviously they knew each other well. 'Alright Mr Johnston,' he snapped, 'that's enough of that. There's enough comedians without you startin'.'

My new-found friend looked at me cheerfully as he tipped his cap to the back of his head, then nodded at the clerk. 'Ah, yeh alright mate,' he said with a wink, 'take no notice of 'im, 'eez norra bad bloke really. Just depends 'ow yeh take 'im, like. By the throat's as good as any!' he added thoughtfully.

Those in the queue who heard the remark burst out laughing, but I didn't join in. I was worried stiff at the prospect before me. My whole world had turned upside down, and without money or a job there was no way I could help Mam. I felt suddenly desperate as I turned, and pointed out to the clerk that I had never been out of work, and that my card was fully stamped. Surely to God that entitled me to dole didn't it?

'Oh aye,' he agreed, 'they're alright but, as I say, them's the rules. You could try the Social,' he added helpfully.

'Social Security!' I exclaimed. The very thought brought memories flooding back of the old Board of Guardians and the Means Test days. I rebelled. 'I want work, not that, mate!' I snapped furiously. 'Haven't you got any jobs goin'? Anything'll do. I don't give a damn what it is.'

He took a box of cards and began flicking through them as a new voice, heavy with sarcasm, intervened behind me.

'Blimey!' it said, ''es bloody keen in't 'e?'

I was just in the right mood, and this *wasn't* St Benedict's. I whipped round viciously. 'Watch it, mate!' I snapped. 'I'm in no bloody mood for wisecracks, so just shut it, OK. And keep it shut, or I'll do it for yeh!'

The bloke, near my own size and age and as scruffy as I'd seen anyone in the old days, eyed me, then backed off. 'I was only kiddin',' he said sullenly. 'Can't yeh take a bloody joke?'

In my present mood I would dearly have liked to thump someone. He was as good as any and I didn't give a damn what happened as I stared back.

'Don't!' I snapped. 'Don't even flamin' well think about it, OK?'

My first friend smoothed the waters as he gave me a wink and said quietly, 'OK mate, keep yeh shirt on, 'e didn't mean no 'arm.'

Still seething I turned back to the counter without replying, to find the clerk holding a card up.

'Job 'ere you might fancy.' he said. 'Papermill.'

'Doin' what?'

'Lab work. Paper testin'. Done any 'f that?'

With little money left I would have said yes if he'd asked me if I could circle the moon on a broomstick! 'That'll do,' I said.

He took a green card from a drawer and filled it in. 'The address is on it. Just take that along and get them to fill it in whether you get the job or not. Alright?'

I nodded, took the card and, giving the bloke I had rollicked a filthy look, made my way out.

I knew the mill, a few miles outside the town. What the hell the job entailed I neither knew nor cared. I had been dead lucky and dashed home to spread the news. They were as delighted as I was, as I set off for the mill. Within a couple of hours it was all settled. I would start twelve-hour day shifts on Monday, and the wages were more than adequate for our needs. Knowing that Mam would never be left alone, nor want for anything, I started my new job in good heart, although it was light years away from St Benedict's. However, I knew, never having done shift work before, nor worked such long hours, that it was going to be rough, at least for a while. But that was small fish; I had a job, that was the main thing.

My first glimpse of the factory was daunting and the noise appalling. Once inside the 'calendar room', among the huge machines, speech became impossible, even within a foot or so, and my head rang with the cacophony as the person directing me to the lab, high up in the roof of the hangar-like room, tried to communicate. One hand cupped about my ear, I concentrated like mad to hear him, but to no avail. Then he pointed to his chest, went ahead and beckoned me to follow. By the time we had staggered up the stairs and through the door into the lab, I felt punch-drunk with the noise. Forgetting where I was, I shouted in reply when he spoke.

He grimaced. 'OK mate,' he said with a grin, 'I'm not deaf!' I apologised in a normal voice. 'Oh, that's alright,' he said, 'everyone does that when they first come. You'll get used to it.'

I wished I could have been as sure, for the lab we entered was small, filled with little machines, and with a dry, hot and enervating atmosphere. God! Twelve hours a day in this! What had I let myself in for? I brushed the thought aside as I was introduced to my two new work mates. My companion nodded at a medium-sized, broad-shouldered, bearded man of about forty, leaning intently over a machine in the corner of the lab.

'Daley,' he said, ''arry Daley. 'Arry, this is Li Sullivan.' Harry looked up with a grin, deep blue eyes twinkling.

'Hi yeh,' he said, extending his hand without rising. 'Ex-service?'

I nodded, 'Army.'

He laughed, 'Navy me.'

I pointed to his beard. 'Yeah, thought so with that. Pipe Majors only with them in our lot.'

With a grin, he turned back to his task as my other new colleague held his hand out. They were as different as chalk and cheese. This one was dumpy, with a moon-shaped face that was both fleshy and melancholy, from which two beady little eyes peeped from beneath bushy brows. His whole attitude exuded a worried sadness.

My companion grinned as he introduced him. 'This 'ere's Alf, Alf Siddons.' I shook his limp hand.

Harry called across with an amused smile. 'He was in the Army too, Li. Weren't you Alf?'

Alf grimaced fiercely back at him, as Harry rose to go down below. 'Don't you talk t'me about the bloody Army, mate,' he snapped, 'Geeermin's!' he added scathingly. 'The only good'un's a dead'un, mate!'

I looked from him to my companion.

'Ex-P.O.W.,' he explained with a wink. He suddenly realised that he hadn't introduced himself. 'Oh,' he added, 'I'm Joe Williams — in charge of the shift up 'ere.' He turned to Alf again, 'Show 'im the ropes Alf, will yeh? I've gorra go below.'

Alf, lugubrious, slow moving, and a natural pessimist, materialised beside me, holding a white lab coat. ''ere, stick this on,' he advised, then, when I was suitably dressed, he mournfully escorted me, clearing his throat every few seconds with a peculiar click, which nearly drove me mad in the following weeks, round the various lab machines, explaining each in a low, meaningless mumble. My heart sank as my mind returned involuntarily to the broad, beautiful vistas of St Benedict's; the contrast was a torture I thrust savagely aside. This was my reality and come hell or high water I must settle, for Mam's sake.

With Harry's return from below, with a roll of paper for testing, things changed considerably for the better. ''Ow did yeh gerron with 'im?' he queried, as the door closed behind my late guide. 'Bundle of fun in't 'e? Yeh wanna 'ear 'im when 'e gets goin'.'

I ventured a comment on our absent mate. 'Doesn't seem to like Germans very much, does he?

He laughed. 'Oh, yeh noticed, did yeh? He hates 'em! If yeh wanna birr'of fun anytime, just mention Jerries an' 'e'll go off like a bloody bomb. You'll see . . . Anyway,' he added unrolling the paper, 'come on, I'll show yeh the job.' I told him Alf had shown me round. He laughed again. 'I'll bet that was fun!' he opined. 'By the way,' he added, 'did yeh notice anythin' funny?' I looked at him enquiringly. ''is click, y'know.'

'Oh that, yeah, weird, isn't it? What's the matter with him?'

He shrugged. 'Dunno. Drives yeh crackers if yeh lerr'it. Nerves probably, 'e was in the "can" a long time, of course. Got nicked at Dunkirk. Anyway, come on, let's get this lot tested then we can have a natter.' His explanations of the job were business-like and to the point, and I didn't need to be Einstein to pick it up. By the time Alf came back with his roll I felt much happier.

The nearest I had ever come to a factory was on the few occasions Dad had worked in the engine shop down the Yard and I had taken his dinner down in a cloth-covered basin; so this would take a bit of getting used to. But I confess I found it fascinating: the huge machines down below, the different kinds of paper they produced, the testing and a dozen and one things I had never encountered before. The main thing to me, though, was that they seemed a decent bunch of blokes, with all, except Alf, as lively as crickets. By lunchtime I was fairly confident, and by knocking off time I felt I'd been there for months, but there was still a lot to learn, and not only about testing.

Mam was anxious when I got home, mainly about my being shut in all day.

I brushed her fears aside. 'Don't worry y'self, I'll get used to it. The money's good, anyway.'

'Think you'll settle?' queried Bernadette anxiously.

'Of course I will. Forget it. How are you two, anyway? That's the main thing.'

'Oh, we're alright,' said Mam, happier now my first day was over.

'You're sure?'

She smiled at me. 'Of course I'm sure!' she replied, as I headed for the back kitchen to get washed. Bernadette followed to check my dinner in the oven.

'*Is* she alright?' I queried. 'Y'know what she's like. She wouldn't admit it if she wasn't.'

My sister shook her head slowly. 'Well y'know. she's not really herself, but it's early days yet. She won't let me do hardly anythin' for her.'

I put my arm round her shoulders. 'Well thanks for everything anyway. I don't know what I'd do without you!'

She wriggled free and dug me in the ribs. 'Ah go on with yeh. They're all good to 'er! How's Antoinette anyway?'

'Oh, worried y'know, but then, who isn't? But she'll have more than enough to keep her busy. I'll be glad when the weekend comes just the same, to see her.' I was about to ask about Con, but she must have read my thoughts.

'As for our Con,' she continued as though I hadn't spoken, 'well, he's never away! First thing in the mornin' and last thing at night he pops in.' I was pleased and grateful to hear it. 'Honest,' she added, 'he's as bad as you are for worryin'.'

I laughed. 'Ah, go on with yeh. Anyway, tell him I'm settled, will you?'

She nodded and took my dinner out of the oven. 'Oh yes,' she exclaimed, 'I nearly forgot. Dinny called on his way to work this morning!'

I was delighted. 'Oh great. How is he?'

She laughed as I took the plate from her. 'Dinny? Oh he'll never change. Just as cheeky as ever. Just came to see if everything was alright. He's very fond of me mam, y'know. Anyroad, he says he'll pop round over the weekend.'

'Good,' I said contentedly, 'I'll look forward to that.'

The first week, with travelling, twelve-hour shifts, the unaccustomed heat of the lab, and the hellish noise on the mill floor, was murderous, and I dreaded the coming night shift. But, like everything else, I got used to it. I was working, the money was good and, although forced to spend less time with Mam than I would have wished, I had much to be grateful for. Delayed shock hitting her was a worry, but she never complained, although she seemed to doze off a lot more than she used to. It was on the Saturday of my first week that she gave me a terrible fright.

Dinny arrived as promised, and for an hour kept us in tucks about the latest trouble at his work, something about who should mark the white line indicating where the steel plates should be cut. It was a good job Dad couldn't hear it, Lord rest him. He would have had something to say about it. It was a long time after Dinny had gone, as we were sitting listening to a good comedy show on the wireless that we noticed that Mam wasn't making a sound, unusual, as she loved comedy. I glanced across at her after a particularly good joke and nearly had heart failure. Sitting in Dad's chair with her head to one side and her eyes closed, she looked unusually still. I tensed. Antoinette noticed.

'What's up, luv?' she asked. I nodded at Mam. She shrugged, and smiled. 'Oh, she's just dropped off. Stop worrying. She's alright.'

I leaned forward anxiously. 'Mam!' I whispered tensely. She remained still. I felt myself blanching. 'Mam!' I repeated in mounting panic. Still she didn't move. Terrified, I went over and knelt in front of her, then gently shook her arm. 'Mam, Mam,' I whispered, heart pounding. A surge of relief swept me as her eyes fluttered, then opened.

'What's up ... What's the matter?' she asked in surprise.

I laughed, hoping my concern didn't show. 'You nodded off,' I said jocularly. 'Why don't you go up to bed?'

She glanced at the clock. A quarter to ten. 'It's a bit early isn't it?' she queried.

I coaxed her with the fact that we would be going up shortly. Anyway, she could take the portable up and listen to the rest of the show in comfort with a cup of tea.

'Oh alright then,' she agreed finally. 'I do feel a bit tired, and that's a fact.'

I was glad when she was safely tucked up, but it was not to be my only fright during the following weeks. Despite all, she fought back tenaciously and rallied, as things settled down. Within a month I had put St Benedict's behind me, and within six weeks, with a lively crew at work, I was enjoying my job. My only enquiry, prompted by Harry, regarding Alf's experiences as a P.O.W. were met with a fierce rebuff.

'Don't talk t'me about bloody Geeermins!' he snapped back.

I left it at that, but Harry didn't. He played on poor Alf with the same consummate ease that Yehudi Menuhin played his violin, to while away many a boring hour, and never once did Alf seem to realise his leg was being pulled. At times it was hilarious.

*　　*　　*

With the last week in March coming to an end, I felt happier than I had for some time. Mam was bright and cheerful, and it was my last night on the hated night shift. I was always glad when Friday night came round, for a weekend with Antoinette and a few quiet hours with Mam. Yes, it had been a good week. We had had a lot of fun in the long periods between reels, as the toilet paper we were on slowly ground its way along the machines. With the shift already nearing its half-way stage and a set of tests just completed, I settled down about eleven o'clock for a cup of tea, and became engrossed in the difficulties of Mr Pickwick and his erstwhile landlady Mrs Bardell. Less than fifteen minutes into my tale, the phone rang. Harry answered it, and called across the lab.

'Hey Li . . . it's for you.'

'Me?' I answered in surprise. 'Who the hell would want me this time of night?' I rose and took the phone. It couldn't be Mam. No, when I left for work she was as bright as a button, with Aunt Sarah and Aunt Min. 'Yes,' I answered, 'Sullivan here.'

'Oh good,' came the reply, 'come down to the gate. There's a message for yeh.'

'Well pass it on then,' I said, thinking of the bitter cold outside after the warmth of the lab.

'No, you come down,' ordered the voice. 'She's waitin'.'

'She?' I thought. 'OK then,' I said, 'I'll be right down.'
Within minutes I was at the gate, and at the first sight of
the shadowy figure under the gates lights, my heart
plummeted. It was Antoinette. It was Mam!

'What's up?' I gasped, as another figure came into
view. It was Harry from the corner shop. He had
brought her in his van.

'It's your Mother.' she said hesitantly.

'Oh no!' I exclaimed. 'Is she very bad?'

She put her arms round me as she shook her head.
'She's dead my love,' she said simply.

I released myself and stared at her dumbly. 'Mam?
. . . Dead?' She nodded. 'Oh God no! Not Mam. Please!'

She put her arms round me again. 'Come on luv,' she
pleaded, 'try not to upset yourself.'

I was confused, devastated and felt as though my
knees would buckle under me. 'No, just give me a
minute, will you? Sit with Harry in the van. Go on —
please,' I added, as she hesitated. I squeezed her hand
reassuringly. 'Honest, I'll be alright. Go on now, just
for a minute.' She went, and I found myself trembling,
but not from the cold. I felt wobbly as I climbed into
the back of the van, then remembered no more until
Antoinette's anxious voice roused me. For the first
time in my life I had fainted.

The journey home seemed forever, but at last I
walked into the crowded house. Aunt Min, tired and
drawn, folded me in her arms, as she had done so many
times over the years, to bring me comfort.

'Ah, God luv yeh,' she said as she released me. 'Are
yeh alright?'

I reassured her as Antoinette took my hand in hers.
'I'll be alright, Aunt Min, thanks . . . Where is she, Lord
rest her?'

'In bed luv. Now don't upset y'self, will yeh? She's
in God's hands now.' *God's hands!* I thought savagely.
God? What the bloody hell did he know about justice?

'I'll be alright,' I repeated, as I made my way to the

295

stairs. She made to follow. I stopped her. 'No Aunt Min, I just want to see her by myself.' She nodded understandingly. I entered the tiny room and gazed at Mam's strangely peaceful, and now unlined face. Oh Mam. Mam! For so long the centre of my life, mother, guide, mentor, and strict disciplinarian. Stern, yet so gentle in trouble, strong, yet so soft hearted when I needed her. Mam, who had faced so harsh a life with so little complaint and such incredible tenacity, loyal at all times and respected by all!

Pages of the turbulent past flickered through my mind as I sat on the bed, tears falling unchecked down my cheeks. What a cruel reward for her pious forbearance. What savagery, that she should suffer the loss of those she loved in so short a time! As I sat holding that work-worn hand, I felt a raging hatred against the God who had so shamefully meted out this cruel, undeserved justice. She would not approve of such thoughts, I knew, but she could not have known, even in life, of the love I had for her. I also knew that for her sake, my tears would have to be quickly dried, that the boy's heart in a man's body would have to steel itself to the immediate and unavoidable task ahead. In her own words, I would 'have to face up to it.' I would, but, as I held her hand and smoothed the iron-grey locks, I found it difficult to break this last meeting alone with her. But it had to be, and with a final kiss on her forehead, I left her, but only in body. In spirit she could never die. Not Mam, not any of them!

*   *   *

The rituals, for the third time, were mechanical. My farewells had been said in my own way on the night I had been brought home. Even the funeral did not bring me closer to her than I was then, and, when she was once again with Dad and Teresa I returned to a house from which all life had gone, with decisions to make and make quickly, in fairness to my dear and patient Antoinette.

Con and Bernadette thought I should keep the house on to make a home for Antoinette there, but that could not be. There were too many ghosts, too many memories. It would not be fair, even if I had wished it. No, the die was cast. We would start again from scratch to make our lives in our way, but it would be elsewhere. As Mam and Dad would always say, 'if you're goin' t'do something, then do it. Don't haver about!' I took their advice, and within two weeks the tenancy of the house had been given up and we moved back to Antoinette's, where discussions were long and serious. Her parents had the same down-to-earth common-sense as Mam and Dad.

'The decisions are yours,' said her father, when I half suggested going away once Antoinette had finished college.

'Well of course it would be nice if we were close,' replied her mother, 'but as Harry says, it is your lives. But where would you go? Wherever it is, you'll have to get a house, jobs, and everything else.'

'Then there's another thing,' interrupted Antoinette, now on a full week's half-term holiday.

'What's that? I asked.

'Well, I finish in July. If I want a job, I have to start applying now.'

'Now!' I exclaimed. 'Already?'

'Oh yes, and that's not all. Wherever I get a job I must, according to regulations, stay in it for at least two years. So,' she added, 'we'll have to be careful, won't we?'

'It's a puzzle,' agreed her mother, 'and that's a fact. You're sure it wouldn't be easier to stay here? You could perhaps get a place outside the town. Oh,' she added, catching a disapproving look from her husband, 'don't misunderstand me now, Harry, I'm not trying to keep them here, if they want a fresh start. All I'm saying is that it might be easier, that's all.'

Antoinette and I laughed at her slight discomfiture. 'Oh don't worry, we know what you mean, Mother,' she said, 'but I think Li's right. There are just too many memories here, and anyway, I think it's a good idea. We should be on our own.' She laughed lightly, 'That way,' she added, 'if things go wrong, then we'll only have ourselves to blame, won't we?'

'Well,' broke in her father, 'where d'you think you would be happy, bearing in mind that wherever it is, it will be a strange place?'

'Dunno really,' I said, looking at Antoinette.

'What about that place you were at with the Coal Board?' broke in her mother 'You both said how much you liked it, if I remember rightly.'

Antoinette and I looked at each other delightedly. The answer was under our noses. If we could get jobs.

It was settled. Antoinette would apply the moment she got back to college, to the Local Authority down there. If she got an interview we could contact our old landlady, Mrs Green, to put her up for a couple of days, and if things went well, who knows? And so, the capricious wheel of fate swung in our favour. Everything worked out as though pre-ordained. The black clouds rolled gently away and the nightmare faded as the confirming letters arrived. Her interview was granted and the job secured. The sunshine grew even brighter as the Greens offered us accommodation until we could get settled. All that remained outstanding was for me to get a job, but that I didn't even think about, because I was prepared to do anything to get started. As the Good Book would put it, 'so it came to pass' that we entered a land, not of milk and honey yet, for that would have to be earned, but perhaps a land of peace and quiet, though our memories of home and family would never fade.

Backcrack Boy
by Joseph McKeown

'Fight yer own bloody battles!'

That was the best advice Liam's father could give him. It was the only way to survive in the Liverpool slums of the thirties where the Means Test and pawnshop economy was the natural way of life, and where comedy and tragedy walked hand in hand.

To Liam, the Back Crack Boy, growing up meant running with his own street gang, grid fishing, and the horsemuck trade. It also meant a constant struggle for his family to survive with dignity and humour despite their circumstances.

BACK CRACK BOY

THE SAGA OF A BOY AND A FAMILY IN MERSEYSIDE

0552 112933

Liam At Large
by Joseph McKeown

Merseyside 1934

'My name is Liam, I am fourteen. I come from the slums. I have nothing, no skills, little learnin' and no prospects, please mister can you give me a job, ANY job . . . Please, me Mam needs the money.'

'Yeh kiddin' son . . . bugger off.'

He'd worked part-time for pennies since he was nine years old, but now — with his father growing increasingly bitter after years of being laid-off at the shipyard — Liam was expected to contribute to the shrinking family resources.

Baker's boy, wireless shop assistant, shipyard worker, he stuck them all for as long as they'd have him. Long hours, little money — but a gutsy philosophy of hope and loyalty pulled Liam and his Merseyside family through the destitute 30's with their dignity and family unity still intact.

A Sequel To BACK CRACK BOY

0552 12799X

Another Street, Another Dance
by Clifford Hanley

The long awaited, gutsy novel of Glasgow life by the author of DANCING IN THE STREETS.

In ANOTHER STREET, ANOTHER DANCE, Clifford Hanley returns to the warm, sprawling life of the old Glasgow tenements, the street games, the intellectual and political ferment of the twenties and thirties, the hard times and the unquenchable energy that made the city sing.

Meg Macrae, an innocent girl from the Islands, has to learn to cope with the big city, and men, and children. In her triumph, she becomes one of the great heroines of our time, and her youngest son, Peter, is destined for glory.
ANOTHER STREET, ANOTHER DANCE sweeps through the troubled depression years, from Red Clydeside to the Spanish Civil War, and on through the tumultuous events of the Second World War. Above all, it is a tale teeming with blazing characters, vibrant with colour and rich with life.

'His ear for Glasgow dialogue is as brilliant as ever . . . funny, entertaining, compassionate and, in its own thoroughly admirable way, wise'
Glasgow Herald

0552 12455 9

No Mean City
by A. McArthur and H. Kingsley Long

NO MEAN CITY is the famous, bestselling novel of Glasgow's pre-war slum underworld — an underworld startling in its crude brutality. The savage, near-truth descriptions, the raw character portrayals, bring to life a story that is fascinating, authentic and convincing.

0552 075833

Cut and Run
by Bill McGhee

This is a story of the Glasgow slums, its streets, its people, its pubs, gaols, betting shops, brothels, dance halls, and the teeming life behind the grimy walls of the great grim tenements, where lust and violence walk hand in hand.

Bill McGhee was born and raised amid the sprawling squalor he describes, and there is a pitiless authenticity in his picture of the seamy side of a great city seen through uncoloured glasses.

0552 083356

The Smoke
by Tom Barling

When a Maltese assassin buries Archie Ogle, London's
'Godfather', under a collapsed building, thirty years of
peace are swept away as the old gangland loyalties end in a
bitter struggle for supremacy.

Now everybody wants a piece of the action. Eyetie Antoni
dreams of a Mafia empire in the West End. The Troys from
Bethnal Green want Archie's Mayfair casinos while the
Harolds want to destroy the Troys' control of the East End.
The Tonnas from Toronto want Archie's international
money laundry, the Triads see London as the drugs capital
of Europe, and a shadowy City financier plans to forge his
own organisation from the shambles.

Only one man — Charlie Dance, professional villain and
Archie's top gun — stands in the way of all of them. Divided
by greed and the brutal lust for power, they are united in
one common aim — KILL CHARLIE DANCE!

THE SMOKE
sweeps from climax to climax: across the battle-scarred
map of London, through the drug networks of Asia to a final
explosive confrontation in the diamond fields of South
Africa where Charlie Dance makes a last desperate stand.

0552 125040